THE END OF CONSENSUS

THE END OF

CONSENSUS

Diversity, Neighborhoods, and the Politics of Public School Assignments

Toby L. Parcel AND **Andrew J. Taylor**

The University of North Carolina Press ► Chapel Hill

*Published with the assistance of the Z. Smith Reynolds Fund of the
University of North Carolina Press*

Designed and set in Arno and Calluna types by Rebecca Evans
Manufactured in the United States of America

The paper in this book meets the guidelines for permanence and durability of
the Committee on Production Guidelines for Book Longevity of the Council on
Library Resources. The University of North Carolina Press has been a member
of the Green Press Initiative since 2003.

Cover illustration: © Depositphotos.com/schlag

Library of Congress Cataloging-in-Publication Data
Parcel, Toby L.
The end of consensus : diversity, neighborhoods, and the politics of public
school assignments / Toby L. Parcel and Andrew J. Taylor, The University of
North Carolina, Chapel Hill.— 1st ed.
    pages cm
Includes bibliographical references and index.
ISBN 978-1-4696-2254-5 (pbk : alk. paper)
ISBN 978-1-4696-2255-2 (ebook)
1. Community schools—North Carolina—Wake County—History.
2. Community and school—North Carolina—Wake County—History. 3. Public
schools—North Carolina—Wake County—History. I. Taylor, Andrew J., 1966–
II. Title.
LC221.2.N8P37 2015   371.0309756'55—dc23
2014047575

Portions of chapter 7 were adapted with permission from "Race, Politics, and
the History of School Assignment Policies in Wake County, NC," in *Yesterday,
Today, and Tomorrow: School Desegregation and Resegregation in Charlotte*, edited
by Roslyn A. Mickelson, Stephen S. Smith, and Amy Hawn Nelson (Harvard
Education Press, 2015). © 2015 President and Fellows of Harvard College.
All rights reserved.

This book was digitally printed.

WE DEDICATE THIS BOOK TO OUR FAMILIES,
ESPECIALLY TO **Esther** AND **Hanna Cunha**
AND TO **Jennifer Taylor**.

Contents

Tables and Map

Preface and Plan of the Book

Between 1976 and 2009, Wake County, North Carolina, contained a single large and rapidly growing district of schools integrated by race and income or social class. Its students were generally improving their test scores, and it enjoyed a solid reputation. On October 6, 2009, residents in a little over half the county went to the polls to elect school board representatives from their respective districts. By nine o'clock that evening, candidates endorsed by the Democrats and who supported a system-wide student diversity policy had lost in all four races to Republican-backed opponents who had campaigned on a platform of returning the county to neighborhood schools and assignment largely by address. Early the next year, a new Republican-affiliated board majority voted to discard a long-standing policy that attempted to ensure each school's students came from a mix of socioeconomic backgrounds.

This change, as well as other actions by the new board, subjected Wake to national and international media attention. During 2010 and 2011 there were articles in the *New York Times*, the *Washington Post*, and the *Economist* and stories on CNN, Fox News Channel, and MSNBC. The board's decisions were ridiculed on Comedy Central's *The Colbert Report*. Nineteen protesters were arrested at a July 2010 school board meeting. Chair Ron Margiotta attracted controversy when, at a March 2010 meeting, he called vocal opponents of the majority present in the audience "animals" (Hui 2010a). Tempers got so frayed on one occasion that a member of the majority derisively called another a "prom queen" (Hui and Goldsmith 2010). At root was a continually intensifying battle over how the county's children should be assigned to public schools.

Because we are social scientists, these events caught our attention. Parcel studies the role of families and schools in promoting the academic and social well-being of children and adolescents and is particularly concerned with how these institutions invest their social and financial resources in children, decisions that improve academic achievement and social adjustment, factors critical to adult success. Taylor has written about Republican politics and analyzes the political landscape of North Carolina. Both of us understand the central role mass views and behavior play in policy making. Together we began to speculate that those who opposed the district's diversity policy appeared to be reacting against a loss of social capital or valuable social ties and the increasingly frequent reassignments of the county's children from one school to another. We also perceived that the debate had become increasingly politicized, despite a long-standing tradition of bipartisanship and consensus on the Wake school board. We were naturally interested in the importance of race, ideology, and other demographic attributes and political views of the population to these events as well.

By mid-2010 we resolved to pool our expertise and conduct a multi-method study in an attempt to understand more clearly the revolutionary changes in Wake County school politics and policy that had just taken place. We sought guidance from studies of other school districts, both in the South and beyond, particularly those of large urban jurisdictions like Wake. We began scouring media reports and publicly available data relevant to the debate. These initial investigations only increased our curiosity. For one thing, despite the media rhetoric that sharply juxtaposed those who favored "diversity" with those who desired "neighborhood schools," we suspected some Wake citizens might actually appreciate elements of both policies, so that children could attend integrated schools but do so closer to home. We were interested in the dramatic rise of coherent and organized opposition to a school board that had enjoyed significant public support for several decades. And we uncovered some survey data suggesting that Wake's African American community had mixed views of the schools' diversity policy. This seemed puzzling. Given the association between race and socioeconomic status, why were African Americans ambivalent about a policy that was designed to help all children, but most immediately many in their own community?

We also discovered that many of our out-of-state colleagues did not realize Wake County was, at the time, the eighteenth largest school district in the country—by 2013 it had become the fifteenth largest, enrolling over 150,000 children, with further growth projected. Wake's sheer size, we believed, made it worthy of analysis. Prior to 2009 it had been held up as a model for other jurisdictions interested in racial and socioeconomic integration of their schools (Grant 2009). Yet despite these accolades, the story of desegregation and resegregation in Charlotte, North Carolina's largest city, was probably better known (Mickelson 2001; Smith 2004).

After clearing procedures with our university's Institutional Review Board, we settled on a three-pronged approach. First, we began interviewing Wake County elites who were major participants in the debate. Between 2010 and 2012 we conducted a total of twenty-four semistructured interviews, typically one-on-one but occasionally with both of us present. The interviews included current and former school board members, business leaders, and visible but unelected citizen activists who either favored the recently discarded diversity policy or were advocates of neighborhood schools. We also conducted two focus groups, using three general questions about the current debate as prompts. One group, led by Parcel, consisted of seven liberal activists who were part of a pro-diversity citizen organization. The other, led by both of us, consisted of five African Americans, some of whom supported the diversity policy and some of whom were more skeptical. The focus groups enriched our understanding of people's attitudes about Wake schools. All sessions were transcribed and coded line-by-line to reveal common themes (Charmaz 2006).

Our second approach was to conduct a survey of Wake County residents. The goal here was to evaluate more systematically some of the ideas that our interviewing and focus groups had suggested. With support from North Carolina State University, we fielded a survey of 1,706 Wake County adults in March 2011. We share the results throughout the book, while the appendix provides greater detail about the survey itself. Briefly, we constructed the questions to reflect various themes uncovered in the first phase of our research, including attitudes toward the importance of neighborhood schools, diversity in student assignments, and the Wake County School Board and its policies. We also collected a great deal of information about respondents' demographic characteristics, family and work situations, and political beliefs. These data portray a heterogeneous group. We oversampled African Americans so as to provide enough cases of this population to permit meaningful analysis. While we lack trend data showing change in Wake citizen attitudes across years, we do have rich cross-sectional data showing how views on key matters vary by important characteristics at a critical point in the public debate.

We also realized that Wake County's experience was a vital piece of the larger state and national picture of public school assignments. How unique were Wake's policies regarding students' race and family income? Was its history of sustained diversification unusual? How did Wake's political dynamics compare with those of other large urban areas or jurisdictions with similar histories and demographic features? Conversations with colleagues from other states were particularly influential in generating these questions. They had difficulty understanding many of Wake's unique characteristics, such as its elaborate system of magnet and year-round calendar schools. Their reactions encouraged us to learn more about our case and to study how typical or atypical it might be.

We therefore deployed a third empirical strategy: we compared Wake's current and historical experience with what we could learn from other case studies of districts that had witnessed desegregation and, in many cases, resegregation.

We derived these case studies from monographs, chapters in edited volumes, and scholarly articles. Based on these content analyses, we were able to group similar cases into a smaller number of categories. We also consulted school district websites to provide additional information. As is the case for the other methods, we provide additional details about this in the appendix.

Plan of the Book

The following eight chapters describe and explain the fracturing of a consensus about public schools in Wake County. They address critical questions, including these: (1) Why was there such strong support for the district's basic diversity policy for assignments until about 2000? (2) What factors brought about a change in public attitudes on school assignment after that time? (3) What role did other ostensibly unrelated matters like growth, large-scale but selective annual reassignments, and year-round elementary and middle schools play in breaking the consensus? (4) How has the public divided over the policy, and do the divisions reflect the heterogeneity in the county based on matters like race, gender, political ideology, trust in government, socioeconomic status, family status, and the depth of roots in the community? (5) How do Wake County's assignment policies, and related population and civic dynamics, compare to that of other urban areas in the country? We conclude with a synopsis of our argument, an update on Wake County school policies, and some speculation about the future.

In chapter 1 we set the Wake story in a larger scholarly context. We begin by reviewing literature stressing the importance of education as a placement mechanism in our society, as well as the importance of diversity in school assignments for promoting upward mobility. We then introduce social capital theory and describe how various types of social capital, including bridging, bonding, norms, and trust, operate within families and among families, schools, and communities. We identify two models of public school assignment: one based on neighborhood schools, the other based on diversity. We then illustrate how heterogeneity in public school assignments and reliance on neighborhood schools relate to social capital in different ways. Families in which adults of low socioeconomic status spend significant time at or traveling to their place of employment and enjoy few connections to their communities and government often lack social capital and find neighborhood schools an appealing mechanism to help manage their work and family life. Conversely, a family headed by more affluent adults with more modest work commitments, strong social networks, and greater trust in government are more likely to have the resources to be accepting of diverse schools and the costs they may bring. We also provide basic information on the size and geography of Wake County, which we believe is an important part of our story regarding school assignment policy change.

In chapter 2 we explore how the county's school system and assignment policy changed after the establishment of a single countywide district in 1976. We describe how the district achieved an early consensus regarding both the importance of diversity and improving student educational outcomes and discuss key strategies, such as magnets, that Wake used to mix public schools. We then study root causes of the dissolution of consensus in an examination of the profound demographic changes brought on by dramatic population growth and the rise of the county's Republican Party and the subsequent increased role of partisanship and ideology in local elections of all types. We show how divisions within the school board along partisan lines affected many issues, including funding and bond issuances. We describe the social and political events beginning around 2000 that set the stage for the 2009 election and, in turn, concerted efforts to change Wake's diversity assignment policy.

Chapter 3 focuses specifically on the school board's general assignment policy. The consensus over Wake schools fractured along several planes, but it was conflict over this issue that is most central to our story. Wake initially assigned students so as to balance schools by race, but as districts across the country came under political and legal pressure to end the practice, it utilized socioeconomic status. Supporters argued that the approach was fair, essential to the system's overall academic achievement, made the area attractive to new-comers, and, after all, involved the busing of only a small proportion of students for diversity reasons. Advocating the neighborhood model, opponents argued that diversity restricted choice, caused hardship by assigning children far from their homes, undermined collective academic performance, and constituted a form of social engineering.

This chapter is presented in a format we employ in chapters 4 through 6 as well. We integrate findings from both media sources and our interviews/focus groups into a historical background to the issue that is the chapter's focus. We follow this with results from our surveys so as to place the qualitative evidence in a larger representative context. In chapter 3, the survey results demonstrate that, although inversely correlated according to media coverage, respondent preferences for diversity and neighborhood schools were not diametrically opposed. Our findings suggest that neighborhood schools had a high degree of support among many citizens, but a subset was also very supportive of diversity. In this chapter we also study diversity preferences by race and show that African American views on school assignment policies were very different from whites' views.

Chapter 4 examines the school board's implementation of ad hoc student assignment decisions up until the watershed election of 2009. As growth accelerated after 2000, citizens became increasingly concerned about its implications for schools. With the board committed to diversity, population growth not uniform across the county, and resources limited, more children from more neighborhoods were reassigned each year. We argue that this generated such deep resentment among county residents that it was eventually marshaled into a fairly cohesive and potent opposition to the board and its policies more generally. The survey data reveal respondents to have had three main concerns about frequent reassignment: they posed challenges to parents, presented dangers to child learning and friendships, and brought unsettling uncertainty to family life. The findings reveal a role for social capital and provide some interesting racial differences.

Chapter 5 is about Wake's considerable use of year-round schooling. Initially this calendar was optional, but in 2006, with an exploding population and limited finances, the school board effectively made year-round schools mandatory in many rapidly growing communities. The policy presented significant challenges to many families and further antagonized school board opponents already sour over assignment and other policies. It motivated them to become better organized, to support particular school board candidates, and to file a lawsuit against the board. As with the general and annual reassignment policies, we use our survey and interview data to show citizen sentiments regarding year-round schools. The results demonstrate that, among other things, wealthier residents with fewer children were more supportive of year-round schools, presumably because they were better positioned to manage the challenges posed by the schedule.

Chapter 6 is about the events of the 2009 school board election and its aftermath. We first examine the 2009 campaign and then cover the new Republican-affiliated board majority's efforts to transform the system's policies, particularly on general assignment. These were not completely successful and were often met with robust opposition. We use our interview and survey data to explain citizen attitudes toward the school board. The findings provide an important part of an emerging picture regarding the lines along which Wake's consensus had dissolved.

Chapter 7 sets the case of Wake County in larger national perspective. We are particularly interested in understanding Wake's often-reported uniqueness. Why was the district able to sustain diversity in school assignments for so long compared to other jurisdictions? We build a typology of school districts based on the characteristics we believe are critical to understanding both the breakdown in Wake's consensus and the efforts to move it away from the diversity assignment policy. Specifically, we content-analyze a large number of urban and suburban jurisdictions examined by the existing literature and sort them into four cells based upon their variation in racial heterogeneity and civic life (or the extent to which residents have reserves of social capital). We also acknowledge the role of population growth/decline and partisan politics in the experiences of these districts. The goal is to understand whether the same kinds of things that transformed Wake have had similar effects elsewhere. We place special emphasis on a comparison with the Charlotte-Mecklenburg district, also located in North Carolina. The analysis helps us show that racial and socioeconomic heterogeneity and a robust civic life make Wake quite different from many other districts. It was able to sustain a diversity policy for an extended period of time while its growing population and more partisan local politics resulted in volatile policy making.

We bring Wake's story up to date in the final chapter by briefly discussing the repudiation of the Republican-backed board in the 2011 and 2013 elections and the events in between. We synopsize the central findings and revisit our main themes with special attention paid to social capital theory. By way of final remarks, we speculate on the future of the county's public schools, particularly with regard to their assignment policy.

Acknowledgments

This book would not be possible without the support of many people. We particularly appreciate that of the leadership in the School of Public and International Affairs and the Department of Sociology and Anthropology at North Carolina State University, which provided several small grants to purchase transcription services and materials and to support graduate students who assisted with the work. We owe special thanks to Maxine Atkinson, who in 2011, as head of Sociology and Anthropology, funded the survey of Wake County adults that is so central to the story we share here. Her successor, Bill Smith, also provided advice and encouragement, as did other NCSU colleagues, including Rick Kearney, Patty McCall, Anna Manzoni, Kim Ebert, Michael Schwalbe, and Martha Crowley. Tom Jensen at Public Policy Polling helped us formulate the survey before he placed it into the field. Melissa Allen and Maja Vouk at Wake County Schools and Julie Crain at Wake Education Partnership helped us locate historical data. Josh Hendrix provided considerable research assistance, including data analysis and management, library work, and manuscript preparation. Through this process he became more of a colleague than a graduate student. Sociology graduate students Erinn Brooks, Jennifer Wesoloski, and Brandon Saunders provided additional research support. Katherine Haddock, an NCSU sociology undergraduate, earned course credit for exploring the survey data on parental views of the diversity policy, thus prompting us to think more deeply about how the attitudes of respondents with children might differ from those of others in the survey.

We appreciate support from Roslyn A. Mickelson, Stephen S. Smith, and Amy Hawn Nelson, who provided feedback on our chapter (with Josh Hendrix) in their edited volume *Yesterday, Today, and Tomorrow*, as well as to Harvard Education Press for granting us permission to reprint parts of that chapter in this book. A number of colleagues read versions of the manuscript or papers derived from the project and offered thoughtful suggestions, including Kevin Hill, Mark Berends, Vinnie Roscigno, Annette Lareau, Roslyn A. Mickelson, Stephen S. Smith, and Patrick Sharkey. Other colleagues provided helpful feedback at professional meetings or in other contexts, including Doug Downey, Brian Schaffner, Claire Smrekar, and Patricia White. Tom Birkland, associate dean for research in the College of Humanities and Social Sciences, gave financial support toward the end of our project. A scholarly reassignment to Parcel for Fall 2014 assisted with the final manuscript. John Gerber helped with final manuscript preparation. We are indebted to the staff of the University of North Carolina Press for believing in this project, particularly Joe Parsons, Chuck Grench, and two of their reviewers who provided feedback on the first version of the manuscript, thus prompting important improvements. We are deeply appreciative of those who allowed us to interview them about these issues, as well as of our focus group participants. We would also like to thank the reporters at Raleigh's *News and Observer* who have covered Wake County public schools so thoroughly over the past four decades. Finally, our families have supported our work to produce this book and have endured endless discussions relevant to it. We are grateful for their patience and encouragement.

THE END OF CONSENSUS

1 ▸ Assigning Children to Public Schools

The story of Wake County public schools is complex and the events of 2009–11 long in development. Initially there was considerable agreement about the governance of schools in the district, but slowly, from about the mid-1990s, deep disputes evolved over a variety of matters. These became particularly fierce by the time of the historic election—and the seating of the county's first Republican-backed school board majority.[1]

The fracturing of Wake's consensus had multiple causes, but it largely broke apart over two differing models of educational arrangements in American life. The first, a traditional model, presents schools as integral parts of communities (Reynolds 1999). Most children receive their education where they live, and the community's schools, which often enjoy considerable autonomy from higher levels of government, become an important part of the fabric of social life as they prepare citizens for productive adult roles and democratic citizenship. The second and competing model views schools as having a broader purpose in society, one tied to democracy in a different way. Whereas in the early part of the twentieth century, schools were tasked with integrating millions of immigrants in the American way of life and preparing workers for various roles in the new industrial economy (Nasaw 1979), more recently they have become vehicles for promoting equal opportunity, an important foundation of meritocracy (Darling-Hammond 2010). Achieving the goals of this "diversity" model necessitates greater centralized control of education than is believed desirable by proponents of the traditional "neighborhood" model.

Why Is School Assignment Important?
The Existing Literature

Although less affluent parents may view schools with indifference or suspicion (Lareau 2011), most adults see education as an important vehicle for their children's happiness and success in life. Since the 1960s, sociologists have studied the role that education has played in the process of achievement (Blau and Duncan 1967; Bowles and Gintis 2002; Breen and Jonsson 2005; Duncan, Featherman, and Duncan 1972; Hallinan 1988), often finding that the role of status inheritance—or children's replication of their parents' work lives—has declined dramatically over time. While in the colonial era sons often took the occupations of their fathers through training at home and apprenticeships (Mintz and Kellogg 1988), by the mid-twentieth century, this model had been fully replaced by an intervening mechanism, formal education, which put greater emphasis on individual initiative and effort (Katsillis and Rubinson 1990). With these changes, sociologists especially began to "unpack" the aspects of education that were most influential on life outcomes, with more recent studies using advanced statistical techniques to separate the effects of school characteristics (like the demographic composition of the student body) from family factors (like the number of parents present in the household and parents' own educational accomplishments) (Campbell 1983; Gamoran 1992; Meyer 1977; Morgan and Sørensen 1999; Raudenbush and Willms 1995; Reisel 2011; Roksa and Potter 2011).

It is fair to say that much of the research has provided support to advocates of Wake's established diversity policy. Some scholars have been very interested in the role race and income—or social class—play in explaining educational achievement. In the modern period, many have focused on the disruption of racial integration in schools by "white flight" and "bright flight," where parents with means relocate children from city schools that often are failing to those, generally in the suburbs, that are more white, more middle class, and perceived to be more successful (Clotfelter 2001; Rossell, Armor, and Walberg 2002; Smrekar and Goldring 2009a). This has led to increasing residential segregation by both class and race, with attendant risks for the resegregation of schools and the reversal of the integration process with implications for all children, but especially for those who are minority and poorer (Boger and Orfield 2005; Clotfelter 2004; Orfield and Lee 2005; Orfield and Yun 1999). Orfield, Eaton, and the Harvard Project on School Desegregation (1996) argue that school desegregation has been dismantled through a variety of mechanisms, including courts' unwillingness to create school boundaries that include sufficient numbers of middle-class children, policy makers' reliance on funding rather than on integration strategies to improve education, and the failure to address the critical relationship between housing patterns and school segregation. Boger and Orfield (2005) maintain that despite numerous early court orders mandating integration, many schools in the South are now actually resegregating. The forces at work in this process include the removal of judicial pressure after systems are declared "unitary" or sufficiently desegregated; tremendous immigration, particularly from Latin America and Asia; and federal legislation such as No Child Left Behind, which places disproportionate administrative burdens on those schools that are performing poorly and already lack resources. Frankenberg and Orfield (2012) point to the suburbs as places where resegregation is occurring most dramatically.

Back in the 1960s, the influential Coleman Report (Coleman et al. 1966) found that disproportionately concentrating minority children in schools was associated with lower levels of achievement, outcomes primarily attributable to socioeconomic differences among the races. These findings strengthened researchers' interest in determining whether it was the context of racial concentration that was consequential or whether differences in achievement were substantially owing to social class composition. Subsequent work has reinforced Coleman and his colleagues' findings regarding the importance of income and social class (Darling-Hammond 2010; Grubb 2009; Kahlenberg 2007; Kozol 2005; Orfield and Lee 2005; Ryan 2010). Mickelson, Bottia, and Lambert (2013) demonstrate the importance of both racial and class heterogeneity in schools, and Gamoran (2001) argues that in the long term, school segregation by income will persist, even though racial integration may continue. Current research on the geography of school inequality uses national data to demonstrate that concentrations of poverty in schools are responsible for most of what otherwise might appear to be racial differentials in achievement (Logan, Minca, and Adar 2012). This research has profound implications for the Wake County case. A southern jurisdiction with a significant population of African Americans, Wake had a policy of diversifying schools along racial lines until 2000. As we shall see, when policies like this were deemed unconstitutional in other school districts, the county shifted gears to integrate schools using income and academic achievement—hence making them socioeconomically heterogeneous.

Just as schools with large poor or minority populations have been shown to struggle, social scientists from a number of disciplines have demonstrated that student bodies mixed by race, ethnicity, and family income perform quite well (Braddock and Eitle 2004; Hallinan 1988; Ladwig 2010; Linn and Welner, 2007; Mickelson, 2014; Rossell, Armor, and Walberg 2002; Vigdor and Ludwig 2008; Wells and Crain 1994; Welner 2006; see Lauen and Gaddis 2013 for cautionary evidence regarding this conclusion). Interestingly, while low-income youth from disadvantaged minority backgrounds benefit the most from diverse student bodies, middle-class white and Asian youths are also better off. For example, Rumberger and Palardy (2005) analyze the 1988 National Education Longitudinal Study data of achievement growth among high school students. They find that the socioeconomic characteristics of schools had important positive effects on the learning of both advantaged and disadvantaged students, independent of the individual student's situation, with the institutional differences being a function of variation in teacher expectations, the amount of homework, course rigor, and students' perceptions of campus safety. Students also benefit socially from attending integrated schools because the interpersonal relationships they build there provide a foundation for positive racial attitudes and patterns of social interaction as they grow up (Braddock and Gonzalez 2010; Pettigrew and Tropp 2004, 2006; Stearns 2010).

Social scientists have focused almost exclusively on the relationship between the composition of schools and student academic achievement. They have devoted much less energy to studying how public schools are organized in the first place. It is this that is the central focus of our work. There are some case studies of how politics and social change in large urban districts have impacted school organization. Ryan (2010), for example, traces the history of desegregation in Richmond schools and argues that boundaries segregating minorities in the city from middle-class whites in the larger county were consequential in the decline of urban schools in terms of achievement levels (see also Lleras 2008; Roscigno, Tomaskovic-Devey, and Crowley 2006). Cuban (2010) addresses similar matters in Austin, Texas, as do Mickelson (2001), Mickelson, Smith, and Hawn Nelson (2015), and Smith (2004) for Charlotte-Mecklenburg. Ravitch (2010) details the political and social forces that resulted in changes in school leadership and organization for New York City and San Diego, among others. Portz, Stein, and Jones (1999) show how differences in what they call "civic capacity" in Boston, Pittsburgh, and St. Louis affected the pattern and extent of changes in the way public schools were organized in those cities.

While these latter studies help to frame our investigation, they rely heavily on archival and interview sources for evidence. Our goal is to tie the Wake County case to theory in a number of social sciences and use a broader range of methods and data. We begin by discussing the concept of social capital and how it underpins our investigation of the diversity and neighborhood school models of student assignment.

Social Capital at Home and at School

Following Coleman (1988, 1990), we understand social capital as resources inherent to the relationships between and among people that facilitate certain outcomes. This definition encompasses multiple levels of social organization, a helpful framework for understanding the Wake case. One relevant level in our study is the family. Familial social capital refers to the bonds between parents and children that are useful in promoting child socialization and as such includes the time and attention parents spend monitoring their offspring's activities and promoting their well-being (Dufur, Parcel, and McKune 2008; Hoffmann 2002; Kim and Schneider 2005; Parcel and Dufur 2001a, 2001b; Parcel, Dufur, and Zito 2010). This is an important form of what is called "bonding" social capital (Putnam 2000). Coleman also identifies "time closure," a resource that encourages family bonding, because when parents are committed to one another and to their children over an extended period of time, their investments are likely to be greater and potentially more effective in socialization. An important part of the viability of social capital, then, is its longevity; when ties between parents and children are fleeting, the capital is greatly reduced.

The school is another level of social organization clearly relevant to our story. Children develop connections, a form of bonding social capital, to other students and teachers at their schools. Coleman (1990) argues these bonds facilitate learning and the acquisition of social norms.[2] As at home, connections among classmates and between children and teachers are more effective when they extend over time, promoting time closure. Scholars have already noted the difficulties schools experience when there is high teacher turnover, thus reducing another form of time closure (Darling-Hammond 2010; Haberman 2005; MacDonald 1999). In his study, Grant (2009, 120–21) argues that high teacher turnover in Syracuse, New York, represented a significant loss of school social capital; by contrast, the stability of Raleigh's instructional staff represented a correspondingly positive asset. Time closure is also reduced when children frequently change schools, often because the family moves. The disruption threatens academic achievement and means that children must either reestablish valuable connections in another setting or, potentially, reduce the effort expended in creating new relationships because they anticipate yet more disruption (DeLuca and Dayton 2009; Grubb 2009).

Putnam's (2000) "bridging" social capital is also important. It describes the connections that occur between settings, in this case the home and the school. For example, some scholars argue Catholic schools facilitate children's achievement because a common religion for students and teachers creates bonds supportive of learning. Although some suggest the effects are modest when appropriate background controls are introduced (Alexander and Pallas 1985; Graetz 1990; Raudenbush and Bryk 1986; Willms 1985), several studies have shown material positive effects of attending Catholic schools (Coleman, Hoffer, and Kilgore 1982; Gibbins and Bickel 1991; Jensen 1986). There is some evidence that if social capital is a "stock of social goodwill created through shared social norms and a sense of common membership," connecting a public school tightly to its immediately surrounding community is worthwhile (Furstenberg 2005, 810).

In addition, children benefit from the social connections that parents have with others such as neighbors, school personnel, and work colleagues (Crosnoe 2004; Dufur, Parcel, and McKune 2008; Johnson, Crosnoe, and Elder 2001; Parcel and Dufur, 2001a, 2001b). These connections can be useful in supporting socialization by creating a broader network that children can access as they integrate into the larger community. The stronger the connections tapping bridging capital, the greater the resources to which children have access. An important form of bridging social capital is "intergenerational closure," which Coleman (1990) defines as occurring when parents know the parents of their children's friends. This enables adults to pool resources in establishing and enforcing norms for children, something that is made easier in stable neighborhoods. The connections also speak to ties among individuals within communities, another form of bridging social capital. To be sure, scholars continue to debate whether social capital built at the community level has positive effects. Putnam (2000) and Murray (2012) worry that declines in social capital have an adverse impact on community functioning, while others find mixed results and question whether social capital at the community level has actually declined and, if it has, whether such changes are consequential (Portes 2000). Still, the notion that individuals are embedded in community networks as a function of frequent contact with and geographic proximity to them is an important one that may indeed be consequential for social outcomes, including academic achievement.

Finally, norms are an important form of social capital. They bind members of social groups together and reflect the values and goals that members hold (Coleman 1990; Portes 1998). We have already noted that much social science literature argues that having adequate numbers of affluent and/or white children in schools and classrooms can help distribute middle-class norms regarding achievement and college attendance to children of lower socioeconomic status who might not otherwise have sufficient exposure to them (Kahlenberg 2001). At the same time, middle-class children learn to deal with peers from a variety of class backgrounds, important preparation for their adult lives (Blau 2003; Gurin, Dey, and Hurtado 2002; Moody 2001; Wells, Duran, and White 2008). It is also often the case that poorer and minority children have such little reserves of social capital that placement in a school with peers from wealthier families, even if it is located far from where they live, may actually help them establish useful relationships.

Trust as Social Capital

Social trust is exhibited when individuals have confidence in the honesty, integrity, and reliability of others. Political trust is displayed when people hold these attitudes toward public institutions. Trust is important to a robust civil society, not least because trusting individuals are more likely to participate in public life (Fukuyama 1995; Hetherington 2005; Rudolph and Evans 2005; Teixeira 1992) and governments in communities characterized by widespread trust perform better (Knack 2002). It is also linked to greater prosperity (Slemrod and Katuscak 2005). Both Coleman and Putnam speak of social trust as an important form of social capital because trust is a pillar upon which social ties are built. Coleman (1990, 195–96) argues that declines in social trust are responsible for reductions in social action by those who have previously been trusted—including makers of public policy. Putnam (2000, 347–49) argues that communities high in social trust are more innovative and better able to weather adverse events (see also Cook, Levi, and Hardin, 2009).

It does seem as though the breakdown in the consensus over Wake schools was at least partially a product of diminished trust in others and the school system and its governing board. Some individuals, particularly whites, are opposed to integration policies and prevent their implementation in a systematic and thorough manner. The opposition stems from social distrust, which is frequently manifested in the form of "threat." This is the idea that as minority racial groups grow and acquire greater resources and political power, spatially proximate whites, who generally make up or are of the same race as the community's elite, respond by advocating policies that protect the status quo (Key 1949). As the size of this threat grows along with an expanding or increasingly powerful minority population, whites feel a greater need to protect existing arrangements (Blalock 1967; Blumer 1958; Bobo and Hutchings 1996; Giles 1977). They use tools of social control like public policy to do so (D'Alessio, Stolzenberg, and Eitle 2002). Economists posit that this is because the dominant group believes it will be able to consume less of a public good if others gain access to it (Alesina, Baqir, and Easterly 1999; Kruse 2005). An alternative but related argument is that members of majority groups feel entitled, and when minorities compete with them for social resources, they derive negative views about those of the other race (Kent and Jacobs 2004, 2005; Lopez and Pantoja 2004).

This feeling can be mitigated by what is called "contact." Individual and direct interaction with members of the minority has been found to be important and can presumably assuage or counteract the attitudes of a majority-race individual evoked by threat (Allport 1954; Jackman and Crane 1986). The more frequent this contact, the lower the animosity toward members of the minority race, either because the direct interaction dilutes the racial fears of majority race members and evokes trust between individuals of different races or because those who are naturally more tolerant of individuals of other races actively seek out relationships with them (Marshall and Stolle 2004; Pettigrew and Tropp 2006; Sigelman and Welch 1993; Stolle, Soroka, and Johnston 2008). As a result, majority-race members who live in communities with large numbers of minorities might have fears reduced if they have significant contact with individuals of the other race (Dixon et al. 2010; Tropp and Pettigrew 2005; Welch et al. 2001). In this view, more intergroup contact will elevate trust, thus building social capital and civil society more generally (Rahn and Rudolph 2005; Rudolph and Popp 2010). As we show, issues of both threat and proximity appear to be relevant to the events in Wake.

Political trust is also important. Events in Wake County developed as the public's trust in governmental and political institutions across the United States was declining markedly. As we shall see, Wake's school board was distrusted by a growing collection of parents with all types of political views. Since people who hold governmental institutions in low esteem generally disdain liberal policies or government intrusion in civic society (Hetherington 2005), purposive racial and socioeconomic integration of schools was viewed with a particularly jaundiced eye. This was at a time when, because of economic conditions accompanying the Great Recession, parents were also likely to be concerned about their children's futures.

Heightened partisanship and ideological division undermine political trust further. The national parties have demonstrated increased levels of interparty polarization and intraparty homogeneity over the past few decades (Abramowitz 2010; Levendusky 2009; Theriault 2008). Greater conservatism exhibited by Republicans and greater liberalism shown by Democrats have been detected in southern politics at the state level as well (Aldrich and Battista 2002; Shor, Berry, and McCarty 2010). White conservatives who were Democrats have become Republicans, while the Democratic Party has become increasingly liberal and African American (Lassiter 2006; Lublin 2004).

The polarization has played out in the educational arena, with Republicans supporting conservative policies, including parental choice, charter schools, voucher programs, and the freedom of parents to homeschool their children, and Democrats continuing their traditional alliance with teachers' unions. Debates regarding curricular changes, especially on evolution and sex education, also have a partisan tone (Howell 2005). In Wake County, however, political differences were driven by assignments.

Neighborhoods and Diversity:
Competing Cultural Models of Public School Assignments

As we have suggested and shall demonstrate in much greater detail later, the principal issue that fractured Wake residents' attitudes about schools was the district's general assignment policy. How should the county decide where children go to school? Large numbers of citizens advocated each of two answers to the question, which we call models.

NEIGHBORHOOD SCHOOLS

The first model is one we have called neighborhood schools. In this model, the commute for students is modest.[3] Children attend elementary schools that are proximate to their homes. Middle and high schools are usually larger and thus may be at slightly longer distances, but again, proximity between the home and place of education remains.

Stability is a key feature of this model. By tradition, families are assured that once their children enroll in a given elementary school, they will attend that school until they are promoted to middle school. There is typically a well-defined set of elementary schools that feed into a smaller number of middle schools, which in turn feed into an even smaller number of high schools. Children from the same family will, as they age, successively attend the same elementary school. This means that families have the opportunity to become well acquainted with the school administration and its teachers and that younger children may be assigned to some of the same teachers their older siblings had. Parents can build relationships at this school from the time their oldest child enters kindergarten to the time their youngest enters middle school. Parents "learn the system" of each elementary, middle, and high school and use this knowledge to benefit all children in the family. If parents remain in the same communities in which they grew up, patterns of school attendance for their children may mirror those they themselves experienced. In these cases, relationships transcend generations. In many parts of the country, neighborhood schools are reinforced as a cultural model that is well established, one that is compelling and that many adults believe is "right" for children.[4] Lareau (2014, 169) estimates 73 percent of children attend neighborhood schools. It is likely that many of Wake's parents attended schools close to their homes while growing up, particularly if they were educated in the Northeast or Midwest. Indeed, some may never have known of other models until they moved to Wake County. Most typically, the jurisdictions to which this approach to assignment is applied are small.

The neighborhood school model is also popular because it provides a strong basis for building social capital between parents and schools and for building social capital at home. Geographical proximity between home and schools places a modest burden on parents in terms of attending school events, volunteering to help in the classroom or with school activities, and visiting the school to meet with teachers as needed, thus building social ties between families and schools, or bridging social capital. Moreover, reasonable proximity to home means that little time is spent traveling to school, thus maximizing opportunities to be at home with the family and promoting bonding social capital. Finally, with neighborhood children attending the same schools, connections from school reinforce community ties and vice versa. This strengthens social capital and provides bridges across race, political affiliations, and attitudinal differences within the community.

Families may see neighborhood schools as a resource to help manage modern life, making the model even more important today. Increased rates of divorce and single-headed households, longer work hours and commutes across large urban areas, pressures to be actively involved in their children's education, and pressures for "concerted cultivation" (Lareau 2011) and "intensive mothering" (Hayes 1996) make neighborhood schools an attractive strategy to manage both paid work and children at home. Having children educated nearby at least reduces the distance between home and school, even if parents' residences and workplaces remain far from one another. Such proximity helps parents manage the "juggling act" inherent in work-family dynamics of today (Bianchi and Milkie 2010).[5]

The neighborhood schools model relies on the notion that attendant students and their parents share norms that are helpful to the integration of children into larger social groups. Simultaneously, however, because neighborhoods tend to contain similar types of housing stocks, the students in their schools are likely to be socioeconomically homogeneous. In this model, residential segregation can bring about school segregation.

DIVERSE SCHOOLS

An alternative assignment model promotes diversity within schools, particularly of the racial kind. As we detail in chapter 7, this approach was not uncommon in the South during the twentieth century. For thirty years, Wake County administered a policy based initially on racial and then on socioeconomic criteria. In doing so, its school board mandated annual reassignments of thousands of children. In some instances, individual children attended multiple elementary schools over time while remaining at the same address. Many middle and high school students had similar experiences. The policy was controversial in part, we think, because parents had difficulty maintaining constructive ties with school administrators and teachers; just as their children became settled in one school, they were transferred to another. Parents, moreover, could not be sure the investments they made in networks at a school on behalf of one child would pay off for younger siblings, who might expect to be assigned to different schools. Wake's explosive population growth and diversity policy meant that numerous children lived as many as ten or more miles from their school. They faced lengthy daily commutes, and because of the distances involved, some parents perceived significant barriers to participation in school activities.

Diversity raises the issue of busing. It is important here to distinguish between the goal of having heterogeneous schools and the implementation strategies Wake used to pursue board objectives. Wake's large geographic area and suburban demeanor meant that bus journeys were frequently long, even for children who were not diversifying campuses. The county also used an extensive system of magnet schools to mix students. Busing was only one of several tactics it used to meet its diversity objectives, and yet, as in many other parts of the country, the strategy became a symbol of the school board's intrusive policies and "social engineering."

The social capital implications of the diversity model are consequential. As we have noted, social ties among children from diverse socioeconomic backgrounds help promote middle-class and pro-education norms in students who might otherwise be insufficiently exposed to these ideas. Such norms can help raise educational aspirations, including attending college. Moreover, middle-class children gain exposure to peers of many types, experience considered important preparation for adult life. In addition to promoting meritocratic principles and greater equality of educational opportunity, there are consequently social capital gains generated by diversity.

The competing models can have varying effects that may depend on the economic and social situations of the adults assessing them. Take, for example, those who head a family and work multiple jobs with lengthy commutes for long hours, are perhaps newly arrived to an area and thus do not know many neighbors, are members of few (if any) local organizations, and feel unconnected to municipal government. These individuals will feel a need to build social capital as they attempt to manage career and family. Neighborhood schools will likely be appealing to them. Moreover, particularly if they have limited financial resources, these individuals may feel unable to meet the challenges of diversity assignments. Compare this situation to a household headed by fairly affluent and well-educated adults with modest commutes and average work hours and who have lived in the area for a long time, hence knowing many neighbors and enjoying strong social networks through their membership in numerous organizations and connections to local government. These individuals are more likely to support diversity in school assignments. They may have a greater appreciation of its benefits to others and own the social and economic resources helpful to paying the costs it might impose on their family.

The Setting

Wake County has just over one million residents and covers 857 square miles of central North Carolina. It is the home of state government, the state's largest public university, and a number of sizable technology and health-care employers. U.S. Census sources show that with a median household income of about $65,000, it is relatively wealthy. As the map illustrates, the county is dominated by the state capital, Raleigh, at its center but is also home to a number of suburban towns that surround the city, including Cary, Apex, Wake Forest, Garner, and Holly Springs, which are all among the top forty most populous municipalities in North Carolina. Its far northern, eastern, and southern reaches are quite rural. Much of Wake's dramatic growth—an issue we discuss in great depth later—has been relatively recent.

Wake's school district is both far greater by population—according to the district's data, it had about 150,000 public school students in 2012–13—and geographic size than the towns, townships, and cities that typically use the neighborhood schools model. This also provides significant challenges to families with lesser stocks of social capital. There can be long commutes to schools, exacerbated for many parents who work in other parts of the large—and some would say sprawling—Triangle region that is also composed of Durham (Durham County), Chapel Hill (Orange County), and the Research Triangle Park. Moreover, according to the county, it experienced a 25 percent increase in the proportion of single-parent households between 1990 and 2010. Because these families frequently find it harder to generate and maintain bonding social capi-

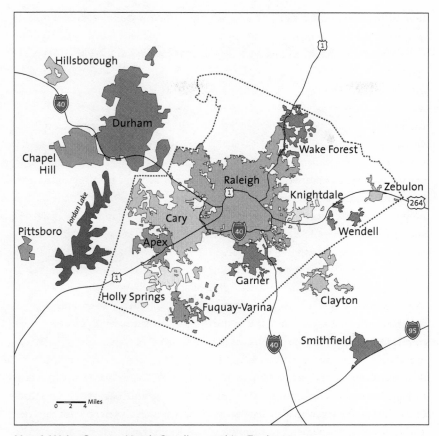

Map 1 Wake County, North Carolina, and Its Environs.

tal than two-parent households, the challenges of commutes, reassignments, and variable school calendars may be particularly acute for them.

Against this backdrop, we now describe the creation and development into the new millennium of Wake's countywide school district. We then analyze the forces that created strain, ultimately leading to the end of consensus and policy change. Subsequent chapters use both qualitative and quantitative evidence to illustrate these dynamics in more detail.

2 ▸ The Wake County Public School System

A SOCIAL AND POLITICAL HISTORY

Before 1976, Wake County children went to public schools in either of two different jurisdictions, Raleigh or one containing the county's smaller towns that ringed the capital city—places like Apex, Cary, Garner, Knightdale, Fuquay-Varina, Wake Forest, Wendell, and Zebulon. Despite their geographical proximity, the two systems were quite distinct and self-contained. Raleigh's was wealthier and its African American children segregated into a small number of predominantly African American schools like Ligon High in the city's southeast. The rest of Wake County was rural and had a smaller per-capita tax base, but residential patterns meant it was more naturally integrated. The two were only formally brought together by the county's board of commissioners, which supplied them with much of their funding.

Serious talk of merger really began in the late 1960s as both the city's and county's schools came under significant pressure to end de facto racial segregation. Only seventy of Raleigh's nearly 5,800 African American students and just seven of about 7,700 in the county were enrolled in predominantly white schools by 1964–65 (McElreath 2002, 331).[1] As the decade wore on, protests across the state against racial division became increasingly frequent, disruptive, and publicized.[2] A study commissioned by Governor Dan K. Moore in 1968 urged the union of city and county school districts throughout North Carolina. In the same year, the U.S. Supreme Court ruled in *Green v. County School Board of New Kent County* that districts were obligated to desegregate in a manner that eliminated identifiable white and African American schools, and in *Alexander v. Holmes* the following year it determined this desegregation should occur immediately. The Johnson and Nixon administrations' Department of Health, Education, and Welfare (HEW) then moved aggressively against jurisdictions deemed segregated. HEW contested the legitimacy of Raleigh's "neighborhood" plan introduced in the spring of 1968, and in 1969 it threatened to terminate $900,000 of annual federal funds to the district (McElreath 2002, 360–70). Following the U.S. Supreme Court's *Swann v. Charlotte-Mecklenburg* decision in April 1971, federal district court judge John D. Larkins rejected as inadequate another Raleigh assignment plan. This one proposed to integrate all of the city's schools so they had a 70-to-30 ratio of white to African American students. Based upon Charlotte's approach, it included a significant amount of busing. HEW also had harsh words to say about Wake superintendent Aaron Fussell's 1968 proposal to integrate his county's schools (McElreath 2002, 356–58). In the summer of 1971, the county board received a letter from HEW asking it to desegregate further by busing students.[3] That August, 3,000 residents packed Raleigh's Memorial Auditorium to lambaste HEW and its suggestions (McElreath 2002, 392–96).

Other issues assisted the nascent drive to merge. Administrative simplification, the consolidation of staffing, and larger economies of scale appealed to those interested in cutting costs. These benefits were discussed in a comprehensive and influential report favoring merger that was requested by the Wake County Board of Commissioners and written by the George Peabody College for Teachers (1969).[4] The general professionalization of education was driving consolidation across the nation (Strang 1987; Tyack 1974), and states, including North Carolina, were making concerted efforts to standardize funding and governing practices (Kenny and Schmidt 1994). It also made sense for the boards to work together on capital campaigns, as they did on a 1973 bond issuance (Christensen 1973).

Race, however, trumped all. Supportive white middle-class Raleigh residents did not so much worry about segregation as feared continued white flight out of the city and the proliferation of private institutions, which would make its public schools largely African American.[5] Many participated in a very public campaign warning that without merger, "only blacks" would be left in Raleigh schools and the city would be "in the same situation as Richmond or Washington" (Lassiter 2006, 296). They argued that standards would drop and the busing of white students to African American neighborhoods in southeast Raleigh would only increase. While the number of African American students had grown by about 15 percent from 1968 to 1975, Raleigh's white student population had declined by more than a quarter (McElreath 2002, 338). Union with towns containing large populations of whites outside Raleigh would mitigate this greatly—while 37 percent of Raleigh's 19,796 students in 1975–76 were African American, only 22 percent of the rest of the county's 33,929 students were (338). In addition, county schools had grown by a third between 1968 and 1975, while Raleigh's had shrunk by 13 percent (338). County residents who favored merger saw Raleigh's superior resources as a way to accommodate population growth.

Merger advocates identified three routes to unification. The first was referendum. Initially both school boards would contemplate a public vote only if additional resources were tied to the merger. In March 1970, however, county commissioners flatly refused the school boards' joint request for a referendum to approve a unification plan consisting of $4.2 million in extra funding and permission to issue bonds worth $29 million. Sensing a general discomfort with merger, even one unburdened by additional financing, opponents like Cary resident George King and his Citizens for the Right to Vote called supporters' bluff and helped place the question on the November 1972 ballot (Marlowe 1972). Business leaders such as Henry C. Knight and the influential owner of Raleigh's *News and Observer* newspaper, Frank Daniels; Wake County commissioner Waverly F. Akins; and Raleigh City School Board chair Casper Holyrod directed a concerted effort to secure its approval. They failed miserably. Public pressure outside of the city intensified with reports that thousands of county students would be reassigned after the two systems were brought together (McElreath 2002, 326–442).[6] Many worried busing would be widespread, and county residents feared merger with Raleigh amounted to takeover by the city (Berg 1972). As the vote approached, support from the Wake board evaporated (Davis 1972). With candidates, particularly Republicans like President Richard Nixon and Senate aspirant Jesse Helms, deriding forced busing vocally from the top of the ballot, the merger was defeated by a margin of more than two to one (Cullen 1972). Only a few liberal white and African American precincts supported the plan, and even there by small amounts.

Taking stock of the experience, merger supporters soon realized that they needed to proceed on one of the two alternative routes. A tripartite agreement between the school boards and the county commissioners looked unlikely after the unsuccessful and divisive referendum. There were, however, some attempts to reconcile undertaken in 1973. State representative Howard Twiggs (D-Wake) worked to bring the three entities together (Berg 1973). Efforts by the Wake school board to synchronize its system with Raleigh's were designed to remove a logistical barrier to unification.[7] All proved fruitless.

It looked, therefore, increasingly as if the third route, legislation drawn up and passed by the North Carolina General Assembly, would be necessary. Merger proponents were strengthened over the year or so following the referendum by data revealing an accelerated movement of families out of Raleigh and quickening growth of the population in the surrounding county: Raleigh schools lost around 800 students in 1974; Wake schools gained over 1,100 (McElreath 2002, 388). Many residents understood that schools were overflowing in places like Cary while classrooms lay empty in urban neighborhoods. Then in 1975, after repeated threats, HEW informed the Raleigh school system it was ineligible for nearly $1 million in funding as a result of the city's foot-dragging on desegregation (McElreath 2002, 427–29).

The county school board began to realize merger was in its interests, too. So as to provide greater representation to distant towns like Fuquay-Varina and Zebulon, three seats were added to it in 1974. This effectively split districts represented by the merger's strongest opponents and helped dilute the influence of representatives from predominantly white and booming jurisdictions, like Cary, that were getting the lion's share of new resources but were doing little to teach African American children (McElreath 2002, 437). In April 1975 Wake board chair and virulent merger opponent Mary Gentry was deposed and replaced by the more accommodating F. Roland Danielson. Understanding that their poor relations were harming the interests of both, the Raleigh and Wake school boards then met on the question of whether to ask the county's delegation to push for merger-enabling legislation during the General Assembly's 1975 long session (McElreath 2002, 439–41). The county board initially demurred, but member Samuel S. Ranzino was persuaded to change his position to favor union. Despite opposition from two of the county's Democratic senators, Bob Barker and William E. Staton, the General Assembly enacted the enabling bill in June (Williams 1975a).

The saga was not over. The new law pushed the issue back to the school boards by imposing merger on them only if they could not agree among themselves. Motivated to complete the task on their own terms, officials in the city and county worked on a proposal that was approved by the Raleigh board unanimously and by the Wake commissioners by a 4–2 vote in August. The next month, after a lengthy and heated public meeting packed with vehement opponents of unification, the Wake school board approved the same plan with minimal and largely cosmetic changes by a 4–3 vote (Williams 1975b). On July 1, 1976, the new 55,000-student, eighty-campus Wake County Public School System was established.

Merger came about for a variety of reasons. Federal and state government pressure over racial integration and escalating population and resource imbalances between Raleigh and Wake were clearly important (McNeal and Oxholm 2009, 1–3). Raleigh political, business, and civic leaders feared the economic effects of continued white flight. Across North Carolina and the South, jurisdictions were responding to racial, economic, and administrative issues in public schools by merging city and county districts. Some cities, like Greensboro, had, with minimal apparent negative effects, effectively been integrated for quite some time (Chafe 1980). There was an established "solution" to "problems" like Raleigh–Wake County's. Supporters made the strategic decision to push an unadorned merger plan that focused on the synthesis of the boards, staff, and schools and left controversial decisions about assignments and resource distribution until later. Human agency no doubt played a role, and newspaper accounts of the episode point to a number of influential people who expended tremendous energy and time seeking unification, as is clear above.

It is the battle over merger, however, that is most important to this study. By 1976 the critical issues were clearly policies to facilitate racial integration and the distribution of resources across schools. With the end of "dual" or essentially all-white and all–African American schools, residents fretted over their children's assignments, generally hoping they would not be bused or have to attend a school with inferior teachers, fewer books, and crumbling facilities. Many merger opponents embraced the neighborhood schools model, while supporters felt unification provided a fairer racial balance within and across district schools and elevated student performance in the aggregate. They tended to advocate diversity. Cleavages fell along several planes, but for the most part merger was promoted by white liberal residents of the city and resisted by white conservatives who lived in the western part of the county. Many poor and middle-class whites were fearful of developments that played on their insecurities, fostered by the era's many social, economic, and cultural changes, including the rising political power of African Americans, a recession and concern that future generations would struggle to prosper, diminishing social capital within local communities, and a sizable increase in hours worked by women outside the home and the concomitant strains placed on family life.[8]

System Building

To some great extent, the divisions over merger would be reprised in the first decade of the 2000s and are central to the story of Wake County's dramatic fracturing in 2009. Immediately following unification, however, the community's leadership and many residents came together to form a quite surprising consensus over school policy.[9] There was a concentrated focus on consolidation, and the system's first superintendent, John A. Murphy, worked diligently to integrate administration and staff and to build the new entity's legitimacy. Murphy was well known for his forceful personality and was popular among staff (McElreath 2002, 531–32). As an experienced educator from the Northeast, he was respected for his expertise and was considered an honest broker in the antagonisms that were sure to linger between those who battled over the merger. Led first by Vernon Malone (1976–77) and then A. Roy Tilley

(1977–78) and John Massey (1978–81), the new board recognized the superintendent's talents and deferred to him on many issues.

The one major programmatic initiative of the late 1970s and early 1980s found broad support. Under Murphy's direction, the county opened its first two magnet schools in 1977—a "gifted and talented" program and an "extended day" campus, both in Raleigh. In 1980 it opened three more, including one outside the city at Apex Elementary. Magnet schools have specialized curricula and offer self-contained courses of study. Families apply and are often accepted after a lottery. Magnets get their name from their capacity to attract students from across a jurisdiction. Murphy and others recognized that by placing these schools in poorer and African American Raleigh neighborhoods, they would also diversify the student body while reversing the flow of white children who were emptying from city schools and causing those in suburban neighborhoods to overflow (Silberman 2001, 146–47).[10] As the superintendent noted in a March 1978 memo to the school board, "The magnet plays an increasingly successful role in the desegregation of public schools" because "it brings together students of different races and backgrounds . . . for educational reasons rather than for the simple exercise of mixing bodies." "In a magnet school setting," he continued, "racial and socio-economic barriers" are brought down more quickly "than they are in settings where forced mixing occurs" (Murphy 1978, 255).

Murphy resigned under an ethics cloud in June 1981.[11] He was replaced by Walter L. Marks, an experienced administrator from New Jersey with a PhD. Marks was energetic and a bold thinker; the same year he came to Raleigh he published an article titled "The Superintendent as Societal Architect."[12] With the board's broad support—the January 1982 vote authorizing the proposal was 6–2—he led a dramatic expansion of the magnet program, one he called "Schools of Choice." In 1982 alone, twenty-seven of them were opened. Although the school system was forced to pay back $489,000 in improperly directed federal grants as a result of his decisions, Marks's tenure and magnet project are often considered a success (Grant 2009, 96–99; Silberman 2001, 146–48).[13] Between the mid-1980s and mid-1990s, the county received in excess of $15 million in federal Magnet Schools Assistance Program grants. It continued to open these schools and broaden their offerings, employing themes like the arts, technology, and international studies.

The magnet expansion was motivated greatly by Marks's interest in curricular issues and the efficient utilization of existing facilities and transportation. But the central goal was to alleviate racial concentration and balance the student populations of schools.[14] The federal government continued to pressure districts, particularly those located in the South, that seemed unwilling or incapable of thorough racial integration. The board demonstrated its commitment to diversity in 1981 when it established a "15/45" policy that mandated no school's racial minority population could be less than 15 percent or more than 45 percent of its student body (Flinspach and Banks 2005, 266–69). As a result, by 1999 only 21 percent of the county's African American children attended a school in which a majority of students were of a minority race. This was in contrast to the national figure of 70 percent (Silberman 1999). The integration was largely attributable to magnet schools, with some African-American children bused to suburban schools. Even after the merger, racial desegregation continued to drive Wake County's policy toward public school assignments. And, unlike many other jurisdictions across the South, it was all done without court order.[15]

The policies of the 1980s and early 1990s were also shaped by the significant growth in population. Between 1985 and 1995 the county grew from 360,000 to 528,000 residents and 57,268 to 81,203 students, the latter representing an increase of 41.8 percent.[16] The influx of people—mainly from the Northeast and Midwest—placed tremendous strains on facilities. In 1985, for the first time since the merger, the county's voters approved a school construction bond issuance, this one for $70 million. Many Wake County residents clearly felt that leaders were not keeping up with demand. Later that year two prominent board members, Mary Gentry—the sitting chair and veteran of the merger battle—and Roy E. Carawan were soundly beaten in their suburban districts where schools were overflowing.[17] Indeed, demand for new facilities was so great that in 1988 the county's residents approved $125 million in bonds to build new schools and renovate existing ones. Turnout for the referendum was light, but of those who did show up at the polls, 85 percent voted "yes." Support was particularly strong in north Raleigh and Cary, two relatively affluent areas witnessing explosive increases in population.

In 1987, at the request of its chair Stewart Adcock, the Wake County Board of Commissioners began to nudge the system to look at year-round schools as a cost-saving measure. Analysts estimated these schools could serve up to a third more students by placing them on as many as four different calendars or "tracks." Instead of following a conventional September to June schedule, year-round schools are open almost permanently with students attending for roughly nine weeks before taking three off. At any one time, all students on one of the tracks are out of school. Year-round schooling was attractive because it would alleviate the intense and constant pressure to build. These schools would also reduce operating costs, a benefit that was particularly appealing to the commissioners, who provided the system with about a quarter of its annual budget. The first year-round school in North Carolina opened in Cary in 1989. By 1995–96 the system had seven multitrack, year-round schools—two at the middle level, five at the elementary—enrolling over 5,000 students. Superintendent Robert Wentz predicted in the 1990–91 school year that at least half of Wake County schools would be on the year-round calendar within a decade.

The significant pressures exerted by population growth could have quite easily divided the school board. Indeed, there was some contentiousness immediately following unification as representatives from the county and city began their work together. The first two formal elections for chair both ended in 5–4 votes—in June 1978, John Massey was chosen only on the third ballot. By 1981 there was discernible concern from board members and residents about overcrowding in north Raleigh and western Wake, and there were lengthy and divisive meetings about the frequent reassignment of children. In an April 1981 board meeting, for example, an effort to stabilize assignments and establish a three-year plan for placing children in schools was narrowly defeated.

For the most part, however, the board maintained its unity. Despite the ignominious endings to the tenures of Murphy and Marks, a philosophy of deference to and trust in superintendents had taken hold. Their successors, Marks's deputy Robert Bridges and Robert E. Wentz, a career education administrator, did nothing to provoke a meaningful reversal. Superintendents managed the schools' business on a day-to-day basis, and the board worked on broad policy matters—"big policy issues"—and acted as "advocates in the community for the school system," as chair John H. Gilbert was to put it later (Silberman 2000a). The popularity of Bridges and Wentz helped make the arrangement work.

Board members tended to be civic-minded citizens or booster types with an interest in education. Craig Lewis, who defeated Gentry, owned a muffler shop. L. Jean Schilawski, who defeated Carawan, was a teacher and school director. Bill Fletcher, a scion of an influential local media family, was a businessman and volunteer. He narrowly lost a race to be the state's superintendent in 2004.[18] John H. Gilbert, who served from 1983 to 1999 and was chair in two different terms, was a political science professor at North Carolina State University. Wray Stephens served even longer, from 1981 to 2001. He was a teacher-turned-owner of a building supplies firm. As was the case throughout the South, Democrats dominated the board, but there was little in the way of partisanship and ideological division. School board elections were nonpartisan, and the political parties neither campaigned for nor formally endorsed candidates.

As described by a veteran of Wake County Democratic politics, "When it came to the school board," an individual's partisan affiliation and views "were issues that were never ever talked about."[19] Republicans Henry C. Knight, head of an electronics firm, and Charlotte Martin each served terms as chair in the 1980s. Divisive votes on who should be chair were rare—from the early 1980s to the mid-1990s, the only annual elections that were contested in any meaningful way occurred in 1986 and 1987.[20] Board members from the period remember it as a time of cooperation and consensus. As Stephens put it in an interview, "When the decision was made, the decision was made; we were one board."[21]

This was reinforced by a unified business community that generally supported the board's policies. In 1983, in conjunction with the school system, the Raleigh Chamber of Commerce formed the Wake Education Foundation (renamed the Wake Education Partnership in 1992), a bipartisan group of prominent business executives and professionals that served to support the schools. The partnership quickly became an energetic promoter and disseminator of the board's policies. It unapologetically defended general assignment policies based on racial diversity. The group's fundamental interest, however, was—and still is—in the health of the local economy. It is rooted firmly in the state's tradition of "business progressivism" and has been guided by "modernizers" or pragmatists less interested in social policy than in fostering the political conditions necessary for prosperity.[22]

The consensus was also facilitated by a widespread belief that the county's schools and students were performing well and improving all the time. In 1998–99, the average SAT scores of graduating high school seniors rose for the fifth consecutive year to forty-three points above the national measure. In the same year, three-fourths of the county's participating schools were considered to have achieved "high [academic] growth" by the state's ABC program, which stands for "strong Accountability, teaching the Basics, and maximum local Control."[23] By the early 2000s, the racial and poor-rich "achievement gaps" had shrunk markedly, a matter viewed by many as a signature accomplishment of the 1976 merger.

As a result, the county's public schools entered the millennium with significant support from a generally contented public. According to a 2000 poll by the Wake Education Partnership, 51 percent of residents gave the schools a grade of A or B (out of choices of A, B, C, D, or Fail), and 58 percent agreed the school system "is improving over time."[24]

The 1990s and Early 2000s: Fissures Appear

Things, however, were about to change. In the early 1990s two important developments began to have major effects on public attitudes about Wake County schools. Indeed, within fifteen years the developments had come together to shatter the consensus that supported the policy of diversity and an educational arrangement organized at a system-wide, rather than at a neighborhood, level.

EXPLOSIVE POPULATION GROWTH

It is not an understatement to say Wake County's population has grown dramatically since 1980. By 2000 it had reached nearly 628,000 citizens, having expanded by 109 percent in twenty years. At a rate of 34.6 percent, Raleigh-Cary was the fourteenth fastest growing of the country's 100 largest metro areas during the 1980s. It increased even more rapidly in the 1990s; at a rate of 47.3 percent, it was fourth nationally. Cary alone more than doubled in size. Proportionally only Las Vegas expanded more in the decade. The school-age population rose by about 4,000 children annually from 1980 to 2000, enough to fill four large new campuses per year.[25]

The growth—derisively termed "suburban sprawl" by many critics (Silberman 2001, 157–60)—inevitably placed considerable strain on the system. To keep up with the new population, the board needed cooperation from county commissioners, who were charged by state law to provide schools with much of their funding. This was not always forthcoming. In 1996 the school board requested $695 million from the county to build fifteen new facilities. Commissioners were willing to give it $400 million (Rawlins 1996). The following year disputes over the operating budget—the school system had asked for a 20 percent increase, which would have necessitated a tax increase—triggered a state-mandated mediated settlement. The resulting agreement allowed the schools to secure a proportion of property tax revenues and required five of the seven commissioners to block a tax increase if new funds were to be directed to schools. County commissioners approved a ten-cent tax hike—eight cents to go to construction, two to operating costs—for the schools under these rules in February 1999. The procedure stabilized the schools' funding stream somewhat but ultimately lasted only until 2002 (Norfleet 2002). The additional taxes it brought about also generated ill feeling among many residents.

Eager to avoid elevating property taxes whenever they could, school board officials and county commissioners looked to other sources of revenue. In March 1997 the board called on municipalities to assess "impact fees" on developers who built new residences (Silberman 1997a). Cary adopted the policy in 1999 and raised around $4 million in twelve years (Hui 1999b).[26] Borrowing, however, was the main source of financing for capital projects. In June 1993 county residents approved a $200 million construction bond issuance by 56 percent to 44 percent. In June 1996 a much healthier 79 percent of voters supported a call for $250 million in construction bonds. Despite a meager turnout of 14 percent, community leaders were thrilled. School board chair Judy Hoffman characterized the public's response as "another statement of their confidence" in the schools (Silberman and Rawlins 1996).

Things had changed dramatically by the time residents considered the next bond in June 1999, a $650 million package that was the centerpiece of what had become a $938 million plan to build and renovate schools. Residents were uneasy with such a huge price tag, particularly on the back of two recent bond issuances. Conservative activists, moreover, continually reminded them that a "yes" vote brought about increases in the property tax (Silberman and Hui 1999). Despite being outspent five to one by a coalition of business and civic boosters called Citizens for Good Schools, the doubters were vindicated. On a relatively large turnout of one-fourth of eligible voters, 65 percent said "no."

The school board was chastened. It and Superintendent Jim Surratt— lauded for his leadership of the successful 1996 bond campaign (Silberman and Rawlins 1996)—had clearly misread the public mood. In response the board reached out to conservative opponents and with them formed a thirty-one-member citizens' advisory committee headed by a local consultant, Jim Talton. The goal was to generate an alternative and presumably scaled-down capital financing plan. The committee came up with $550 million worth of projects, including the construction of fourteen new schools and the renovation of thirty-two others. Tellingly, the proposal did not contain a tax increase. Derived from "a coalition effort of listening to all voices" and considered "an example of what local government is supposed to do," it passed overwhelmingly with the support of 77 percent of voters in November 2000 (Hui and Silberman 2000).[27]

The school system came back for permission to issue more bonds for construction in 2003 and 2006. On the first occasion a $450 million package that contained thirteen new schools and improvements at seventy-seven others was approved by 64 percent of voters. Given that 21 percent turned out in an off year, the result was encouraging for supporters (Hui 2003a). Three years later, however, a significant increase in cost projections, especially for land (Hui and Silberman 2006), had the board contemplating a bond issuance of between $1.375 billion and $1.975 billion. With the public skittish, the headline number was reduced (Coleman 2006). Still, at $970 million it was huge, particularly for a proposal that contained just seventeen new schools and the conversion of twenty-two others. The proposal also included a property tax increase of about $70 on $150,000 of value. Although proponents, led by the Friends of Wake County, spent $500,000 on an advocacy campaign, the opposition was so considerable that the bond squeaked by with only 53 percent of the vote in what was a very good election for Democrats (Hui 2006d).

In the nine academic years between 1992–93 and 2000–2001, Wake opened twenty-three elementary schools alone. Building new facilities and expanding and renovating existing ones constituted just part of the effort to deal with population growth, however. The county's new residents occupied new communities and transformed existing ones so much that the board was forced to reassign several thousand students annually. This created a pervasive sense of uncertainty and instability about schooling, particularly in the fastest growing parts of the county. As early as 1993, so many Cary residents had been affected by the annual reassignment process that the town set up a commission to examine ways in which the school system could improve it (Brown 1993). In 1995 Apex was hit hard. The next year the focus of reassignments switched to north Raleigh in a conscious effort to protect Apex and Cary (Silberman 1996a). By 2002, however, it was Apex's turn again (Hui 2002a). In 2003 reassignments focused on southwestern Wake and particularly Holly Springs (Hui 2003b). Indeed, in the years between 2003 and 2009, a total of about 45,000 students were uprooted from their schools and sent to another (Hui 2008a). Often they made way for newcomers who had just moved into recently built subdivisions. Sometimes the affected students went to schools that were farther away from home. The policy was extremely controversial and, as we shall discuss in chapter 4, played an important role in fracturing the consensus and generating support for the neighborhood schools model.

An increased reliance on year-round schools was another growth-management strategy. After the defeat of the 1999 bond, the successful 2000 proposal included a rather ambiguous commitment to more year-round schools where attendance would require parental consent. Between 1995–96 and 1999–2000 the county opened three elementary schools (kindergarten–grade 5) and one middle school (grades 6–8) on a year-round calendar. Two other elementary schools were switched from the traditional calendar. The Capital Improvement Program passed by the voters in the bond referendum of 2006 contained a pledge to accelerate the construction of year-round schools and to convert existing traditional calendar schools to the year-round format. With the board's decision to separate year-rounds from the magnet program in 2005, the system was ready to assign children to these campuses as an alternative to their traditional calendar option or, in some cases, as their only school. The effect was to make year-round mandatory for many residents in the western part of the county.

The expansion of year-round schooling was dramatic. By 2009–10, 33,157 students were in forty-two year-round elementary schools and 10,925 students were attending nine year-round middle schools. It was also painful. Just as the annual reassignment ritual mobilized parents against the board and its policies, so did the decision to make year-rounds compulsory for some. Opponents became organized and even went to the courts. As we shall discuss in chapter 5, year-round schooling contributed significantly to the shattering of the consensus.

Efforts to accommodate population growth were complicated by Wake's continued commitment to diversity. As early as 1996 there was concern among board members that concessions made on reassignment plans to aggrieved white families were undermining efforts to integrate the county's schools (Silberman 1996b). "Reverse busing," in which children from relatively affluent areas are bused to schools in poorer ones, became a controversial feature of the process (Hui 2002b). As we shall see, the decision to remove year-round schools from the magnet admission procedure in 2005 was driven, in part, by diversity concerns.

Wake originally defined diversity strictly in racial terms. In the late 1990s this approach came under significant legal pressure when the federal Fourth Circuit Court of Appeals ruled against race-based student assignments in Charlotte and Maryland.[28] As a result, the Wake board changed its policy in January 2000. Now the aim would be for schools to have no more than 40 percent of their students receiving free or reduced-price lunches and no more than 25 percent of them reading below grade level (Kahlenberg 2007, 11–12; Silberman 2001, 148–52; Wake Education Partnership 2003, 9–11).

On the surface, the decision was dramatic. Wake revolutionized the way it integrated schools and thought about student assignment. Residents seemed pleased. The percentage of respondents to a Wake Education Partnership survey that gave the school system a grade of either A or B increased from 46 percent to 54 percent between 1998 and 2004.[29] There were tangible academic accomplishments as well (Finder 2005).

But it is difficult to say whether the academic improvement was a product of the new policy. The composition of student populations across schools changed to increase proportions of poorer students in some schools. According to the system's own numbers, in 1999–2000, 17.6 percent of elementary schools had more than 40 percent of students on free or reduced-price lunches.

The figure increased to 31.1 percent in 2007–08. The proportion of minority students in some schools also increased.[30]

The new definition of diversity certainly did not change the debate about assignment either. Residents continued to talk about educational arrangements in the language of racial diversity versus neighborhood schools. There were the same arguments about academic achievement and busing. This is a point we shall explore in chapter 3 when we examine the county's general assignment policy in more detail.

It is important to make one last observation here. The massive population growth and its influence on school calendars and assignment policies had important effects, particularly on the reserves of social capital at families' disposal. The uncertainty surrounding children's schooling frequently interacted with the pressures of modern life to place great strains on parents' work and personal lives. The heterogeneity and sheer number of newcomers diluted any sense of community. Growth also congested roads and other public services, lengthened commutes, and reduced the time parents could spend with their families and at their children's schools (Garreau 1991; Lindstrom and Bartling 2003). We explore further the roles that social capital and family and work played in the fracturing of the consensus at various points later in the book.

A NEW LOCAL REPUBLICAN PARTY

The early 1990s also sowed the seeds of a revolution in Wake County politics. Raleigh and its environs were never extremely liberal or, at least within the context of the one-party South, Democratic. Jesse Helms, a father of sorts for the local Republican Party, was a two-term Raleigh city council member first elected in 1957 who made his name presenting editorials on network-affiliated WRAL television in the 1960s. In 1972 the county played its part in securing Republican statewide victories in presidential, gubernatorial, and, with Helms, U.S. Senate elections—Wake, for example, was one of only five counties east of Greensboro to support the party's candidate for governor, Jim Holshouser. In 1976 it was one of fourteen in North Carolina—and just three outside the traditionally more Republican western half of the state—to support Gerald Ford for the presidency. This was consistent with developments in the rest of the South where Republicans made breakthroughs in suburban rather than socially conservative rural areas (Lublin 2004).

Wake resisted a complete embrace of the Republicans, however. Although both grew and urbanized dramatically in the 1980s, Raleigh was not Charlotte. Its economy was based not on banking but on government, education, and the professions. Whereas North Carolina's Queen City had a strong tradition of

Republicanism dating back to the Civil War, Raleigh had little of one. In 1984 Wake supported former Democratic governor Jim Hunt in his titanic battle with Helms for the latter's Senate seat.[31] A majority of its voters supported former Charlotte mayor and African American Democrat Harvey Gantt as he lost to Helms in 1990. In 1992 the county went for Bill Clinton as the state gave its electoral votes to George H. W. Bush.[32]

It did not go unnoticed, therefore, when in 1993 Tom Fetzer became the first Republican mayor of Raleigh in living memory. Fetzer's surprising victory in a runoff against council member Barlow Hergert gained Republicans an important foothold in the area. It was orchestrated by the chair of the county party, Tom Roberg, who, despite inheriting a small and rudderless group earlier in the year, worked assiduously on a sophisticated "get-out-the-vote" strategy (Rawlins 1993). Roberg's effect on the county party was so great that by early 1995 he would ensure—with assistance from others like State Representative David Miner of Cary—a formally organized Republican presence in 80 percent of Wake's precincts (Rawlins 1995). The county party's convention that year attracted 700 attendees to celebrate the establishment of what Fetzer called "a base camp to assault the pinnacle" of local politics (Eisley 1995).

Fetzer was mayor for six years, mixing a young, energetic, and modern style with traditional conservative politics he had shown as an aide in Helms's National Congressional Club, a sophisticated and highly successful political organization that from its base in Raleigh used innovative media strategies to elect ideological allies to national office.[33] Fetzer's focus on low taxes and fighting crime and his personal appeal and significant skills as a political organizer helped make Republicans a force in the city for some time.[34] Paul Coble, who was first elected to the council with Fetzer in 1993, served as mayor from 1999 to 2001. As a nephew of Helms, Coble knew Fetzer well, and the two worked together closely. Coble went on to become chair of the Wake County commissioners in 2011.

In 1994, the year after Fetzer's first victory, Republicans took control of the North Carolina House for the first time in almost a century. They also won a majority of the state's U.S. House delegation and captured the seat centered in Wake, where former Raleigh city police chief Fred Heineman beat four-term incumbent David Price. The county was now quite clearly washed over by a Republican tide that had swept much of the South. Wake seemed to be especially suited to what commentators have called the "suburban strategy," after Richard Nixon's 1968 effort to appeal to southerners' conservative values without talking directly about race (Black and Black 2003, 210–22; Edsall and Edsall 1991, 74–98; Lassiter 2006, 225–41; Scher 1997, 101–6).[35] Whereas many rural North Carolina counties were drawn to the Republican Party's message on states' rights in the 1970s and 1980s (Christensen 2008, 203–7), Wake supported more pragmatic Republicans who placed an emphasis on economic, not social, issues (227–34). Most of its residents wanted low taxes but also seemed to support strong public education and were uncomfortable with any allusions to religion or skin color, however coded or faint.

In the inevitable splintering that resulted from such rapid growth of the state party, the county's Republicans more often than not sided with "corporate boardrooms" over "fundamentalist churches," drank "Chablis" rather than "sweet tea," and preferred Governor Holshouser and his supporters and protégés—including Senator Jim Broyhill and the other Republican governor of the era, Jim Martin, who won in 1984 and 1988—over Senator Helms and his (Christensen 2008, 230–32). This was no doubt largely attributable to the massive influx of people from outside the South. Of the roughly 20,000 people Wake County added to its population per year in the 1980s and 1990s, 12,000 came from elsewhere. According to the 2000 census, just five years earlier 18 percent of migrants had been living in a U.S. state other than North Carolina, and 4.5 percent had been overseas. Precise figures are difficult to obtain, but a large majority of those who moved into the county from out of state surely came from the Northeast and Midwest. The fact that they relocated mainly to places like Apex, Cary, and north Raleigh also helped suburbanize the county greatly. It was becoming the kind of place that, in Shafer and Johnston's analysis (2006), was making the South's politics much more like those in the rest of the country.

The Republican rise was fueled by an injection of capital as well as people. Probably nobody provided more financial support than local retail magnate and former state legislator Art Pope. Pope's family gave critical financial aid in the early 1990s to the John Locke Foundation, an influential right-of-center think tank based in Raleigh. Pope personally gave to Republican candidates for office and began to invest in the conservative and libertarian movements, as well as their ideas (Mayer 2011; Miller 2009). By 2010, estimates suggested he had been responsible for directing about $17 million in contributions to political causes (Christensen 2010).

By the mid-1990s the Republican Party was poised to shape the county's education policies. For the candidates it supported in the 1995 school board races, it constructed a semiformal platform of orthodox conservative positions like reduced busing and greater choices in assignments (Silberman 1995). After that election, Republican board members felt confident enough to push for greater power. Bill Fletcher, Bill Fisher, and J. C. O'Neal challenged the Democratic board members' choices for chair in 1995 and 1996. In 1997, with support from Fetzer and other local Republican leaders, candidates Robert L. Luddy and Stewart Joslin ran energetic campaigns that were critical of the board (Silberman 1997c).[36] Republicans also held a majority on the county commission in the late 1990s, and from his perch as chair of that body Gary Pendleton did much to coordinate the party's efforts to influence policy making at the local level, including on schools.[37] In 1999 State Representative Russell Capps's Wake County Taxpayers' Association and Chuck Fuller's North Carolina Citizens for a Sound Economy led the successful effort to defeat the $650 million school bond proposal. Candidates they backed took prominent businessman Tom Oxholm and influential sitting board member Wray Stephens to runoffs in that fall's elections. By 2003 the party had entered municipal government and nonpartisan elections with great vigor. It began formally endorsing candidates in local races as a matter of course. Its fund-raising and voter mobilization efforts were more professional and systematic as well.

Following a battle over the speakership of the state House in late 2002 and early 2003, North Carolina Republicans fell into what was essentially a civil war fought largely along ideological lines.[38] David Miner, who was in his sixth term in the House and had been a "pioneer" for the Bush 2000 presidential campaign, was defeated in a particularly divisive primary. In 2005 conservative Republicans—many of whom were connected to a group called Assignment by Choice, which opposed busing and a diversity policy in school assignments—supported Curt Stangler in an effort to remove Bill Fletcher from the school board. A Democrat-backed candidate, Eleanor Goettee, took advantage of the Republican infighting. Although opposition on the right had been muted in the 2000 and 2003 bond campaigns, in 2006 a loose coalition led energetically by Americans for Prosperity and western Wake parents upset by the expanded use of year-round schools fought vigorously against the $970 million proposal and very nearly defeated it (Hui 2006d).[39] By 2007 the county's Republican state legislative delegation featured Miner's conqueror, Nelson Dollar; Marilyn Avila, one of the John Locke Foundation's very first staff members; and Paul "Skip" Stam, the party's leader in the House—all widely considered to be staunch conservatives.

These efforts helped Wake County Republicans coalesce around a position on schools. As was the case across much of the country, social and religious conservatives took on issues like the curriculum and pushed for a loosening of restrictions on in-home instruction—by 2000, Wake had 1,400 home schools registered with the state—and freedom for charter, private, and parochial institutions (Deckman 2004, 10–30). Others to the right of center echoed positions taken by national conservative leaders on issues like performance testing and vouchers (Shober 2012). Bob Luddy, the 1997 school board candidate and local businessman, became an informal leader in this regard. He gave extensively to Republican and conservative candidates for local and state office. In 2007 Luddy opened a series of schools, called Thales Academies, based on Direct Instruction and "a curriculum infused with the values of our Founding Fathers and grounded by the Judeo-Christian and Greco-Roman heritage of Western Civilization."[40]

It was issues like busing, property taxes, and public school assignment that motivated most rank-and-file Republican and right-of-center residents of the county, however. The tremendous influx of population meant that schools were overcrowded and students regularly took instruction in trailers rather than in brick-and-mortar classrooms. New schools were built annually, forcing frequent reassignments of children. Roads and other public facilities became crowded, placing greater strains on social and family life. Much of the sense of community perceived by residents had eroded. The tremendous diversity and change in the population also likely reduced trust in government.[41]

Coming into the 2009 elections, Wake County Republicans were organized, funded, and motivated enough to take on what they perceived as a liberal board and its harmful policies. Their efforts were likely to resonate with large numbers of parents who lived in western Wake and north Raleigh and who held residual resentment against the board for its policies on reassignments and year-round schools. They were likely to be assisted by a general political mood stoked by the emergence of the conservative Tea Party movement (Skocpol and Williamson 2012; Zernicke 2010). Under the leadership of county chair Claude Pope, they had recruited energetic candidates with a singular coordinated message. The deep economic recession had intensified an antiestablishment mood and people's fears for their and their children's futures.[42] The era of consensus was over.

Conclusion

This fracture ultimately split the county open during and after the watershed 2009 election, when a new cohort of combative Republicans won a majority on the school board.[43] They worked assiduously, although not with rapid or complete success, to replicate the neighborhood schools model in Wake. They pushed out a recalcitrant superintendent and battled a ferocious backlash from supporters of the status quo.

Three main issues forced this divide: ad hoc and frequent reassignments of groups of children, the greatly accelerated and often mandatory use of year-round schools, and, of course, the system's general assignment policy itself. Although these issues did not mobilize the same sets of people and sometimes cut across recognized groups rather than between them, for the most part they divided more conservative and Republican residents who lived in western and southern Wake and north Raleigh from more liberal, Democratic residents who lived inside Raleigh's "Beltline." Citizens' groups that formed on both sides of the cleavage and business interests, although still largely in favor of Wake's diversity model, tried to find some common ground between them. As we shall see later, race, class, and gender played interesting and often un-recognized or counterintuitive roles in residents' attitudes about the conflict and the policies that had ignited it.

We explore the fracturing of the consensus in more detail in the next three chapters. We look first at the controversy generated by the general reassign-ment policy.

3 ▸ A Focus of Conflict I

WAKE SCHOOLS' GENERAL STUDENT
ASSIGNMENT POLICY

Intense disagreements about the conflicting cultural models of public education were a leading cause of the breakdown of Wake County's consensus in
the 1990s and first decade of the 2000s. On one side, many board members
and liberal activists from groups like the Great Schools in Wake coalition saw
diversity—effectively the status quo in the county for the twenty-three years
before the watershed 2009 elections—to be in the interests of each individual
student, as well as of the system collectively. They believed it was critical to a
strategy to elevate academic achievement, a goal stressed by the state during
the 1980s and 1990s through its investments in K–12 teachers and the development of new curricula, standards, and evaluation (Darling-Hammond 2010,
141–46). As we noted in chapter 1, liberals cited research that viewed heterogeneous schools as critical to academic success and meritocratic principles. Such
schools build social capital to benefit all children, but particularly those from
minority and lower socioeconomic backgrounds.

Around the turn of the millennium, however, there were concerted efforts
to repudiate these assertions. Conservatives advocated neighborhood schools,
stating the arrangements fostered a sense of community around children's educational experience, hence generating another form of social capital, one more
attentive to mutually reinforcing bonds between neighborhoods and schools.
Under this model, students do not waste time in transit and parents can more
easily play an active role in their children's schooling. They also pointed to
studies that find policy-mandated racial desegregation has no perceptible effect
on the educational performance of minority students and may, on occasion,
reduce it (Armor and Rossell 2002). Believing that good teaching explains a
significant proportion of a child's academic advancement that is influenced
by the classroom, conservatives found laissez-faire assignment policies, like
neighborhood schools, just as effective as others. They touted research that
demonstrated that mandated diversity can be counterproductive by accelerat-
ing "white flight" from communities (Orfield 1988; Rossell and Armor 1996).

By the late 1990s these opponents of activist assignment policies saw the federal courts coming to their side. U.S. district judge Robert Potter declared Charlotte-Mecklenburg's race-based busing policy illegal in September 1999, echoing conservatives' sentiments that diversity treated children not as "individual students but as cogs in a social experimentation machine."[1] More crucially, in *Parents Involved in Community Schools v. Seattle School District* (2007), the U.S. Supreme Court ruled that using race as the means of assignment was impermissible and that diverse schools and classrooms did not constitute a compelling state interest.

From Racial Diversity to Socioeconomic Diversity

Prior to 2010 the unified Wake County Public School System had implemented two general assignment policies for its students. Both were modeled on what proponents called "community" schools, where the community was operationalized as countywide and the idea that campuses with heterogeneous populations were most desirable. The first policy was race-conscious. In 1981 the county moved to assign children so that elementary, middle, and high schools had student bodies that were no less than 15 percent and no more than 45 percent minority—effectively meaning African American at the time, although by the end of the 1990s the calculation came to include, at least informally, Latinos as well. By 1998, 80 percent of schools had met this target. By 1999, only 21 percent of the county's African American students went to schools that were majority-minority. The policy made Wake somewhat unique in the South, where the number of African American children who attended schools where more than nine in ten students were minority grew by about 30 percent between 1988 and 2001 (Orfield and Lee 2005).

The initial diversity policy had two components. As discussed in chapter 2, the district established a magnet system so as to draw white students to schools in African American neighborhoods in Raleigh. These schools offered instruction that was attractive to many families, even though children often had to travel considerable distances and were not always provided with transportation. The policy's second part involved the busing of minority students to schools in white suburban neighborhoods—largely in north Raleigh and towns in the western part of the county. By 1998, 4,000 out of the approximately 25,000 minority students enrolled in the system were bused to schools in predominantly white neighborhoods so as to maintain the required racial mix (Hui 1999b).

This initial form of diversification faced, at most, muted opposition. The policy was effectively made by consensus and quietly administered by successive superintendents and their staffs. In 1999, however, the system initiated steps to overhaul it. That year, not only did Judge Potter issue his highly publicized ruling on Charlotte-Mecklenburg but federal courts also handed down decisions severely questioning the constitutionality of assigning children to public schools in Maryland and Virginia on the basis of their race (Boger and Bower 2001).[2] Other urban schools had already met the requirement of a "unitary" system and were therefore no longer subject to court-mandated racial desegregation orders.[3] Anticipating legal action to its policy, the Wake school board moved to use a different measure in student assignments. Initially established for magnet schools and then quickly applied to the entire district after January 2000, it adopted a policy of assignment by income rather than by race. It was an approach advocated by influential proponents of diversity such as the Century Foundation's Richard Kahlenberg (2007). The new policy set targets for schools to have no more than 40 percent of students receiving free or reduced-price lunches and no more than 25 percent reading below grade level. These figures were readily available to staff, thus facilitating policy implementation. All mention of race was stricken entirely from the formal policy. Superintendent Jim Surratt called it a "momentous decision" (Silberman 2000b).

Some African Americans worried their children would be affected as a result of the focus on income, and to some extent they were proved correct. The number of schools with greater than 45 percent of their population African American doubled in the years following the January 2000 decision (Houck and Williams 2010). Indeed, although on the surface the switch from race to economic standing seemed semantic—Cynthia Matson, founder of the advocacy group Assignment by Choice, spoke for many when she called the "economic diversity" policy "a proxy for race" (Finder 2005)—they were not identical metrics. Around 38 percent of the county's minority students were reading at or above grade level and did not qualify for free or reduced-price lunches, while 13 percent of whites performed below grade level and did qualify for such assistance.

The new assignment policy was not always easy to implement. The board found it difficult to meet targets as the number of students eligible for free and reduced-price lunches continued to increase (Epps 2007). But it seemed to have no immediate negative effects on academic achievement. In fact, data revealed that Wake County continued to make gains. In 1998, under the direction of Superintendent Bill McNeill, the county adopted what was billed as its "first-ever measurable goal for improved student achievement in the public schools" (Wake Education Partnership 2002). The endeavor was formally called "Goal 2003," and, using third- through eighth-grade end-of-year test data, it was to have at least 95 percent of students at or above grade level in reading and math.[4] Between 1998 and 2003 the proportion of white students in grades three through eight who were reading at or above grade level rose from 90.6 percent to 96.6 percent. The corresponding figures for African Americans went from 57.6 to 78.3 and for Latinos 66.5 to 78.2. Similar gains were made in math.[5] The scores were significantly higher than those of minority students in the Charlotte-Mecklenburg school system.[6]

Whether a function of the socioeconomic diversity policy or not, the schools' performance leveled off and then began to dip slightly after 2003 (Williams and Houck 2013). Wake's academic achievements were still strong compared to those in the rest of North Carolina, but its composite scores on the state's ABC program, based largely on end-of-grade testing, dropped; only 2.5 percent of schools were not meeting expected academic growth in 2003, while more than 14 percent were not doing so in the years between 2005 and 2008.[7]

Support for diversity in assignments, however defined, was evident in our conversations with some local elites and those most closely identified with this very public issue. Many pointed to the benefits it brought to children of both races and all socioeconomic circumstances. "In terms of their education and the knowledge that they [the students] are gaining and what is happening as a result of the busing, it has been positive," was a typical response from interviewees who supported diversity.[8] A former Democrat-affiliated school board member put it slightly differently: "I think the children from southeast Raleigh need to be exposed to other kinds of cultures, and I think our [middle-class] children need to be exposed to people from other areas; the research shows too that the middle-class children are not held back by having those experiences."[9] Such assets are said to extend beyond children's immediate educational experiences. As one liberal activist mentioned in a focus group, "By not educating their [white and middle-class/affluent] children in a diverse environment, when they go to work in places, wherever they may be, whether it is IBM or in a doctor's office or wherever, they are going to be at a disadvantage."[10]

Another mentioned the prosperous neighborhoods that the less affluent children might see on bus rides: "If those [less affluent] children did not ride the bus, they would not have the opportunity to see all the things that they would have an opportunity for in life and . . . get to talk to other people, then actually get invited to someone's house and then [become acquainted] with children that have all of those things." The activist also identified some of the "willing and brave" middle-class parents whose [children] "were invited to southeast Raleigh, Rush Street, where [less affluent] children were coming from, and it was like, [their children discovered that]'Wow, I did not know that everybody did not have what I had.' It was a real lesson."[11]

The Battle over Diversity

There had been antibusing entities—like the Concerned Parents Association in Charlotte—in many parts of the country since the early 1970s, but Wake County had not really seen them. Moreover, and as noted in chapter 2, most conservative candidates for school board prior to 2009 ran campaigns that emphasized right-of-center positions that were at best only tangentially related to the county's assignment policy—such as the efficient use of resources and curriculum issues. Ron Margiotta, the lone conservative voice on the board since 2003, was best known for his vigorous opposition to mandatory year-round schooling and tended to avoid discussions of diversity and neighborhood schools (Hui 2009d).

By the late 1990s, however, local critics of the diversity assignment policy began to organize. A number of groups, with names such as Assignment by Choice (ABC), Take Wake Schools Back, Wake Cares, and Wake Schools Community Alliance, were formed. Their positions varied—some emphasized parental choice, others favored neighborhood schools, still others maintained a broader critique of the school board—and they were of different sizes, functions, and effectiveness, but the underlying message was essentially the same. Wake County's school assignment policy needed to change, and families needed to lobby energetically for transformation and to support candidates who would bring it about. In 2003, for example, ABC joined with Christian conservatives to try to elect school board members who would push for neighborhood schools (Hui 2005). Two years later, three candidates expressly advocated for the neighborhood model, even if it was not the focus of their campaigns. One of these candidates, Horace Tart, a critic of the existing board majority more generally, won a seat. Another, Curt Stangler, lost largely because ABC had contributed to a civil war among Cary Republicans.

Our more conservative sources emphasized the themes of this effort. They were more in favor of neighborhood schools, and their comments reflected several different concerns. Some argued that long bus rides were bad for children. A conservative community leader said, "I see young children standing out there in the cold and dark at 6:30 in the morning, and it is totally obnoxious that any polite society would do this to the children. It is not safe, it is not fair, and it certainly is not fostering any good educational system; people generally want good schools close to home."[12] A conservative school board member in 2010 argued, "There seemed to be far too much busing going on, far too many people that were close to a school but were taking an hour and forty-five minute rides. Usually, in my van [that would be] thirty-five to forty minutes."[13] This basic position resonated with residents more broadly. A survey of Wake County residents we administered in March 2011 (introduced more thoroughly below) revealed that 62.3 percent of respondents "strongly agreed" that a bus journey of more than forty-five minutes was too long.

Other supporters of neighborhood schools worried about creating positive connections between children and education generally: "Really, if you think about elementary school, you know a lot of it is creating a love for school, and so if you are putting a heavy burden on a child and they are going to school hungry and they are having to get up extra early—you would think [this situation] would potentially, in some students, create more of a negative taste for education and send them down the wrong road."[14] The neighborhood model, it was argued, should also nurture strong relationships between the entire family and the children's school. "I do go back to when I was growing up," said one conservative activist. "We had ownership of our school system and we were proud of it. I don't get this sense of pride [here in Wake]."[15] When children live far away from where they are educated, another argued, "parents are unable to play the kind of role that they want to ... in their kids' schools. ... They cannot be in PTA; they cannot involve themselves."[16]

A number of diversity's opponents argued that the policy did not further the system's principal goal of providing children with a good education. One African American community leader stated, "I just don't think diversity, shipping kids around, really matters as much as them getting a good education, and at the end of the day, there is a job."[17] Several others believed the debate itself was detracting from the school system's basic responsibility. An African American parent at a focus group made this point when she said, "The child still has to know that two plus two equals four. I don't care—Democrat, Republican, independent, Tea Party. They have to get what they need, and our kids are failing and no one is addressing the issues. In my opinion they are busy—the chairman [of the school board] is trying to figure out who is going to win, who is going to lose, but our kids are the losers."[18]

Supporters of diversity, of course, had their responses to this emerging support for the neighborhood model. Some believed the effort was racially tinged and was designed to roll back years of progress. One white liberal activist put it this way: "It is not OK to segregate our schools. It is not OK to deliberately create high-poverty schools and claim that you are going to have all these fixes, whether it is funding or innovative programs, etc. It is just wrong, and that is why I am in this debate. My children will be fine regardless of where they go to school because I have the ability to make it fine for them, but not everybody has those resources, and it is not OK with me to leave other kids behind."[19]

A former top administrator in the schools suggested such pro-diversity sentiments were rare: "In fact, the real issue was not necessarily assignment; the real issue may be who is in my school that I do not want in my school, or who is in my neighborhood that I do not want in my neighborhood. But political correctness would not allow you to say it in those terms. The real issue was the fact that these kids from poverty, these minority kids, we don't want in our schools because in some ways they bring our property values down. So you are approaching it in trying to come up with solutions over here and the real problem is over there. Therefore you do not come up with solutions for that problem [race, poverty] because they are not telling you that is exactly what is going on."[20]

Analyzing Residents' Views of the General Assignment Policy

In March 2011, Public Policy Polling conducted a telephone survey of Wake County adults on our behalf. We posed numerous questions about Wake County public schools, including many on student assignment policies. The response rate was 8.1 percent for a total N of 1,706, a rate that is good considering the length of the survey and the fact it was automated. We oversampled African Americans and weighted the data in line with the county's basic demographic characteristics as revealed in the 2010 U.S. Census. Additional details about the survey can be found in the appendix.

We first explored the perception that positions in favor of diversity and neighborhood schools could be placed on a single dimension. Media coverage of the diversity debate after 2009 repeatedly referred to citizens as either favoring it or the neighborhood model of assignments. In late September 2009, for example, the region's most influential newspaper, Raleigh's *News and Observer*, presented the upcoming election as an opportunity to vote for candidates who would support neighborhood schools instead of the long-standing diversity policy (Goldsmith 2009a). After the election, there were frequent media references to "anger" as a sentiment that drove election results in changing the board majority from pro-diversity to pro–neighborhood schools (Goldsmith 2009b). In March 2010 the *News and Observer* reported the board had voted to end the school assignment policy based on diversity in favor of one based on neighborhood schools, explicitly juxtaposing the two approaches (Hui and Goldsmith 2010b).

We measured these sentiments using several survey questions. Four referred to support of *neighborhood schools*. Respondents were asked whether they strongly disagreed, somewhat disagreed, neither disagreed or agreed, somewhat agreed, or strongly agreed with the following: (1) "Having children in neighborhood schools makes it easier for parents," (2) "School bus rides over 45 minutes are too hard on young children," (3) "Children learn best when they attend school with children from their own neighborhoods," and (4) "I am willing to pay higher taxes to build more schools so more children can attend school closer to home." To measure support for *diversity*, we used another four items, two of which were "Children learn best when they attend schools that are racially diverse" and "Children learn best when they attend schools that are economically diverse." The other two items repeated this wording but referred to *classrooms* instead of *schools*. Again, responses were scored on the "strongly disagree" to "strongly agree" scale.

Contrary to conventional wisdom, statistical analysis suggests that two separate dimensions underlay these items, one for support for neighborhood schools and another reflecting support for diversity. Respondents' positions were not diametrically opposed and anchored at each end of a single continuum. Indices measuring survey responses to each component of these dimensions do reveal a negative correlation, but it is not especially strong ($r = -.398$, where -1.00 is a perfect negative correlation). As we shall demonstrate shortly, moreover, a quantitative model of attitudes about diversity did not provide results that were the mirror opposite of respondents' views on neighborhood schools.

How should this be interpreted? We believe that most Wake County citizens favored neighborhood schools. This may be because the model is traditional in our society or because they attended such schools when growing up. The attitude may also reflect sensitivity to the challenges that other schooling models present for contemporary families—especially those with limited reserves of social capital. Regardless, we believe a subset of the respondents who favored neighborhood schools as a cultural model also strongly valued diverse schools and classrooms. For these respondents, socioeconomic and racial diversity at school were important, even while they continued to believe that neighborhood schools provide advantages for children and parents.

The existing literature suggests who might favor and oppose the assignment policies derived from the two models. Considerable scholarship documents racial differences in support for diversity generally, with whites less approving than other races, despite some convergence over time (Bobo 2001; Schuman et al. 1997; Tuch and Hughes 1996). Older respondents may also be less supportive, given their political socialization occurred at a time when diversity was not as highly valued (Firebaugh and Davis 1988). We therefore would expect older and white respondents to be less supportive of diversity in children's school assignments.

We also would anticipate higher social class, as reflected in earnings and education, may provide some insulation from the issue of diversity in children's school assignments; individuals can rely on socioeconomic resources to promote their children's well-being and thus feel less concerned about the specifics of school assignment policies that may trouble parents of fewer means. Indeed, research has shown that because such policies result in greater competition for resources, lower-income whites oppose government efforts at racial integration more than do their wealthier counterparts (Branton and Jones 2005; Oliver and Mendelberg 2000; Taylor and Mateyka 2011). Elevated levels of education, moreover, are traditionally associated with more liberal racial views (Banks and Valentino 2012; Federico 2004; Sniderman, Brody, and Tetlock 1991; Sniderman and Piazza 1993). Thus we would expect wealthier and better-educated individuals to be more supportive of diversity as a basis for children's school assignments. We also would expect women to be more supportive of diversity as a basis for children's assignments than men (Howell and Day 2000; Hughes and Tuch 2003; Spanierman, Beard, and Todd 2012), especially in the South, where racial attitudes are more polarized between white men and women (Hutchings, Walton, and Benjamin 2010; Kuklinski, Cobb, and Gilens 1997).

We used several other measures in our analysis. All other things being equal, we would expect respondents with school-aged children to feel the perceived adverse effects of diversity—such as distant schools and the sharing of classrooms with lower-performing students—more than those without school-aged children (Hetherington 2005). Perceptions of the amount of busing for the purposes of socioeconomic heterogeneity might have motivated views about the assignment policy. As alluded to earlier, the district estimated that the percentage of children from the entire system who were bused to comply with the assignment policy was only around 3 percent. Presumably those who believe it is considerably larger than that are more likely to oppose diversity.

We also documented the extent to which the school assignment issue in Wake had become politicized. We would expect Republicans and conservatives to argue against diversity and Democrats and liberals more likely to support it. We therefore employed a measure of political ideology. Despite the fact that at the time of the survey the assignment policy was being administered based on socioeconomic diversity and not on racial diversity, it remained a racially charged issue. We therefore used a measure designed to unobtrusively capture whites' basic views of African Americans. Here we looked at attitudes toward Martin Luther King Jr.—an icon of expanded rights for African Americans—as a proxy for such attitudes (Griffin and Bollen 2009).

Other aspects of social organization in Wake County could also be consequential. We noted in chapter 2 that newcomers to the area often had different views of politics and public affairs. They were brought up in different social milieus. Just after the 2009 school board discarded the diversity policy, Steve Ford, an editor at the *News and Observer*, argued that the longer people had lived in Wake, the more supportive of the diversity policy they were. He wrote:

> If you had grown up in Wake County or elsewhere in the South, you had an on-the-ground understanding of how appalling it was for other Americans to be treated as second-class citizens. You saw how tolerance and accommodation worked to the community's benefit. Thoroughly integrated schools—a goal that Wake wisely had set for itself as it moved to a single, countywide school system in the mid-1970s—were a point of pride and a symbol of unity.
>
> If you moved here from the Northeast, you might have brought your own set of progressive values. But you would have seen racial tensions in your former home that were a corrosive force many communities were ill-equipped to deal with.
>
> The tendency back there was for municipalities to wall themselves off, typically on the basis of income. . . . It's not surprising that folks moving to Wake County from such places would bring with them a certain set of attitudes and expectations. And that when they got here, many would settle in the newer suburbs of Cary, Apex, Holly Springs and Wake Forest, if not the sprawling stretches of North Raleigh.[21]

Ford's sentiments reflected the pervasive perception that Raleigh's longtime residents were progressive on issues of race relations in ways that newcomers were not. His remarks constituted a thinly veiled reference to Republican school board members Ron Margiotta and John Tedesco, who had arrived in Wake from New Jersey relatively recently and who favored the neighborhood schools model. We included measures of the length of time a respondent had lived in Wake and the South to evaluate Ford's proposition.

We have shown that opposition to the diversity policy was thought to be particularly strong in the western part of the county while white citizens in central and east Raleigh had incentives to support it. Recall that diversification and magnets resulted in a material reduction in the proportion of poorer and minority children in central and east Raleigh schools and an increase in affluent and white children attending schools inside the "Beltline" that surrounds central Raleigh. The diversity policy therefore effectively made schools inside the Beltline more middle class. So we included in our survey indicators of whether or not a respondent lived in central and east Raleigh or in Apex, Cary, Holly Springs, Morrisville, Wake Forest, or north Raleigh, which we derived from respondent zip codes.

We also looked at the proportion of African Americans and Latinos who lived in a respondent's zip code. If white respondents who lived in neighborhoods with higher percentages of minorities tended to approve of diversity in assignments, we can demonstrate results consistent with what is called racial "contact" theory. As we noted in chapter 1, this states that repeated and meaningful interaction between individuals of different races reduces animosity between them. If, on the other hand, white residents of such neighborhoods tended to oppose the diversity policy, we might suggest there exists evidence for the theory of racial "threat," the idea that greater and more visible interracial competition for public resources results in antagonism toward African Americans.

We used two variables designed to capture the extent to which an individual's reservoir of social capital affected his or her attitudes toward school assignments. Consistent with our views on income and education, we would expect those with greater amounts of social capital to be more likely to support diversity and less likely to support neighborhood schools than those with fewer such resources. The first variable was the number of organizations to which a respondent belonged. Integration into the broader community through church, club, and other group membership has become an established indicator of social capital (Putnam 2000). The second was an index taken from three questions about the extent to which respondents trusted government at the federal, state, and local levels. High values were indicative of greater amounts of trust.[22] Our data, like those from earlier studies of the topic, show an individual's trust in all types of government to be strongly correlated (Wolak and Palus 2010). As Hetherington (2005) notes, moreover, trust in government is closely related to ideology—with liberals intrinsically more trusting—but it is theoretically distinct. Indeed, our indicators of trust and ideology are correlated only at −.282.

Finally, we added two explanatory variables in the second of the two specifications reported for this analysis. These were the total number of hours worked a week by the respondent and spouse, if applicable, and the length of their combined commutes in minutes. Both evaluated the basic proposition that residents with greater demands on their time and effort would be more supportive of neighborhood schools that make it easier for parents to involve themselves in their children's education. Longer commutes and work hours may limit family bonding as well as bridging to other community members.

Part of our analysis focuses specifically on African Americans. Although previous polls have revealed African Americans to be supportive of busing for reasons of diversity, as far as we know there has been no large-N survey and subsequent analysis of the determinants of minority attitudes about school assignment. This approach will permit us to compare the determinants of African American and white views of diversity and neighborhood schools.

Results

Table 3.1 reports the results of an ordinary least-squares (OLS) regression model of respondents' scores on the diversity and neighborhood schools indexes described above. The sign of the coefficient indicates the nature of the relationship of the measure with the outcome or dependent variable and is only reported when the relationship is statistically significant. Positive signs mean the outcome and measure move in tandem, a negative sign that they move in opposite directions.

The results of the diversity models are interesting and largely anticipated. Note that the diversity index ranges from 4 to 20 and has a mean of 14.45 and a standard deviation of 4.69. The most robust findings are generated by the measures of basic demographic characteristics, ideology, and racial attitudes. Younger residents, African Americans, women, those most approving of Martin Luther King, and liberals were much more likely to support diversity—indeed, the move up from liberal through moderate to conservative on a 3-point ideology scale resulted in a reduction of 1.73 points in the diversity index. Note also that respondents with children of school age tended to oppose diversity more so than those without them. This suggests that a respondent's proximity to the effects of the assignment policy was important. Perceptions played a role as well. The more inaccurate a resident's estimation of the percentage of Wake County public school students bused for the purposes of diversity, the more he or she opposed the assignment policy.

The second set of columns reports the results of an analysis where the dependent variable was support for neighborhood schools, or a respondent's score on that index. Like the diversity index it generated high values—the mean is 14.59, the standard deviation 3.8, and the range 4–20—suggesting a

Table 3.1 OLS Regression Predicting Diversity and Neighborhood Schools
(N = 1,706)

	Diversity		Neighborhood schools	
Variable	Model I	Model II	Model I	Model II
White	−	−	+	+
Female	+	+	NS	NS
Age	−	−	+	+
Has school-age children	−	−	+	+
Annual household income	NS	NS	−	−
Educational attainment	NS	NS	−	−
Length of residence in Wake	NS	NS	−	−
Lives in western Wake, etc.	NS	NS	NS	NS
Lives in central/east Raleigh	+	+	NS	NS
Neighborhood % minority	NS	NS	NS	NS
Conservative ideology	−	−	+	+
Very favorable toward MLK	+	+	−	−
Perception of busing	−	−	+	+
Number of organizations	NS	NS	−	−
Trust in government	+	+	NS	NS
Total household commute		+		−
Total household work hours		−		+

Note: (+) sign indicates that the relationship is statistically significant and positive, (−) indicates that the relationship is statistically significant and negative, and NS indicates that the relationship is statistically insignificant. If the cell is blank, the variable was not included in that model.

kind of natural approval for both diversity and neighborhood schools that is consistent with our argument that they do not form the poles of a single dimension.

We uncovered a series of important and interesting findings. First, on the whole, results demonstrating support for neighborhood schools do not mean diametric opposition to diversity. It is true that whites, conservatives, and those with children of school age supported neighborhood schools. Those who held King in high esteem opposed them. It is also interesting that those who inaccurately inflated the proportion of children bused for diversity purposes also favored neighborhood schools. We suggest this is a product of a post hoc justification for a position against diversity and for children attending schools close to home. Respondents may have been genuinely uninformed about the amount of busing undertaken in Wake but provided an answer to this survey question consistent with their view of the assignment policy arrived at from other experiences and attitudes.

Women, who were supporters of diversity, took a position on neighborhood schools that was indistinguishable from that of men. African Americans were opposed to the neighborhood model. This finding is consistent with many views expressed by African American participants at a focus group we held in February 2011. As we have indicated, several saw the battle over diversity as distant from their everyday lives and complained their children were being used as pawns in a political game between liberal and conservative white elites. Others showed support for neighborhood arrangements in principle, believing that the approach would be preferable if their schools were brought up to the standards of those in the suburbs.[23] The imposition of neighborhood assignments on their current situation generated almost universal disapproval, however. As one respondent put it, "Neighborhood schools mean the people that live in nice neighborhoods are going to always do better."[24]

Second, indicators of social capital had some robust effects. The length of commute and workweek variables performed quite well in both the neighborhood schools and diversity models. Respondents with longer work hours did indeed favor neighborhood schools, although the substantive effect was small, with a thirty-hour increase in the family's workweek resulting in just over a half a point increase in the neighborhood schools index. Interestingly, however, the total commute measure acted in the opposite way. It is possible that residents with lengthier commutes lived farther from schools anyway and already "priced in" their situation when considering the survey's questions. Those with shorter commutes balked at the idea of having to get their children to distant schools. Moreover, although organizational membership was not important to the diversity models, a greater number of affiliations tended to make respondents less supportive of neighborhood schools. Note also the effect of the trust in government measure. It is clearly the case that those who trusted government supported the diversity policy, although trust's effect on neighborhood schools was not significant. In fact, when all other things were equal, a move of two points up the government trust index scale resulted in an increase of nearly one point in the diversity index. An argument based on socioeconomic status is assisted by the fact that those with higher incomes and higher levels of education—and therefore greater resources to mitigate the negative effects of little time for family needs—were less supportive of neighborhood schools.

Note two other interesting findings. Whereas the length of time a respondent had lived in the county was unimportant to attitudes about diversity,

Table 3.2 OLS Regression Predicting Diversity by Race (*N* = 1,593)

Variables	Whites (*n* = 1,156)		African Americans (*n* = 437)	
	Model I	Model II	Model I	Model II
Female	+	+	+	+
Age	−	−	−	−
Has school-age children	−	−	−	−
Annual household income	NS	NS	+	+
Educational attainment	NS	NS	NS	NS
Length of residence in Wake	NS	NS	NS	NS
Lives in western Wake, etc.	+	NS	NS	NS
Lives in central/east Raleigh	+	+	NS	NS
Neighborhood % minority	NS	NS	−	−
Conservative ideology	−	−	−	−
Very favorable toward MLK	+	+		
Perception of busing	−	−	NS	NS
Number of organizations	NS	NS	+	+
Trust in government	+	+	+	+
Total household commute		+		NS
Total household work hours		NS		NS

Note: (+) sign indicates that the relationship is statistically significant and positive, (−) indicates that the relationship is statistically significant and negative, and NS indicates that the relationship is statistically insignificant. If the cell is blank, the variable was not included in that model.

those who had resided in Wake for a shorter period of time had a greater affinity for neighborhood schools. The result was the same when we substituted a measure of the length of time lived in the South in an unreported analysis. This suggests it was the resonance of that cultural model with the views and experiences of newcomers rather than any special aversion to diversity that is important in understanding the role of migrants in the school assignment debate. Second, whereas residents of central and east Raleigh supported diversity more than others, they did not oppose neighborhood schools particularly. We will discuss a possible reason for this below.

In Table 3.2 we separate white and African American respondents and reveal the results of specifications of their attitudes toward diversity assignment. The results in the first column, for whites, reveal few differences with the overall model. There was a positive King effect, which suggests racial animus influences attitudes toward diversity. Moving from the collapsed categories of "unfavorable" and "somewhat favorable" impressions of the civil rights leader to the "very favorable" category in a binary measure had the effect of pushing the average respondent up about two points on the diversity index.

White residents of central Raleigh showed considerable support for the diversity policy, even after accounting for other factors. The motivation for this is not entirely clear, although it may be that these residents were aware that the policy had the effect of reducing the proportion of poorer and minority children in schools near where they lived and of increasing it for suburban schools. In other words, support for a global diversity policy was in some ways merely opposition to heterogeneous schools for their own children. Newly elected and Democrat-affiliated school board member Jim Martin seemed to portray this position when he complained at a January 2012 meeting that under the assignment plan adopted by the previous Republican majority, his son's urban middle school would receive a larger number of minority students from a nearby elementary school (Hui and Goldsmith 2012).

It is also interesting that despite the perception that they were the policy's principal opponents, white respondents in western suburban towns, Wake Forest, and north Raleigh were more likely to support the diversity policy than those who lived elsewhere. Given that Raleigh city residents were also supportive, we can conclude that whites in other parts of the county—the southern and eastern, less affluent towns—were, in a relative sense at least, its strongest critics.

As with whites, the African Americans who looked on diversity most favorably were young, female, and liberal. Greater trust in government also predicted support for the diversity policy for both races. Four other findings about African American attitudes deserve attention. First, note that those who lived in areas with larger proportions of African Americans and Latinos tended to be less welcoming of diversity. It was from these areas that minority and less well off children were generally bused to suburban schools. Second and somewhat related, poorer African Americans were also relatively lukewarm on the policy. The income variable's performance may suggest that more affluent African Americans understood the importance of heterogeneous schools to their economic success and had greater capacity to pay the costs in social capital brought about by having their children receive education some distance away from home. Third, like their white counterparts, African Americans with children of school age were less likely to support the diversity assignment policy than those who did not have them.

Finally, African Americans who were immersed in public life as members of a relatively large number of organizations were much more supportive of diversity—for every organization an African American respondent was a member of, he or she rose nearly four-tenths of a point on the diversity scale. This is consistent with the argument about social capital's impact on attitudes about assignment. It also speaks volumes about racial differences in views about diversity. Whereas organizational involvement and affluence did not affect white attitudes, it was the more engaged and economically better off African Americans who supported the policy of purposive assignment to mix schools by race and income most vigorously.

Conclusion

After the two school systems in Wake County were unified in 1976, leaders pursued racial integration by setting targets that no school would have a student body that was less than 15 percent but no more than 45 percent minority. There was general consensus around the policy, implemented by using magnets to attract whites to central Raleigh and by busing minority children to majority white schools in the suburbs. In 2000 the standard shifted from race to socioeconomic status and achievement, such that schools would have no more than 40 percent of their students receiving free or reduced-price lunches and no more than 25 percent of them reading below grade level.

In the years before the 2009 election, the diversity policy, as it became known, began to attract opposition. Viewed as fair and beneficial to children of all backgrounds by many, it was increasingly criticized for undermining performance, forcing long bus rides on children, and limiting parental and community involvement in school by others. Some opponents formed groups to push for a general assignment policy based on the neighborhood model. Their cause was joined by conservatives and a strengthening county Republican Party. The diversity issue, as we will share in more detail later, became a centerpiece of the school board election campaigns in 2009.

Our quantitative findings, designed to help us understand what kinds of residents supported diversity and neighborhood assignments, are consistent with much of the popular assessments of the conflict. Women, African Americans, liberals, and younger individuals tended to be diversity's most ardent supporters. However, we also report results contradictory to conventional narratives and uncover previously neglected explanations for people's attitudes. Despite the media's characterization of the competing views of the general assignment policy, for example, support for diversity did not necessarily mean commensurate opposition to neighborhood schools or vice versa. Although newcomers to the county did approve of the neighborhood model more than longtime residents did, they were not materially less supportive of diversity. We show that perceptions of the existing scope of the assignment policy's busing greatly influenced people's views, and residents most directly affected by decisions about public education—that is, those with school-aged children—were most opposed to diversity and welcoming of neighborhood schools. Residents with lower levels of education tended, as predicted, to be more supportive of the neighborhood model. Again somewhat counter to popular perception, white residents in the western and northern suburbs were more likely to support diversity than those who resided elsewhere. Among African Americans, higher income individuals were particularly likely to embrace diversity. Greater reserves of social capital, as measured by indicators like commute length and trust, also caused citizens to embrace the diversity policy more strongly, while higher numbers of community connections discouraged support for neighborhood schools.

4 ▸ A Focus of Conflict II

ANNUAL STUDENT REASSIGNMENTS

One of the most dramatic consequences of Wake County's rapid growth in the 1990s and early 2000s—the number of residents under age eighteen increased from 100,000 in 1990 to about 260,000 in 2010 (U.S. Census Bureau 2010)—was the need to build new schools or add classroom space to existing facilities. As noted in chapter 2, the county was granted authority to borrow for expansion, mainly in the form of new construction, by voters who approved a number of bond issuances. But even though forty-four elementary schools, fifteen middle schools, and twelve high schools were added between 1991 and 2010, the school board struggled to keep up with the demand for seats. School board member Beverly Clark equated the effort in 2007 to pushing against a "tsunami" (Hui 2007).

The endeavor was hindered considerably by escalating land prices, especially after 2000 (Hui and Silberman 2006). Housing development policy that was frequently described as "sprawling," particularly in liberal quarters, compounded the problem of acquiring reasonably inexpensive real estate to build schools proximate to large numbers of potential students.[1] The county's different municipalities encouraged building to different degrees, and the process of securing land for housing was uncoordinated. With development the responsibility of municipalities and schools governed at the county level, residences were constructed with little regard to the geographic placement of existing public schools, and because subdivisions often concentrated residents of similar socioeconomic status, this posed significant problems for the system's diversity policy as well. Some campuses, moreover, were better able to expand physically than others. Newer facilities tended to have more land on which to place temporary structures, generally in the form of trailers—twenty were added to one north Raleigh facility alone (Silberman 2001, 146), and in 2004–05 there were 709 in total across the county.[2] This accelerated and uneven growth forced the school board to undertake yearly efforts to reassign children to different, but not always brand-new, schools.

The lack of capacity was particularly pronounced in the western towns and north Raleigh, where the county's new residents tended to settle, and it was these areas that experienced most of the annual reassignments. At first, in the early 1990s, the school board proposed reassigning around 1,000 students a year. By 1997 this had reached 1,800, and in the decade following 2000, the figure often exceeded 5,000 annually. In 2003 the board looked to other places for reassignments and moved 2,300 children who lived in Holly Springs, a town in southwestern Wake. As we shall see in the next chapter, the board's effort to move large numbers of schools to a year-round calendar only added to the number of students who had to be transferred every twelve months. In 2006 it reassigned 9,300 children and in 2007 moved another 10,760.[3] In 2008, just prior to the great rift in the county's school politics, the board suggested that more than 14,000 students be moved for the coming academic year.

The school system did attempt to mitigate the effects of annual reassignment. In 1997, as it was experiencing the first concerted resistance by affected residents, the board permitted some parents a limited choice among schools for their reassigned children. It also began capping enrollments at some schools, a strategy used repeatedly in the fast-growing areas of western Wake during the early 2000s (Hui 2003a). The intention, in the words of board member Bill Fletcher, was to shift "the burden of growth to those who choose to move into the area" and reduce the need to reassign currently enrolled students (Silberman 1997b). In 2002 policies were altered to allow more students selected for reassignment to remain at their current school so long as they could provide their own transportation. At the same time, a "grandfathering" calculus was utilized to avoid the movement of rising fifth, seventh, eighth, eleventh, and twelfth graders who had been at their current school for some time and were scheduled to age out of it relatively soon anyway (Hui 2002a). In December 2008 the board rather dramatically recommended changing the schools of more than 25,000 students over three years so as to terminate the annual reassignment process entirely. Under this revised model, no additional reassignments would be made until 2012. In 2009 it suggested the first group—6,500 students in total—should comprise only elementary-age children so as to minimize disruption for older students.

For many residents unsettled by the continual upheaval in their lives and focused on the education of their children, these efforts provided little consolation. In fact, there are numerous media reports of affected parents being deeply angered by reassignments. In 1996, for example, Walter Tote, a north Raleigh resident and parent of a student designated for transfer, emotively told the board, "I want you to come home with me tonight and explain to my child why he has to go to a different school" (Silberman 1996a). Such feelings were heightened in those who saw their children transported to schools that were farther away than their current one or who lived close to a recently built facility that was being utilized by newcomers to the county. A comprehensive online survey of Wake residents done by the school system in 2010 provides some hint as to why parents resisted the process and fretted about change. At a time when people were supposedly displeased with K–12 education in the county, 94 percent of the 39,000 respondents were "satisfied" or "very satisfied" with their child's school (Hui 2010a). This suggests that parents were pleased with their children's current situations but worried about change.

Although parents whose children were moved could appeal the transfers, the procedure by which this was done did little to assuage discontent. The board did grant many of these requests in formal meetings with appellants, but its decisions often seemed arbitrary. While for board members already dealing with an escalating workload in their part-time positions the appeals process was indubitably laborious, for parents it often seemed critical to the future success and current happiness of their children. To many pleading families, members seemed aloof, disinterested, and sometimes arrogant as they plowed through the many cases. Apex parent Karen Stiles told a reporter after she had appealed a reassignment decision, "They just come here and talk to us so they could say they listened to us. Did you see them talking to each other during the meeting? They weren't even paying attention" (Jordan 1995).

A lack of sympathy on the part of board members might have been attributable to what they considered reassignment's most obvious cause: unrestricted growth. Democrats repeatedly fought what they saw as excessive development at the municipal level, often to no avail. The result was a genuine effort to alleviate the consequences of growth but a certain unwillingness to accept responsibility for reassignment. As one former board member put it, "These children are jerked around from school to school because of population growth, and that is what it was. The busing was not intended primarily for diversity but just to fill in these schools, and I am sure we might have been able to do it better if we had had more time to think about it. There was a year I think we opened twelve schools. So, of course, when the school is built, we have to fill it, and in order to fill it you have to move children from nearby schools."[4]

Parents' sense of powerlessness was exacerbated by other characteristics of the reassignment process. Until late in the first decade of the new millennium, the communities and numbers of students affected did not form any kind of pattern. The data used by the board and the system's staff were not publicly available. Plans were also generally announced close to or after the deadline to transfer to a magnet school in the upcoming year (Hoxby and Weingarth 2006, 15). Not surprisingly, the uncertainty and opacity added to the general sense of unease.[5] Even the response to the announcement of the multiyear mass reassignment proposal made in late 2008 was negative. Before any list of designated transfers had even been discussed, board members and school system staff were quickly bombarded with e-mails and phone calls from irate parents (Hui 2008a). A conservative activist reported to us an extreme case of parents' reaction to reassignments: "Approximately sixty kids got reassigned [to a particular school], and . . . by the end of the year, only twelve of them were left. [The principal] literally said that she was having to call their homes on a regular basis and threaten legal action just to get those kids to school, and she had no idea what happened to the other forty-eight."[6]

Organized Opposition to Annual Reassignments

The board's strategy to "spread the pain" so that a number of communities shared the burden of reassignment naturally increased the geographical scope of the opposition to its policy. When a neighborhood's children were targeted for reassignment, parents often created organizations, with varying degrees of formality and effectiveness, to fight the decision. In 2007 and 2008, for example, parent groups formed spontaneously to oppose reassignments of children at the Davis Drive and Farmington Woods Elementary Schools in Cary (Hui 2008a). This activism was often assisted by municipal policy makers. Although Cary's efforts in 1993 to investigate ways of improving the reassignment process ended with a shrug and a faint appeal to the county commission for more money (Brown 1993), a decade later, under Mayor Ernie McAlister, Cary considered suing the school board on behalf of residents negatively affected by the policy (Hui 2003a). In 2002 the mayors of Apex, Cary, and Garner collaborated to form a thirty-three-member citizens' task force whose responsibility it was to advocate for fewer annual reassignments. Apex's mayor held a special meeting for residents concerned about transfer policies in January 2006. The goal was to coordinate an official town response in opposition to the school board's decisions on the issue. By 2009 numerous officeholders in suburban Wake municipalities were involved in a broad lobbying effort to reduce the movement of their residents' children between schools (Hui 2009a).

These groups and their views had residual effects. Entire neighborhoods were soured on the school board by their experience in the annual reassignment process, and a quiet opposition frequently remained after the original dispute receded. More important, the groups merged into others and later provided much of a sophisticated, potent, and programmatic opposition to the board. They fused their positions on annual reassignment with policy stances on diversity and year-round schooling that were also antagonistic to the status quo. Assignment by Choice (ABC), for example, was founded by Cynthia Matson in 2002 largely as a response to her personal experience with what she considered the ad hoc and irrational nature of the assignment process (Grant 2009, 129–31). ABC worked with disgruntled Apex parents in the same year to fight a student transfer plan in the town (Hui 2002b). It later became a staunch and effective opponent to both the diversity and mandatory year-round policies (Flinspach and Banks 2005, 277; Hui 2005). Although, as we shall see, better known for their battles against mandatory year-round schools, the Wake Schools Community Alliance and Wake Cares were also conceived in the general unhappiness that many Apex and Cary parents felt about the reassignment of their children. They later channeled their frustration into the broader effort to bring about change.

In fact, by the 2009 election, the annual reassignment issue had become closely tied to the diversity–neighborhood schools debate. This was not a fabricated connection. For many years, the system's promulgated policy was to reassign students in response to population growth and overcrowding so as to some extent recognize the importance of proximity to school but with the purpose of maintaining the system's fundamental goal of racial or, after 2000, socioeconomic diversity (Hui 2002b). As early as the mid-1990s there was a concerted effort by some on the board to prevent the granting of many reassignment appeals on the grounds that they undermined racial balance in schools (Silberman 1996b). Moreover, researchers have estimated that in a number of years the proportion of reassignments of low-income children to schools where relatively few existing students received free or reduced-price lunches was actually quite significant (Hoxby and Weingarth 2006, 14). In 2004–05, for example, more than 10 percent of the 4,500 children identified for transfer were to be sent from poorer neighborhoods in Raleigh to increase the number of poorer students at suburban schools in the western part of the county. In 2002 the board made its first attempt to use "reverse busing" in its assignment decisions. That year it proposed to transfer more than 100 students from Apex Elementary, most to Swift Creek Elementary around nine miles away where the student body was appreciably less well-off. After significant pressure from the parents of the reassigned students, the plan was abandoned.

The issues of annual reassignment and socioeconomic diversity were particularly intertwined for Garner parents. Residents of the town just south of Raleigh complained repeatedly to policy makers that their schools had become a target for annual transfers of low-income children so as to reduce the proportion of students receiving free or reduced-price lunches in parts of central Raleigh. With more than 50 percent of their children formally classified as low-income, some Garner schools in 2007 had a much greater proportion of such students than did the town's aggregate population. One leader of discontented parents, Paul Capps, estimated that over 3,000 Garner children had fled its public schools as a result—by choosing magnets in Raleigh, selecting private institutions, homeschooling, or changing residence (McMahan 2007). Perhaps unsurprisingly, Garner was to become an important place in the 2009 school board election.

The connection of the annual and broader reassignment policies was apparent even to affected parents whose children were moved for purposes other than socioeconomic heterogeneity. Many reassigned students were transferred to schools farther from their homes than their current school, often disrupting their friendships, family life, and general educational experiences. Moreover, the geographic nodes that identified where a school's attendees lived often seemed random and arbitrarily selected. They shifted constantly. In this light, the idea of schools with fixed catchment areas and attended by neighborhood children—a model continually juxtaposed with diversity—was tremendously appealing.

Annual Reassignments, Family Life, and the Worries of Citizens

The interviews and focus groups we conducted allowed us to gain some understanding of residents' views about annual reassignments and why they found frequent changes worrisome. From this and quantitative analysis of the survey data, we suggest three basic concerns that surrounded frequent student transfers within the Wake County school system, all of which help explain the unpopularity of the board's actions on this matter.

The first concern is that reassignments posed significant *challenges* to families, both parents and children. Often, the challenge was a function of proximity. As noted in chapter 3, long bus rides are generally viewed as detrimental to students' academic performance. As a former superintendent noted in an interview, "I was having a forum over at Moore Square Middle School and it was about 200 . . . predominantly African American parents . . . and I will not forget the parent who stood up and said, 'Well, we do not understand why we have to put our five-year-old on that bus and ride for an hour and twenty minutes to a school that is a [significant] distance from the house,' and they proceeded to talk about the hardships of things of that nature."[7]

Others also suggested that having children attend school far from home challenged their capacity to meet parental responsibilities. One African American interviewee recalled an unusual storm Wake County experienced on January 19, 2005. Although only half an inch of snow accumulated, icy roads and early dismissals created traffic delays of many hours. Some students ended up spending the night at their schools. She said, "But that assignment [plan], how far is [too far]? For the parent, how quickly can I get to my child? That was exhibited when we had that freak storm. How quickly can I get to my child in an emergency, from [my] workplace or home?"[8]

Distant schools can make it more difficult for parents to involve themselves in their children's education. Parents across the socioeconomic and political spectrum tied the notion of proximity to parental responsibility while also indicating consequences for students. A board member from the Republican majority suggested that it was single mothers who "are some of the hardest hit people" because "they don't have the help they would like from someone else."[9] A middle-class community activist said, "I remember [school board] election day of that October [2009], it was raining like hell. We were out early at six o'clock in the morning, and these kids were standing out here in the rain waiting to catch a bus, no shelters, you know. I never cared for it even when my kids were in [school]. I did everything I could to make sure that they went to schools in this community because I wanted to be able to go over there and jack them up if they did something wrong."[10]

The challenges posed by reassignment also include adjustment to new schedules, new cultures, and new relationships. Mothers and fathers instinctively understand the burdens placed on families and parenting during a child's transition as the result of family relocation or the promotion to middle or high school. When these costs must also be paid because policy makers have moved children to a new school, parents inevitably become resentful and resistant. Another activist parent spoke to the challenge inherent in multiple reassignments and how they led to parents being "burned out."[11]

The second view is that reassignments presented *dangers* to children's academic performance and social well-being. Much of this thinking was tied tightly to attitudes about diversity and neighborhood schools. Proponents of diversity felt minimal reassignments for the purposes of maintaining socioeconomic heterogeneity were clearly worth the cost, while opponents worried more about the costs to children from reassignments. However, even diversity's advocates were aware that repeatedly transferring the same children was detrimental to their education. This philosophy undoubtedly contributed to the policy of subjecting different towns and neighborhoods to reassignment each year and, in turn, to the inadvertent spread of anti-board feeling that contributed to the fracturing of the consensus described earlier.

Indeed, regardless of a resident's preferences about the general assignment policy, there was a clear concern that moving children from school to school on a frequent basis was not good for their education and social development. This is demonstrated by the views of an African American parent at a focus group: "I will use the word 'repulsive,' and the reason I say it is repulsive is because I am tired of all of this sitting on the backs of the children. . . . It is the children that you are busing; it is the children that you are manipulating. . . . It [should not be] on their backs to take the long bus ride or be pulled out of your class."[12]

The third concern was that the reassignment process created *uncertainty*. The process by which the system shifted children was complex. Staff generated proposals based upon previously established principles, and then the board considered them before promulgating its decision. Parents were presented an opportunity to make their case against their children's reassignment to the board. It is not surprising that when the diversity general assignment, magnet school, and year-round policies were appended to the annual transfer process, parents were extremely confused and, as a result, afraid of the entire seemingly byzantine and mysterious way in which the county matched children with schools. One liberal activist described the general feeling about the procedure: "People . . . do not understand exactly how students are assigned, how schools are run, when bell times are, how you get to exercise your choice that is available through year-rounds or magnets. You know, there are a lot of new people, a lot of frustration, and a lot of reassignment."[13]

The confusion was hardly alleviated by the system's propensity to alter the attendance areas, or residential nodes, for schools frequently and what appeared to be randomly. One involved parent stated, "The discontent that I was hearing was the unbelievable inconsistency in feeder patterns. People would not know from one year to the next where their kid was going to school, and not only would they not know where they were going to go this year, they did not even have a sense of, OK, well, you will go to this elementary school, this middle school, and then this high school. It switched with no rhyme or reason."[14]

Inevitably, there was also a pervasive belief that the process was opaque. A conservative activist said in an interview, "Even his [Chuck Delaney, assistant superintendent] closest assistant did not know how to decipher the algorithm that was set up in the computer [to determine] where these kids were going. It is a domino effect. You take one kid out, and [others are put in]. It made no sense. It was not manageable. You need something that is more transparent, easy to understand."[15]

From this came a feeling that the process was "rigged." In talking specifically about magnet assignments, one African American parent complained, "I got news for you, it [the magnet school lottery] ain't any open lottery. It has criteria after criteria as to whether or not you make the cut to even get in, and the biggest criteria is are you coming from a low F&R [free or reduced-price lunch] school."[16]

Who Worried Most about Reassignments?

In order to discern which residents particularly exhibited these concerns, we used the survey introduced in chapter 3 to ask questions about the challenges, dangers, and uncertainty of reassignments. We utilized two questionnaire items to measure the dimension of challenge: (1) "Reassigning children even once during elementary school creates challenges for parents," and (2) "Reassigning children even once during middle school creates challenges for parents." Notice that these two items both refer to the challenges that these assignment policies mean for parents, which underscores the importance of this issue not only to children's education but also for those who have responsibilities to manage households and provide for families. Four items reflected the concept of dangers: (1) "Reassigning children even once during elementary school inhibits learning," (2) "Reassigning children even once during elementary school inhibits child friendships," and (3) and (4), which are middle school versions of these statements. The final dimension reflected the uncertainty that the process of reassignment created for both children and families. Two items capture this concern: (1) "The uncertainty surrounding possible school reassignments creates problems for children," and (2) "The uncertainty surrounding possible school reassignments creates problems for parents." Interestingly, while 63 percent of participants were likely to somewhat or strongly agree that reassignments created problems for children, 82 percent gave the same responses when asked whether reassignments created problems for parents. These findings reinforce the claim that adults' preferences about transfers were shaped as much by what these policies meant for parents—who were often managing both work and family—as by their implications for children's learning and social well-being.

We deployed what is essentially the same model used in chapter 3 to examine the determinants of residents' attitudes about the challenges, dangers, and uncertainty of reassignment. We added a binary variable to denote whether or not a respondent had a child who had been reassigned to a new school outside of the usual process of moving or promotion. Our expectations were that residents with relatively large pools of social capital were more likely to be tolerant of reassignment and not as concerned about its challenges, dangers, and uncertainty. We also expected that respondents with children of school age would feel more threatened by reassignment and, because of the issue's politicization throughout the previous decade, that conservatives would be particularly sensitive to its effects. It may be that African American respondents equated reassignment with efforts to diversify schools and therefore were less opposed to it.

We paid particular attention to the role of gender in these analyses. Recall that in chapter 3 we found that women were more supportive of diversity as the basis for the county's general assignment policy, while men and women were equally supportive of neighborhood schools. Prior research suggests that the work involving parental decisions regarding where children go to school is highly gendered and supports an expectation that mothers take on more of the burden of managing children's assignments than do fathers (David, West, and Ribbens 1994; Gewirtz, Ball, and Bowe 1995; Reay and Ball 1998). Some scholars argue mothers' liability for deciding where children go to school is part of women's "total responsibility" for their offspring's emotional, social, physical, moral, and intellectual development (Griffith and Smith 1991). A man, on the other hand, is more likely to view his participation in paid employment as his primary responsibility and school choice as one aspect of caregiving that is his wife's duty or, in the case of divorce or more informal partnership, his children's mother's responsibility (Reay and Ball 1998). As a result, when parents are in a position to affect school placements, where children end up may reflect the extent to which women are engaging in "good mothering."

As such, we believe it is often mothers who exert the most labor in becoming informed about schools through informal social networks, by visiting campuses and websites, and through the use of other strategies to maximize their children's opportunities as well as to quell anxieties about their well-being—or what Hochschild (2000) refers to as the "emotional ecology" of women's care for children (Reay and Ball 1998). Based on these arguments, we expected women in Wake County to be more likely than comparable men to perceive the challenges in managing children's school assignments, to worry about the dangers to child learning and friendships from reassignments, and to perceive uncertainty surrounding the process of reassignment.

Table 4.1 OLS Regression Predicting Challenges, Dangers, and Uncertainty of School Reassignment (*N* = 1,706)

Variable	Challenges	Dangers	Uncertainty
White	+	+	+
Female	+	+	+
Age	NS	NS	NS
Number of school-age children	+	+	NS
Has a child reassigned	NS	NS	NS
Conservative ideology	+	+	NS
Annual household income	–	–	–
Educational attainment	–	–	–
Total household commute	NS	NS	NS
Total household work hours	NS	NS	NS
Number of organizations	NS	NS	NS
Trust in government	–	–	–

Note: (+) sign indicates that the relationship is statistically significant and positive, (–) indicates that the relationship is statistically significant and negative, and NS indicates that the relationship is statistically insignificant.

Table 4.1 shows the results of the model when applied to the challenges, dangers, and uncertainty indexes. The method is again OLS, and increases in the outcomes mean that respondents perceived greater levels of challenges, dangers, and uncertainty.

The results of all three specifications of the model are very similar. The first thing to note is that, as expected, women were considerably more likely to perceive the challenges, dangers, and uncertainty of reassignments. When all other measures were held constant, being female accounted for a 0.33-point increase in the challenges index (range 2–10, mean 7.81, standard deviation 2.22), a 0.63-point increase in the dangers index (range 3–15, mean 10.84, standard deviation 3.40), and a 0.65-point increase in the uncertainty index (range 2–10, mean 8.23, standard deviation 1.95). Whites were also more concerned. As we noted, this might be because minority respondents saw reassignments in terms of the costs necessary for diversifying schools and therefore had greater tolerance for paying them. All other things being equal, a white respondent was likely to score 1.28 points more on the dangers index than his or her African American counterpart.

Whereas coefficients of the measure of time spent at work and commuting never reach a level of statistical significance, the performance of the education and income variables suggests that those with socioeconomic resources were better equipped to meet the demands of reassignments. For example, the higher a respondent's education, the less worried he or she was that transferring schools could undermine a child's academic performance and social well-being. A respondent who graduated from college could be expected to score 1.64 points lower on the dangers index than one who did not graduate from high school.

The performance of the number of school-aged children variable is interesting as well. It makes sense that the more children a survey respondent had, the greater the sensitivity to the costs of reassignment's challenges and dangers. A hypothetical addition of three children to a respondent's household moved him or her up a full point on the dangers index. The variable is not statistically significant in the model of uncertainty, though. The same results are generated by the ideology measure, with conservatives being less willing to accept challenges and dangers but showing no demonstrable effect of ideology on uncertainty. These findings might suggest a greater concern with the outcomes of reassignments than with the process by which they are made—although, as noted earlier, conservatives were frequently keen to point out the lack of transparency in the board's policy making in the years leading up to 2009.

The indicator of whether a respondent had experienced a student transfer previously had no measurable effect. It may be the case, therefore, that parents anticipate that the costs of reassignment relative to any benefits will be greater than they actually turn out to be. As we saw earlier in the chapter, the vast majority of Wake County residents approved of their child's current assignment, regardless of how it came about. Alternatively, already reassigned parents might have believed they were less likely to be candidates for transfers in the future and, having already paid these costs, viewed the issue as purely hypothetical.

Trust was also relevant. It is clear that although citizens do not receive insulation from building connections via organizational memberships, higher levels of political trust reduce concerns about challenges, dangers, and uncertainty. Again, as with mandated assignment to diversify schools, those who trusted government were more willing to allow it to direct transfers of students between schools.

Table 4.2 permits additional understanding of racial differentiation in perceptions of challenges, dangers, and uncertainty. Two findings are in common by race. They also hold across all three measures. First, women of both races were markedly more concerned about challenges, dangers, and uncertainty than were men. We interpret these findings to suggest that women of both races were exercising significant "emotional capital" surrounding children's school assignments (Allatt 1993; Bourdieu 1998; Nowotny 1981). Note from chapter 3, however, that women support diversity more than do men. Despite

Table 4.2 OLS Regression Predicting Challenges, Dangers, and Uncertainty of School Reassignment by Race (N = 1,593)

Variable	Challenges		Dangers		Uncertainty	
	Whites	African Americans	Whites	African Americans	Whites	African Americans
Female	+	+	+	+	+	+
Age	+	–	NS	NS	NS	–
Number of school-age children	+	NS	+	NS	NS	NS
Has a child reassigned	NS	NS	NS	NS	NS	NS
Conservative ideology	+	–	+	NS	NS	–
Annual household income	NS	–	NS	NS	NS	NS
Educational attainment	–	–	–	–	–	–
Total household commute	NS	NS	NS	NS	NS	NS
Total work hours	NS	NS	NS	NS	NS	NS
Number of organizations	NS	NS	NS	NS	NS	+
Trust in government	–	NS	–	NS	–	NS

Note: (+) sign indicates that the relationship is statistically significant and positive, (–) indicates that the relationship is statistically significant and negative, and NS indicates that the relationship is statistically insignificant. Whites (n = 1,156); African Americans (n = 437).

their greater concerns about the costs of reassignment, women tend to believe in diversity more strongly.

Second, higher levels of education appeared to insulate respondents of both races from these concerns. We infer that those with more education had greater understanding of the intent and implications of assignment policies and were willing to tolerate their implementation because of that understanding. In addition, these respondents may have had greater resources to use in managing the challenges and uncertainty that implementation entails. Higher-income African Americans were less worried about challenges than their lower-income counterparts.

In contrast, additional findings point more strongly to racial differentiation in policy attitudes. Greater trust in government provided insulation against perceptions of challenges, dangers, and uncertainty among whites but not among African Americans. Older white respondents were more concerned with challenges, while younger African Americans were less concerned with both challenges and uncertainty. Higher numbers of school-aged children increased white perceptions of challenges and dangers but had no effect among African Americans. Among whites, conservatives tended to exhibit these worries; among African Americans, liberals did so.

Conclusion

Annual reassignments contributed greatly to the conflict over Wake County schools that erupted so dramatically in 2009. They often involved thousands of students and, over the course of two decades, affected many neighborhoods. They came to be viewed as an intrinsic feature of the diversity policy, and residents often felt incapable of anticipating them and powerless to prevent them once they had been announced. Many residents believed reassignment plans to be arbitrary in their formulation and callous in their execution.

We argue that residents viewed the annual reassignment process as presenting three types of problems, those that we call challenges, dangers, and uncertainty. Challenges refer mainly to the perceived costs felt by the families as parents had to deal with disruption and new routines, although parents also discerned challenges for their children. By dangers we describe the perceived effects on children's school lives and academic performance. Uncertainty may reflect the capriciousness and opacity of the reassignment procedure and the randomness of its outcomes, about which Wake County residents frequently complained. It also reflects the burden families felt during the prolonged process of moving groups (or nodes) of children between schools.

Our analysis of who held these views demonstrates that, as for demographic characteristics, it was less-educated poorer women with larger families who were most sensitive to the costs of reassignment. Conservatives, who had increasingly viewed the annual reassignment policy as a critical failure on the part of the Democrat-controlled school board, were concerned about these issues too. Perhaps viewing reassignments as a necessary condition for diversification, African Americans tended to be more tolerant of school transfers than their white counterparts—although our qualitative evidence suggests that some African American parents did worry about the burden that reassignments placed on their children. Finally, higher levels of trust in government reduced concerns with reassignment, again suggesting this form of social capital helped residents accept and absorb the burdens of Wake's active assignment policies.

5 ▸ A Focus of Conflict III

YEAR-ROUND SCHOOLS

The rather ad hoc annual reassignment process was just one strategy used by the school board to manage explosive growth and resource constraints. Another more innovative and possibly politically consequential response was year-round schools.[1] Following an investigation of the benefits of year-round schooling in the mid-1980s, Wake County opened its first such campus, Kingswood Elementary, in 1989–90. Initially conceived as part of the broader magnet program, year-round schools split their classes into four "tracks" or schedules; at any one time, all students on one of the tracks are out of school. The effect is to create a calendar in which the school year is divided into quarters with roughly four nine-week sessions punctuated by four three-week breaks. All students receive time off over Christmas and New Year's and a week over Independence Day to allow their movement between grades. High school athletics and the other personal and academic demands on older children mean Wake County operates year-round exclusively at the elementary and middle levels. However, the school board did slowly establish what is called a "modified" calendar for a small number of magnet schools such as Southeast Raleigh High. These schedules reduce the length of the summer and increase the number and duration of breaks throughout the year but do not place students on multiple tracks.

The research on the academic effects of year-round schooling is mixed. Downey, von Hippel, and Broh (2004) demonstrate that gaps in achievement between certain demographic groups of students widen during lengthy breaks. Some policy makers in Wake seemed also to have been influenced by work done in the 1990s that showed that children learn better under the year-round calendar, presumably because they needed to spend less time reviewing material and sharpening skills lost over the summer (Alexander, Entwistle, and Olson 2007; Cooper et al. 1996; Kneese 1996). Additional research, however, has suggested that these gains are negligible at best and that no individual demographic subgroup benefits from the year-round schedule (McMullen and Rouse 2012).

Regardless, the principal reason year-round schools were introduced in Wake County was economic. Such campuses cost about $100,000 more a year to run because of the additional pay for support staff and expenses for maintenance, but on a per-child basis they are significantly cheaper than schools that use a traditional calendar (Hui 2009c). By operating throughout the summer, a year-round facility can accommodate around 25 percent more students.

At first, year-round schools grew slowly in the county. In the decade following their introduction at Kingswood, several opened with or phased into multitrack schedules, including West Lake in Apex and Durant Road in north Raleigh, where new year-round elementary and middle schools were constructed almost side-by-side. In the mid-1990s Green Elementary and Wilburn Elementary in Raleigh were the first to be converted from traditional to year-round magnet schools. It was not until 2006, however, that the schedule became a hallmark of Wake County. In the 2006–07 and 2007–08 school years, eight new year-round schools were opened and twenty-one converted from the traditional calendar. By 2009–10, 29 percent of all Wake County students and 41 percent of those enrolled in elementary and middle schools went year-round.

The approach had become controversial long before then. Initially, the dispute was not about the calendar but about the demographic character of the student bodies of year-round schools. Year-round schools were considered to be magnets, and as such parents applied to have their children admitted to them. Students were usually not assigned on the basis of residence, a process that would have allowed the district to apply its diversity rules.[2] The result was that throughout the 1990s students at year-rounds were disproportionately white and affluent. Three factors seem to have contributed to this. First, minority and low-income parents were uninterested in traversing the application process or, as sometimes suggested in news reports, found the costs of child care outside of the summer prohibitive.[3] Second, minority and low-income parents were likely deterred by the location of new year-round campuses in the fast-growing suburban parts of the county, such as Adams Elementary in Cary, Jones Dairy Elementary in Wake Forest, and Lufkin Middle in Apex. For many, the prospect of providing transportation—busing was not guaranteed—to magnet schools some distance away was tremendously unappealing. Finally, some observers suggested that white middle-class parents deliberately chose year-round options because they knew such schools would have few minority and low-income students. In fact, there was such strong competition for open slots that in 2005, 29 percent of applications for year-round schools were rejected (Hui and Goldsmith 2010). One former school board member put it this way: "When we started the year-round program as a voluntary program, lots of people opted out of traditional schools that had high numbers of children that did not look like their own, which reduced diversity in those schools and created these little primarily white islands in the school district. The schools that those students and families left were incensed by that."[4]

With an eye to the broader diversity policy, some on the school board began to fret publicly. John Gilbert remarked as early as 1992, when only five application-only year-rounds had opened, that operating such schools "on a voluntary basis" had "complicated desegregation" (Silberman 1992). Superintendent Jim Surratt observed in retrospect that "there's no question year-round schools were becoming an avenue for some parents to avoid desegregation" (Silberman 2001, 156).

The board's response was to change the policy so they could steadily assign year-round schools to children from neighborhoods that were disproportionately minority or low-income. Between 2001 and 2005, nine existing year-round elementary and middle schools were given "base" students in addition to their successful applicants. The assigned or "base" students tended to live some distance from their schools and were minority or low-income. Timber Drive Elementary in Garner, for example, began receiving English as a Second Language (ESL) Latino students from Raleigh in 2001 (Hui 2001). At the time, the proportion of its students receiving free or reduced-price lunches had fallen below 9 percent, whereas the figures at most neighboring schools on traditional calendars were above the system's high-end target of 40 percent (Silberman 2001, 157). By 2005 the board's policy had narrowed the dramatic differences in the populations of traditional and year-round schools. In that year 21 percent of the county's year-round school students were low-income compared to 27 percent of the entire population. As we shall see, critics of the school board soon came to understand the strategy.

Not all affluent white parents embraced year-round schools, though. Most schools on the new calendar were opened as such, and because population growth was largely in the suburbs, places like Apex, Cary, and north Raleigh housed appreciably more of them. By 2001–02, of the twelve year-round schools, only one was proximate to downtown Raleigh and the poorer and minority neighborhoods of the southern and eastern parts of the city. That August, the board moved to convert existing traditional calendar schools in more heterogeneous neighborhoods so as to diversify the aggregate student population in year-rounds. Board members soon discovered, however, that opening new schools on the alternative calendar was considerably easier than conversion when they targeted two schools, Stough Elementary and Carroll Middle, for the year-round schedule. Stough had a student population about one-fifth ESL and one-third on free or reduced-price lunches, while Carroll had considerably fewer ESL children but slightly more with low incomes. Both sit just north of the Raleigh "Beltline," a kind of unofficial boundary between the city and suburbs. Faced with intense opposition from the schools' more well-to-do parents, the board backed away from its proposal and ultimately abandoned it (Hui 2001).

The Stough and Carroll episode stung, but with population growth escalating and the system unable to construct new schools to keep up, the board and its staff were forced to revisit the conversion issue three years later. In the fall of 2004 the system's policy makers floated an idea to convert up to thirty-six elementary schools to the year-round calendar, an effort quickly abandoned in the face of public opposition. In June 2005 the board offered a new, but marginally more modest proposal to convert "only" twenty schools to the year-round calendar. They planned, however, to assign students to them while providing their parents with no feasible alternative traditional-calendar placement in the public school system. It was pushed more forcefully than the original plan and undertaken with a significant move to separate year-round schools from the magnet program. The board concluded that Wake schools had reached their capacity, and a new strategy was required to keep up with population growth. Administrators believed they were approximately 9,600 seats short of what was required for the 2007–08 school year (Hui 2006a). As member Patti Head explained at the time, economic and demographic realities meant the county "may have to shift from traditional schools being the backbone to year-rounds being the backbone" (Hui 2005).

The result was that in 2006–07, four year-round schools opened with both designated and applicant students and one with designated students only. In 2007–08, twenty-one traditional schools were converted to the year-round calendar with assigned students only. This sea-change effectively constituted mandatory year-round schooling in many neighborhoods in the county's suburban communities. Parents recognized that this new system left them with unappealing choices: they had to either send their children to a year-round school or have them go to a traditional one, often with an unattractive starting time and long commute. One parent who campaigned energetically against year-rounds said in an interview, "For example . . . they converted the school Salem Elementary [to year-round], which had a starting time of . . . 9:30 a.m. So they made their 'opt out' school Davis Drive Elementary, which had a starting time of 7:30 a.m. So kids from Raleigh would have to get on the bus at . . . six-something in the morning."[5]

Organized Opposition to Year-Rounds

Indeed, there was significant resistance from many who were affected by the new policy. Groups of parents formed rapidly to protect the traditional calendar at their children's schools. The most active and influential, like Stop Mandatory Year-Round, Wake Cares, and Save Our Summers Wake County, were located in Apex and Cary. Leaders such as Allison Backhouse, Kathleen Brennan, Dave Duncan, and Patrice Lee organized similarly situated parents and assiduously worked to influence public debate about the issue of year-rounds. They soon found an advocate in board member Ron Margiotta of the eighth district, which covered Apex, some of Cary, and Holly Springs; he increasingly became a vocal, if lone, opponent of the majority and its decisions on year-rounds (Hui 2009b). They also received some support from the Republican-controlled county commission. In January 2007 the commissioners rewrote the spending plan for the bond issuance approved the previous fall by Wake County voters so as to speed up the construction of new schools and undercut the board's argument for year-rounds. Once they realized their new plan would increase aggregate costs for the projects promised in the bond, however, the commission reversed itself (Beckwith 2007). Still, the episode was a reminder of the burgeoning antagonism between activists and Republican local officials on one side and the school board on the other.

There were several arguments that sustained the movement against mandatory year-rounds and attracted numerous allies among the county's residents. The first was unfamiliarity with the concept of this kind of school calendar. One focus group participant noted, "At this engagement meeting where I was in February 2010, citizen after citizen came up and said, 'I do not want mandatory year-round, I moved here four years ago from so-and-so, I moved here three years ago, I moved here six years ago.' All these folks had moved here since 1999 [and] did not understand why we had year-round schools."[6] Like the diversity assignment policy, year-round schools clashed with the traditional neighborhood model so ingrained in newcomers to the county.

Another argument stemmed from the *requirement* that children attend year-round schools. A conservative activist noted, "I . . . ran across very few people that said they like mandatory year-round. I ran across people that liked year-round schools, but as soon as you put 'mandatory' in front of it, nobody is going to say that they like it."[7] Another referred to how the change to year-round schools was "unsettling" for parents: "I think their [parents'] attitudes were somewhat hardened by the year-round. So first, we [the schools] are going to move [to] year-round, and then we [the schools] will put your kids in different tracks. . . . So when you combine all of those things together it is unsettling for parents. They began to think, 'What is the school doing to us? We are allegedly getting a free public education, but we are paying a high price to get it.'"[8]

In addition, there was the sentiment that the board was deliberately picking on suburban schools in the western part of the county. The feeling was, in the words of one opponent, "Just because I happen to buy a house here, why am I the one that is forced into this situation?"[9] Of the eighteen elementary schools switched to a year-round calendar in the mass conversion of 2007–08, six were in Apex and Cary and another two in southwestern parts of the county— Fuquay-Varina and Holly Springs. None was inside or near the Beltline, which for many suburban conservatives had come to symbolize a bastion of white liberal elitism.

The final argument focused on the calendar itself. Some parents worried about losing family and vacation time during the summer and about managing personal lives with the possibility of several children on different academic schedules (Hui 2005). More forcefully, several critics of mandatory year-round schools suggested at the beginning of the large transformation in 2006 that the policy would bring about mass retirements and resignations from teachers unhappy with their new schedules. A poll taken in May 2006 showed that 20 percent of teachers would contemplate leaving if they had to work on a year-round calendar (Hui 2006b). Opponents also predicted that parents and children would leave for private schools or move out of the county entirely to seek public schooling elsewhere. Many of them argued that the board should ask for the bond scheduled in the fall of 2006 to be increased so as to accommodate the accelerated construction required to maintain traditional calendars as an option for parents (Hui 2006c). None of the dire forecasts proved correct, however. Despite the intervention of the financial crisis in 2008, population growth continued after 2006, albeit at a reduced rate. Teacher turnover rose marginally immediately following the implementation of the policy, but in the next few years elementary and middle school turnover rates settled at levels lower than they were for high schools, none of which utilized the year-round calendar (Jackl and Lougee 2012).

Wake Cares pursued an additional strategy to prevent the institution of mandatory year-rounds: in May 2007 it sued to prevent twenty-two schools from converting to the calendar as the board had proposed for 2007–08. The suit, arguing the board's policy was in violation of state law, was initially successful. Superior court judge Howard Manning Jr. ruled in May that students did not have to attend year-round schools unless a parent provided "informed consent." In response, the system sent letters to 30,000 parents with students assigned to year-rounds asking them if they wanted their children to remain at their designated school. It stated, however, that the administration could not provide details of students' traditional calendar options should the parents decide they did not want their children to attend the original year-round. The uncertainty over alternative placements caused significant consternation and heightened criticism from mandatory year-round opponents (Hui 2007). Of the families given the option of declining the year-round assignment, only 2,771 took it (Hui 2008b). Interestingly, and to the concern of proponents of the diversity policy, although roughly 90 percent of parents effectively granted their consent, of those who did not, 65 percent had children receiving free or reduced-price lunches (Hui 2009b). The following year, an estimated 1,700 families scheduled to go to year-round schools took preemptive action and decided to go through the formal application process to secure another assignment for their children in magnet programs rather than submit themselves to the "opt-out" process and an uncertain traditional calendar alternative (Hui 2008c).

The school board appealed Manning's ruling, and in May 2008 the decision was overturned. With the system now legally able, at least in the short term, to assign students to year-round schools without parental consent, it immediately stated it would honor only existing, and no future, opt-out requests (Hui and Epps 2008). Wake Cares responded by taking the appellate court's decision to the North Carolina Supreme Court. In a 5–2 decision made public in May 2009, the high court confirmed that the system did not require consent from parents to assign children to year-round schools. Now that mandatory year-round opponents realized their only recourse was to change board policy through political means, the verdict served to motivate them for the upcoming October 2009 election.

Despite the failure of the Wake Cares lawsuit, the mandatory year-round policy faced headwinds, even before the transformative election of the fall. The financial crisis and resultant recession that began in 2008 tempered the influx of newcomers to the county somewhat. This altered projections about the need for seats. Board members also continued to worry about overcrowding in traditional schools and the disproportionately high number of low-income students enrolled there. In March 2009, even before the state supreme court's ruling, Ron Margiotta was able to secure the support of three colleagues for a proposal to begin converting some year-round schools back to the traditional calendar (Hui 2009b). His narrow one-vote defeat suggested there had been a significant rethink about the policy among many in the leadership of Wake County schools.

The opponents of mandatory year-round schooling were hardly political professionals, but they proved adept at bringing media attention to their fight and fusing it to a burgeoning and broader push to stand up to the board and its policies. The new calendar was certainly the gateway into the movement for many. As one conservative activist put it, "My wife and I both actively spoke out against mandatory year-round schools, and that is how we started to meet up with some of the other schools' dissidents."[10] In Margiotta and some municipal policy makers, particularly on the county commission and on Apex and Cary town councils, the activists found influential allies. Soon issues of the mandatory year-round calendar, diversity, and annual reassignments and the loose but increasingly formal organization that had grown were beginning to galvanize many Republicans and conservatives into a cohesive bloc. It helped that the connections between issues were obvious to many in the expanding movement. As a leader of Wake Cares put it, mandatory year-round schools raised "many flags" for people, leading them to ask, "What was driving this need to convert so many schools in one isolated area?" The answer for many was the assignment policy, or in this individual's words again, "the need to reach our 40 percent threshold of diversity."[11]

Those involved in school board politics recognized the seriousness of parental concerns. One interviewee said, "Year-round mandatory anything creates a lot of anxiety and resentment, and I think the district's attempt to do multitrack year-round to manage growth and to keep cost down in terms of facility had, I think, the effect of intens[ifying] the opposition to the district."[12] Even more pointedly, one former school board member noted, "Converting [to year-round] is suicide for a school board member. You are going to tell me that I have to be on that, or if not, I have to transfer ten miles away? I am going to kill you. You are disrupting my life; I am going to kill you. It becomes that personal for every mom and dad out there. . . . You are messing with their schedules, and the reason is all financial."[13]

Analyzing Residents' Views of Year-Round Schools

Since the debate over year-round schools seems to have contributed greatly to the split among the county's residents, it is worth analyzing attitudes toward the policy. Our survey asked a single question about support for year-rounds: "How would you rate Wake County's year-round calendar for elementary and middle schools?" Just over 41 percent of survey participants responded with

Table 5.1 Ordered Logistic Regression Predicting Respondents' Rating of WCPSS Year-Round Calendar (*N* = 1,706)

Variable	Model I	Model II
White	NS	NS
Female	NS	NS
Age	+	+
Lives in western Wake/north Raleigh/Wake Forest	+	+
Number of school-age children	–	–
Has a child in year-round school	+	+
Conservative ideology	–	NS
Annual household income	+	NS
Educational attainment	+	+
Total household commute hours	NS	NS
Total household work hours	NS	NS
Number of organizations		NS
Trust in government		+

Note: (+) sign indicates that the relationship is statistically significant and positive, (–) indicates that the relationship is statistically significant and negative, and NS indicates that the relationship is statistically insignificant. If the cell is blank, the variable was not included in that model.

scores of 7, 8, or 9 (which represented the most favorable responses) and only 13.7 percent with scores of 1, 2, or 3. These findings demonstrate that attitudes toward the year-round calendar were, overall, quite positive and suggest that the real conflict over year-round schooling had more to do with its mandatory status in certain communities than with the calendar itself. A Civitas poll in September 2009, for example, found that 68 percent of respondents believed "parents should be able to choose to send their child to either a year-round or traditional calendar school," and 28 percent believed that "the school system should be able to assign students to year-round schools even if the parents disagree."[14]

Table 5.1 shows the results of an ordered logistic regression with support for year-rounds designated the highest scores. There are several interesting findings. It is not surprising that individuals with children in year-round schools were supportive of the calendar since, even in 2011, a majority of children in these schools were there by choice. Indeed, the variable's performance is consistent with a former school board member's observations that "people like the status quo" and "do not like a [year-round] school until they are in it, and then they seem to think that it is a pretty good place."[15] It is also consistent with the counterintuitive positive and statistically significant coefficient of a binary variable indicating whether the respondent lived in western Wake's suburban towns, north Raleigh, or Wake Forest, the areas most impacted by the implementation of the mandatory year-round policy. For example, the model predicted that of ideologically moderate white women with an average income, age, education, commute, and workweek and with a school-aged child not in year-round school, those who lived in these suburban areas had a 38.5 percent chance of being in the group of residents most supportive of year-round schools (or providing a response of 7, 8, or 9 to the question). Those who did not live in the west, north Raleigh, or Wake Forest had just a 34.1 percent chance of having the same position. Despite these communities' reputations for opposition to the new calendar, there was measurable support for it among their residents.

There are also findings to bolster the proposition that age and socioeconomic status matter. Older, higher-income, and better-educated respondents—or those who face fewer challenges in managing work and family obligations—liked year-round schools. So as to demonstrate the effect of age, the model predicted that a sixty-year-old white woman of average income, education, workweek, and commute length who lived in the suburban communities described above and did not have a child of school age had a 42.8 percent chance of being in the group of residents most supportive of year-round schools, her thirty-year-old counterpart just 35.9 percent.

The more school-aged children a respondent had, the less likely it was that she would be supportive of year-round schools. Adding a school-aged child to an average thirty-five-year-old white suburban woman with one already, for example, decreased the chances she would be in the group of Wake residents who most liked year-rounds by 3.2 percentage points, to 30.5 percent. Two factors may be at work here. First, year-round school assignments run counter to neighborhood schools as a cultural model. Many families with multiple children might have had successful experiences with traditional schools. They may have been reluctant to adjust to a different calendar or may have been more likely to view the year-round approach as inferior. Second, the possibility of having children on various school calendars is a disconcerting one. Different schedules limit to a few weeks per year the time whole families can vacation together. They make finding affordable child care during "track-out" periods more challenging and likely to disrupt family life.

It is important to note that respondents seem to have come to their views about year-round schools based upon their ideological positions. Conservatives were much less likely than liberals to support the calendar. A conservative white suburban woman of average age, income, education, workweek, and commute length with a school-aged child not in year-round had a 33.3 percent

Table 5.2 Ordered Logistic Regression Predicting Respondents' Rating of WCPSS Year-Round Calendar by Race (*N* = 1,593)

Variable	Whites (*n* = 1,156)		African Americans (*n* = 437)	
	Model I	Model II	Model I	Model II
Female	NS	NS	–	–
Age	+	+	NS	NS
Lives in western Wake, etc.	+	+	NS	NS
Number of school-age children	–	–	–	–
Has a child in year-round school	+	+	+	+
Conservative ideology	–	NS	NS	NS
Annual household income	+	+	NS	NS
Educational attainment	+	+	NS	NS
Total household commute hours	NS	NS	NS	NS
Total household work hours	NS	NS	NS	NS
Number of organizations		NS		NS
Trust in government		+		+

Note: (+) sign indicates that the relationship is statistically significant and positive, (–) indicates that the relationship is statistically significant and negative, and NS indicates that the relationship is statistically insignificant. If the cell is blank, the variable was not included in that model.

chance of being the most supportive of the year-round calendar, her liberal counterpart a 44 percent chance. Some might argue year-round schools hinder choice and opposition to them is therefore consistent with conservatism, but such schools also save taxpayers' money, another important tenet of that philosophy. In short, although year-round schools are not an obviously ideological issue, our findings suggest that the great split sorted political conservatives and liberals into opposing camps on this matter.

The second model demonstrates that trust in government had measurable effects on attitudes about year-round schools. Increasing the trust score of an average thirty-five-year-old white woman with one child who was in year-round school from 6 (about one standard deviation below the mean) to 10 (about one standard deviation above the mean) increased the probability she would like the year-round calendar (that is, provide a response we coded as a 7, 8, or 9) from 59 percent to 77.3 percent. This again suggests that those who trusted government were more willing to permit it to implement policies that moved education away from traditional approaches to schooling.

Table 5.2 reveals attitudes about year-round schools broken down by race. There were few strong a priori reasons to believe views of year-round schools would differ by race, and for the most part, the results confirm this. Still, notice that among African Americans, income and educational attainment produced null findings. It may well be that economic resources did not adequately buffer minority families from the social costs of year-round schooling to the degree they did whites—only about 37 percent of African Americans in this analysis gave a 7-, 8-, or 9-point response to the year-round question, whereas just over 44 percent of whites did. In a similar vein, the finding that African American women were markedly less supportive of year-rounds than African American men may reflect the disproportionately large amount of parenting they provide within their families. Whereas older whites were supportive of year-round schools, age made no difference to African Americans.

Conclusion

We have seen how Wake year-round school assignments began in 1989 as a cost-saving measure. When district leaders discovered that such schools were less diverse than those on traditional calendars, however, they implemented strategies to promote their socioeconomic integration. Year-round schools began as an optional magnet program but by 2006 had become mandatory in that many students, particularly in the suburbs, were assigned to them as a base. Continued population pressures accelerated both the opening of new schools on the year-round calendar and the conversion of existing traditional schools to it. Two forces were therefore at work: growth and the school board's commitment to diversity. The aggressive approach, ultimately reinforced by a favorable North Carolina Supreme Court ruling in 2009, prompted political activism from citizens, particularly parents in the western, and directly affected, part of the county. After their lawsuit failed to prevent district officials from making mandatory year-round assignments to public schools, activists turned their attention to changing school board policy via the ballot box.

Our survey results place these developments in broader perspective. Residents with children in year-round schools tended to like them. So did the more educated and those with higher incomes and smaller families, just the kind of people with the reserves of social capital often necessary to meet the challenges of the schedule. Conservatives, on the other hand, did not. Since ideological arguments for or against year-round schools seem tenuous, we believe liberal and conservative positions on the issue were really driven by broader debates about public education and general attitudes about the Wake County school board.

6 ▶ The Great Split

ELECTION 2009 AND ITS AFTERMATH

The Wake County school board consists of nine members, each representing a contiguous and relatively compact district in the county for a four-year term. Prior to 2014 the elections were held in odd-numbered years with four seats up in one cycle and five in the next.[1] In 2009 there were four contests, for the seats in the first, second, seventh, and ninth districts. Although only one sitting member of the board, Ron Margiotta, had emerged as an ally of conservatives and an opponent to the majority's policies, control of the county's school system was up for grabs. This was because all four contested districts were being defended by members associated with the status quo and the Democrats. The only incumbent standing for reelection was Horace J. Tart in the second district. Liberals and their allies had recruited Lois Nixon, Rita Rakestraw, and Karen Simon to run to replace the retiring members—Lori Millberg, Patti Head, and Eleanor Goettee.

Republicans and school board opponents therefore faced the extremely difficult task of winning every contest if they were to assume control. All four districts were in somewhat conservative-friendly territory, however, and the candidates who emerged as standard-bearers for their cause appeared competitive. Chris Malone, a case officer for an insurance fraud investigator, ran in the first district, which covered towns running east from Wake Forest through Rolesville and down to Knightdale, Wendell, and Zebulon; John Tedesco, the chief development officer of the nonprofit Big Brothers and Big Sisters of the Triangle, was the candidate in the second, which covered Garner and most of Fuquay-Varina; Deborah Prickett, a program manager in the state's Department of Public Instruction, stood in the seventh district, which stretched from Morrisville east to suburban northwest Raleigh; and Debra Goldman, a parent volunteer and certified firefighter, campaigned for the seat in the ninth district in Cary.

Goldman, Malone, Prickett, and Tedesco cohered as a team committed to overturning the policies of the school board. A deep cleavage formed between them and Margiotta on one side and their principal electoral opponents—

Rakestraw in the first, Tart in the second, Simon in the seventh, Nixon in the ninth—and the four remaining school board members not up for reelection on the other. The divide was primarily a function of clashing policy positions. We have discussed the principal issues that had driven public school politics in the county for about a decade in the preceding three chapters. There were clearly deep differences between the two sides on annual reassignments, mandatory year-round schools, and, most dramatically, the use of socioeconomic diversity in general assignment practices. By stating in September that "parents want stability, calendar choices, and consideration for the individual students," Deborah Prickett was not only claiming that the group was vindicated by public opinion but also succinctly characterizing the basic division between the camps (Goldsmith 2009a).

The two sides' positions on these issues were interesting. As noted earlier, diversity had been the subject of an intense national debate about race and public schools for a long time. The opposing camps in this well-rehearsed discussion were clearly delineated by ideology. The criticism of the annual reassignment policy was not ideological, however, and seemed to be more a method of questioning the existing board majority's judgment and approach to equity. Given the prevalence of reassignment over the preceding fifteen years, this connection made sense to a large number of the county's residents, as the analysis of the survey in chapter 4 demonstrates.

The Democratic board members' opponents were also mobilized by the general feeling in suburban communities that residents were being "picked on" by the mandatory year-round policy. Still, if anything, year-round schooling is a conservative position since, on a per capita basis at least, it reduces state and local education expenditures. To the extent conservatives have traditionally talked about school "choice," it has been about allowing interested parents access to public resources to educate their children privately—something that is often thought of in the form of a "voucher"—not selecting between individual public schools with different calendars (Howell and Peterson 2002). Opposition to mandatory year-round schools may perhaps be seen as "conservative" only in that the policy interferes with traditional family life.

It is therefore not entirely accurate to characterize the polarization in 2009 as one of ideologies. The combatants were frequently as dogmatic as typical ideologues, but they were not as consistent with their policy preferences. Those who wanted neighborhood schools, rejected mandatory year-rounds, and vocally decried existing annual reassignment practices were, as we have seen, generally conservative. Their adversaries tended to be liberal. The basic positions taken by both candidates and voters, however, could be more correctly defined in terms of support for or opposition to the sitting school board majority.

Moreover, it is notable that right-of-center residents were brought together by positions that were not directly related to school funding, curricula, testing, the educational system's contribution to economic well-being, and the relationship between public and private schools. Across the country, these were often the issues that divided activists at the local level into competing political and ideological groups (Kirst and Wirt 2009). Although some of these issues had been important to the general debate about the direction of public education in Wake County over previous years—the funding issue dominated public discussions of the important bond issuances of the 1990s and early 2000s, for example—they were hardly talked about at all in 2009.

The division was undoubtedly deepened by the intense personal animosity felt by individual activists toward many of their opponents. These feelings were probably exacerbated by the Internet, where people could quickly, anonymously, and very publicly communicate their views about personalities on the other side.[2] Many of the board's critics had been provoked by what they considered to be the arrogance and insensitivity of decision makers who unfeelingly transferred children from school to school in what they saw as social engineering of breathtaking magnitude. There was a pervasive feeling, discernible in our interviews and survey, that policy makers had lost touch with the needs of parents and students.[3] One conservative activist reported that it "seemed like every week, every other week ... if there was not a major thing that came up, the school board would do something ... to anger the constituents."[4]

The board's "Wacky Wednesday" policy established in the months leading up to the 2009 election furnishes a small but neat example. Just before the start of 2009–10, the board, without consulting the community, hastily announced that schools were to be dismissed one hour early every Wednesday so as to provide teachers opportunities to work together on collaborative projects and professional development. The decision left many working parents hurrying to arrange additional child care. As one conservative, who actually supported the practice, noted in our interviews, "The 'Wacky Wednesdays' was another [thing that the school board did to anger constituents]. We had a very positive experience with that the year before. My son ... has some challenges in school, and over at Davis Middle they were already doing those [Wacky Wednesdays], and I could see how those sessions really helped the teachers come up with the strategy to teach my son. I think that people really reacted very badly to that whole Wacky Wednesday thing. That all happened in a space of about six weeks. We went from nobody had heard of anything about it to it got rammed through the school board. Then parents had to very quickly react . . . 'What do I do now?'"[5]

From the other side, the board's supporters viewed their adversaries as self-interested and economically advantaged individuals with little compassion and understanding of the world beyond their own personal experiences. This myopic view threatened the economic and social health of the county and educational prospects of thousands of students. Opponents of the diversity policy, in particular, were thought to be prejudicial against minorities and perhaps even racist.[6] Several critics felt the appeal of neighborhood schools was purely "convenience," not academic achievement. Rita Rakestraw argued that the money contributed by conservative donors like Bob Luddy and Art Pope was an effort "to re-segregate our schools and focus solely on parents' convenience, not student achievement" (Hui 2010b), while one liberal African American activist told us that the opposition to the board in 2009 was based on "a selfish kind of individualistic approach to resolving the issues of people that have been inconvenienced."[7] Many also claimed the Republican-supported candidates were inexperienced ideologues whose election would end a quarter-century-long tradition of pragmatic governance by smart, hard-working, and civic-minded individuals from both parties.[8]

Of course, the schism did not form in a vacuum. The Wake school board elections of 2009 should be viewed in light of the heightened partisanship and polarization that was taking place in national, state, and county politics more broadly—a subject discussed in some detail in chapter 2. Still, although nationally there had been bitter partisan and ideological battles over control of K–12 public education in many jurisdictions—particularly involving Christian conservatives (Deckman 2004, 83–122)—most school board elections were still low-key affairs generally decided in favor of incumbents and by parochial issues and the strength of the local teachers' unions (Berkman and Plutzer 2005, 112–27; Deckman 2004, 123–34; Hess and Leal 2005).

One important consequence of the 2009 campaign's connection to the broader political context was what we might call its "professionalization." Parties formally endorsed slates of candidates. The voter mobilization efforts on both sides were extensive as the local political parties and many members of the citizen groups that had emerged over the years—such as Wake Cares and Stop Mandatory Year-Round opposing the board and Great Schools in Wake supporting it—went to work stuffing envelopes, knocking on doors, and pounding keyboards. The amount of money contributed to the campaigns was transformative. More than $340,000 was spent by the candidates and parties on the election, around $190,000 in favor of the Republican-affiliated candidates. Approximately 20 percent of the money to oust the sitting majority came from Pope, Luddy, and their families (Hui 2010b). The election also saw the emergence of political action committees in Wake school politics, such as the anti-board Take Wake Schools Back and Wake Schools Community Alliance, led by Allison Backhouse, that raised around $50,000 for its cause (Hui and Goldsmith 2009). Some liberals believed the 2009 election constituted an effort by national groups affiliated with the Tea Party to take over Wake's schools (Stover 2012). Many of these activities had taken place in previous Wake school board elections, but they had never remotely approached the scale seen in 2009.

To close observers, it quickly became clear that the campaign would prove difficult for candidates allied with the board majority. A broad backlash against "Obamacare," the health-care overhaul legislation at the time being considered seriously by Congress, had adversely affected public attitudes about the Democratic Party. A September 2009 Civitas poll of North Carolinians showed 40 percent "strongly" opposed to the legislation. A Public Policy Polling (PPP) poll in the same month revealed Obama's approval rating falling precipitously in the state and that 51 percent of residents disapproved of the job he was doing as president.[9] With the election coming during the deep recession that followed the financial crisis of the previous year, Wake County residents were also likely despondent about economic conditions and the future in a manner that presumably focused their attention on their children's education as a path to future economic success. According to a PPP poll in December 2009, the category "the economy and jobs" was the "most important" of seven major issues to 54 percent of North Carolina respondents.[10]

Surveys done specifically about the public schools and the board election brought even worse news for the status quo. Another Civitas poll fielded in September 2009 reported that although the public supported diversity in the abstract, a slim majority of 51 percent "strongly" opposed the extant policy of "assigning students to schools based on achieving diversity instead of sending students to the school closest to their home."[11] At roughly the same time, PPP found that even larger majorities objected to the assignment policy in the districts where seats were being contested. Most strikingly, PPP discovered that only 49 percent of Democrats and 46 percent of African Americans supported it (Goldsmith 2009b). Kimberly Coleman may have spoken for a number of southeast Raleigh residents when she complained that busing for diversity placed unfair demands on minority and low-income families and that "if it's not going to be equal, just put us back in our neighborhood schools" (Collins 2009).

Board opponents understood this dynamic well and focused their attacks on the general assignment policy as the campaign intensified. The board majority's response demonstrated recognition of this development too. Keith Sutton, who was not up for reelection in 2009, characterized the dying days of the campaign as a "referendum on diversity" (Collins and Hui 2009). As PPP's Dean Debnam put it, "The issue that had the juice was the neighborhood school issue" (Goldsmith 2009b).

The election ultimately proved historic because it brought about the unified county system's first Republican-affiliated and conservative-leaning school board majority. Goldman, Malone, and Prickett won convincingly, none of them receiving less than 58 percent of the vote. Of the nearly 6,600 votes cast, Tedesco fell forty-three short of being elected outright and was subject to a runoff that was requested by the second-place finisher in his district, Cathy Truitt. Tart, the incumbent and supporter of the diversity policy in the second district, trailed in third with just 22.8 percent of the vote. The issue of the new board's policies, however, was not in dispute, since as soon as she declared her intention to call for a second election, Truitt announced, "Forced busing is dead" (Hui 2009c). Regardless, Tedesco beat her quite decisively in the second ballot in early November, capturing more than three in four of the slightly more than 8,700 votes recorded.

It is true that voters in only four of the county's nine districts were able to express their views about the board's policies in 2009 and that at 11.7 percent, the turnout was low by any reasonable absolute standard. Still, it was much higher than it had been in 2005 when the same seats were previously contested and slightly higher than in 2007 when the other five were. There was no denying the county had witnessed a sea change in its politics and was about to witness something similarly revolutionary in the policies that governed its public schools.

The "Republican" Board, 2009–2011

The new board majority moved quickly to change existing policies. After electing Ron Margiotta chair as their first order of business, the Republican-affiliated members effectively ended the regulation mandating year-round schools in January 2010. However, even this proposal, one on which most observers believed the majority was unified, did not pass without controversy. Debra Goldman moved to revise the measure to terminate the policy by replacing rather stark language about its abolition with some that essentially called on the school system to make every effort to bring it about. Her stated rationale was that the existing proposal did not explain the mechanism by which the county might bring an end to mandatory year-round schooling. Goldman's alternative passed 5–4, with all her Republican colleagues in opposition. A disappointed Margiotta noted that Goldman had effectively broken a promise made by all those in the majority to vote together (Hui and Goldsmith 2010). Thus began a term in which Goldman emerged as the vacillating member of the otherwise cohesive majority and, therefore, the crucial swing vote on several issues.[12]

The policy that had drawn the most attention in the 2009 campaign was, as noted, the general assignment plan. Just after they were seated, the members of the new majority set to work dismantling and replacing the socioeconomic diversity mandate. John Tedesco was selected to chair a committee charged with constructing a new policy using principles grounded firmly in the neighborhood schools model that Republican candidates had campaigned on during the previous fall. His effort was met immediately with stiff resistance from liberals. As early as January 2010, the state NAACP promised a legal fight to maintain the diversity policy. Led by its chair, Reverend William Barber, it also worked to mobilize political pressure. Vowing "not to sit back and watch our schools, without any challenge, go back to segregation" (Collins 2010), Barber, activists, and academics from a disparate array of groups like Great Schools in Wake and the student-led N.C.HEAT (Heroes Emerging Amongst Teens) organized a series of high-profile demonstrations at school board meetings that led to arrests and garnered a great deal of local and national media attention. The board's efforts to transform the assignment policy and the resistance to them were the subject of articles in publications like the *New York Times*, the *Washington Post*, and the *Economist* and of a story on the show of liberal television satirist Stephen Colbert. In February the Wake County Public School System superintendent, Del Burns, announced his resignation, citing opposition to the board's work on the general assignment policy as the primary reason. Waiving existing rules that the superintendent should have a doctorate and be an educator by profession, the board selected Tony Tata, a retired brigadier general and former chief operating officer of the District of Columbia schools, as his replacement.

By this time the new board was facing a barrage of criticism about its operations. Many of its opponents accused it of being driven by politics. One liberal activist developed this thought by talking about her past involvement with the school board:

I can remember . . . every single school board election [in which] I
supported candidates for school board. I worked for and was on the
fund-raising committee for a young man called Tom Fetzer back in
the day. I had no clue if Tom Fetzer was a Republican or a Democrat. I just knew that Tom Fetzer supported things that I cared about
from the school system. In my own school [election] district . . . ,
Elizabeth Martin was the representative. I adored her. Come to find
out—guess what?—she was a Republican; I am a Democrat. She did
not know I was a Democrat; I sure did not know she was a Republican. These were just issues that were never even talked about when
it came to school board. We would talk about things instead—[like]
Bill Fletcher and Eleanor Goettee are running for school board. . . .
You go to listen to what they have to say. Eleanor Goettee was a retired
teacher. I adored her. She was a Democrat. I did not know that. I supported Judy Hoffman; I supported Roxie Cash. I worked my tail off
for Tom Fetzer. These people were all Republicans. I did not know
they were Republicans. This is how it used to be in Wake County.[13]

By contrast, the board majority installed after the 2009 election was viewed
as tremendously ideological. A leader of an advocacy organization neatly expressed the views of many critics: "When it was a functional board, I often
did not know who the Republicans were, who the Democrats were. They had
healthy debates around these very complex choices. Now, it is not about Republican and Democrat; it is really about people who have that ideology, and
they are not letting the facts get in the way of the ideology. So they are making
these global statements that are just not supported by the facts. The facts are
the facts. The consequences of the direction [in which] they are currently
heading are going to be pernicious for this community and pervasive in the
impact from neighborhood to neighborhood."[14]

Such comments reflect the perception that the new board majority was
uninterested in data, instead arriving at decisions because of deeply entrenched
predispositions. Speakers at a focus group of liberal activists believed the
board's policies "were put into place with no data, no statistics to support anything," and "with no research, and when research [was] presented to them . . .
they [were] very dismissive of it."[15] As a former board member put it, "Elected
officials [on a] board, whether it is city, county, or school board, they figure,
'Well, we got elected; we must know what we are doing,' and some of them
[are] a lot worse than others. The current board majority is really bad about

that. . . . Unfortunately, some folks on the current board do not care to read that [research], and they are told by somebody else: 'Oh no, there is a product somewhere where [a given policy] is working, 400 kids in Chicago in a little school that spends $20,000 a year [total], those kids can graduate.' That does not mean it can happen universally."[16] The new board also stood accused of shackling senior staff and disrupting the day-to-day administration of the system. One leader within the education community worried that "there isn't the trust in the staff anymore; [the board is] fighting over micro-decisions as well as macro-decisions."[17]

Finally, some observers were concerned that the board was not practicing what a Democratic board member called "transparency" and "inclusivity."[18] An activist within the African American community asked, "Why aren't we included?" when assessing the board's deliberations.[19] Interestingly, these concerns were echoed by some on the other end of the political spectrum. One conservative activist said, "Now they [board members] are attacking each other and accusing each other of heinous violations of the school board ethics policy. John Tedesco is a very ethical person, but he took ownership of building this new assignment model. I think he did an absolutely horrible job of communicating what he was working on to the public; I do not think that John did a very good job listening to stakeholders. He very much created the impression at his community meetings that he was willing to listen, but he was not really willing to consider input from other people."[20]

This criticism seemed to have some effect. Crucially, an April 2010 survey revealed the county's business community to be evenly split over the efforts to change the assignment policy. Many feared the controversy surrounding the reform would deter business investment (Goldsmith 2010a). Although the board had voted in March to adopt a Tedesco assignment plan based upon a neighborhood schools model that split the county into sixteen "zones," the majority was checked when in October Goldman introduced an ultimately successful motion to halt its implementation (Hui and Goldsmith 2010a). Although it was clear she was under significant pressure from many of her Cary constituents who wanted revisions to proposed feeder patterns into some schools, the behavior not surprisingly earned her the opprobrium of fellow Republicans. Tedesco famously called Goldman a "prom queen" during the ensuing spat (Hui and Goldsmith 2010b).[21]

By this point, the business community, mainly in the form of the Greater Raleigh Chamber of Commerce and the Wake Education Partnership, had offered an alternative to the zonal plan. It promised to gain support from both sides of the political divide and, more critically, Goldman. Proposed in the summer of 2010 by Michael Alves, a consultant who had been brought in to assist the board on the chamber's dime, it was called "controlled choice" (Goldsmith 2010b). Essentially modeled on an approach used in Massachusetts in the 1980s, it allowed students to go to a public school of their parents' choosing so long as seats were available. Children were not assigned to base schools. The response from the board was generally favorable, and members, together with staff, crafted two options for the new assignment policy they called the "blue" (or "Community-Based Choice") and "green" (or "Base Schools Achievement") plans. Superintendent Tata then worked, after public consultation and the use of online simulations, to focus the board on the blue option, which would provide students with the choice of at least five elementary schools, two middle schools, and two high schools, based upon where they lived. Families could keep their current assignment, and younger siblings would also be able to attend the same school.

The new policy was released in its final form as Wake County residents went to the polls in October 2011 to elect five members to the school board who would sit for the following two years. As we shall see in chapter 8, that election brought about a new, more liberal and "Democratic" majority and another change in policy direction. However, and controversially with the support of two retiring members of the minority, Ann McLaurin and Carolyn Morrison, Tata's "controlled choice" plan was adopted by a 6–2 vote just two weeks later, on October 18. It would be left to the new board to implement it.

A final note about this decision is in order here. The two years of Republican or conservative rule on the school board are thought of as revolutionary. In many ways, it is hard to argue with that characterization—indeed, it is a central premise of this book. But the intense rhetoric and highly charged politics of the period were not reflected in the speed and magnitude of policy change undertaken in 2010 and 2011. Specifically, it took the new board its entire term to formulate a new general student assignment plan that still awaited implementation and, at best, could only loosely be described as based on the neighborhood model—although the choice component was clearly consistent with conservative values. Second, at least in terms of race, Wake County's decision to move to diversification on socioeconomic principles was already having a fairly large and resegregating effect. During the five years immediately following the shift away from school integration by race in 2000, Wake's "imbalance" index for minorities had grown by one-third to 12 percent (Clotfelter, Ladd, and Vigdor 2013).[22] Although features permitting students to stay at their current schools and providing parents with choices within the area of the county

Table 6.1 Ordered Logistic Regression Predicting Respondents' Rating of WCPSS School Board

Variable	Entire sample (n = 1,706)	Whites (n = 1,156)	African Americans (n = 437)
White	+		
Female	–	–	NS
Age	+	+	–
Length of residence in Wake County	–	NS	–
Has school-age children	+	+	NS
Trust in local government	+	+	+
Conservative ideology	+	+	+
Annual household income	NS	NS	–
Educational attainment	–	–	NS

Note: (+) sign indicates that the relationship is statistically significant and positive, (–) indicates that the relationship is statistically significant and negative, and NS indicates that the relationship is statistically insignificant.

where they resided may well have accelerated this, we will never know the real effects of the Republicans' policy because it was quickly rescinded.

Evidence from the Survey

Because it was being conducted during March 2011, our survey sheds some important light on residents' attitudes about the Republican-controlled board at the time it was orchestrating significant changes to policy. One question asked was, "How would you rate the job the current school board is doing?" The average of all respondents on a scale of 1–9 was 4.08, reflecting low opinion in an absolute sense. We again use ordered logistic regression to understand the determinants of respondents' opinions with the usual and intuitive political and demographic controls included in the model. Table 6.1 reveals the results.

The results in the first column were largely as predicted. Conservatives, whites, and older residents supported the board more than did liberals, non-whites, and younger adults. Women tended to oppose the board. Note, interestingly, that all other things being equal, better-educated residents were more likely to disapprove of the job it was doing. Those with children of school age were more likely to support the Republican-backed board and, presumably, its policies. As implied by the general discussion about new residents, recent arrivals into Wake were also more complimentary of the new board.

We used an indicator of attitudes toward only local government to measure trust here. It is clear that those more trusting of local government affirmed the board's performance. Those with trust in government tend to be more liberal in their politics (Hetherington 2005), but here it may be that individuals' trust in local government was shaped by the new school board. With the considerable media coverage and salience of Wake County public school governance, residents were possibly shifting their entire view of local government in response to their feelings about the board and its actions. This was indubitably facilitated by respondents' naturally malleable and performance-based attitudes about local government (Rahn and Rudolph 2002).

The reported results do not tell us much about substantive effects, however. To provide some idea of the influence of several of these explanatory variables, consider that a white woman without a child of school age and of average amounts of all other attributes accounted for in the model had a 47.7 percent chance of giving the board its lowest scores of 1, 2, or 3. For a man with identical characteristics, this fell to 40.7 percent. The predicted probability for the same responses from an African American man was 65.3 percent. The effect of having a child of school age decreased the predicted probability that a white woman would give the board its lowest approval score by 6.2 percentage points to 42.4 percent. If she had lived in Wake County for less than three years, that white female respondent without a child of school age had a 37.7 percent chance of providing the most disapproving responses to the question; this figure increased to 48.8 percent if she had lived in the county for more than fifteen years but not her entire life.

The remaining columns of Table 6.1 show respondents' views of the school board by race; some interesting differences in the attitudes of whites and blacks are revealed. Attitudes among whites mainly mirrored those of the larger sample, but gender and being a parent of a school-age child had no measurable effect on African American attitudes. It is interesting that African Americans who had lived in Wake County for some time—and presumably grew up with the diversity policy—had worse views of the school board than did those of more recent domicile. In addition, whereas older residents tended to be the most supportive of the board among whites, age had the reverse impact on African American attitudes. Long-term residents and older African American respondents may have been more attuned than younger counterparts to the personal benefits of the long-standing diversity policy and thus more fearful of its demise. The attitudes of higher-income African Americans may have had similar roots.

Conclusion

Until 2009 there were few major policy disputes among Wake County school board members, and they received significant support from the public. But that year Wake County Republicans and conservatives built upon the political, economic, and demographic developments of the previous two decades to coordinate an effort to take control of the body. A growing belief that decisions about transfers, year-round schools, and especially assignments designed to diversify student bodies were wrong mobilized grassroots support for their endeavor. Candidates running to replace the status quo were likely also assisted by a growing sense of economic insecurity among residents, declining public support for Democrats generally, families' depleting stocks of social capital, and a pervasive sense that the current board was insensitive to mass opinion. The result was a new Republican-backed majority and a clear departure from the way things were done in the past.

It is unsurprising that residents were split in their support for the Republican-backed board along cleavages practically identical to those detected in their views on the diversity, annual reassignment, and year-round policies. The three issues had combined to bifurcate many of the county's residents into polarized camps. On one side sat conservatives; on the other, liberals. The population was also divided, albeit on occasion less starkly, by race, gender, income, place of residence, levels of trust in government, and whether or not an individual had a child of school age.

There is no doubt that 2009 marked a significant change in Wake County public schools politics. Interestingly, however, the school system's policies did not change as dramatically as many thought they would. Most important, there was not a clean break from assignments based upon socioeconomic diversity and a turn to ones determined solely by where students lived. This was at least partially attributable to the energetic reaction of the new board's opponents, motivated by both the majority's policy proposals and governing style. It was likely also a result of economic and demographic developments brought on by the financial crisis and resulting recession. The new board and its vociferous critics did make sure, however, that the 2010–11 period would not bring a return to the halcyon days of consensus.

7 ▸ Is Wake Different?

We believe the Wake County case is important. But is it typical, or perhaps unique? Why was Wake able to sustain diversity in public school assignments for many years while other districts have not? Have other jurisdictions experienced such contentious politics surrounding assignments? In this chapter we compare Wake with a number of other urban and suburban jurisdictions to set the county's experience into a broader national context. We place these districts into a four-cell typology that helps us understand more about Wake's public schools compared with other systems in North Carolina, the South, and beyond.

Wake in the Context of Large U.S. Urban School Districts

Earlier we remarked upon the significant size of Wake County's public school system. Table 7.1 shows that as of 2012–13, Wake was the fifteenth largest school district in the United States.[1] Four of the top ten districts were in Florida, which, like Wake, has countywide districts and has experienced strong population growth over many years. Of the top fifteen districts, thirteen are located in the South or West. Most of the top twenty districts have experienced enrollment growth over the last few years; Los Angeles, Chicago, Houston, Philadelphia, and San Diego are the exceptions. Wake's rate of expansion outstrips them all, however. We include some of these large districts in our comparative analysis and return to how Wake fits into this group at the end of this chapter.

A Typology of School Districts

Existing analyses of student assignment policies in K–12 education rely largely on case studies. The advantage of this approach, of course, is that it provides a rich (or "thick") amount of detail. Case studies allow analysts to use multiple sources of evidence (Yin 2008). Because of the intense focus on a single example, however, comparisons with others are frequently neglected or given little attention. This research strategy typically pays little heed to external validity. Literatures built on case studies are often heterogeneous in approach because contributors frame questions and invoke theory differently.

Table 7.1 Population Estimates of the Twenty Largest School Districts in the United States

Name of district	State	Enrollment 2012-13	Enrollment change 2010-12	Enrollment % change
New York City	NY	993,903	20,137	2.0
Los Angeles	CA	655,455	−11,796	−1.8
Chicago	IL	402,665	−7,597	−1.9
Miami–Dade County	FL	354,236	6,830	1.9
Clark County	NV	311,238	1,489	0.5
Broward County	FL	260,234	4,093	1.6
Houston Independent	TX	202,842	−852	−0.4
Hillsborough County	FL	200,287	5,934	3.0
Hawaii	HI	183,251	5,062	2.8
Orange County	FL	183,021	7,035	3.8
Fairfax County	VA	180,616	6,137	3.4
Palm Beach County	FL	179,494	4,835	2.7
Gwinnett County	GA	160,744	930	0.6
Dallas Independent	TX	158,570	2,043	1.3
Wake County	NC	149,508	6,219	4.2
Montgomery County	MD	148,780	4,757	3.2
Charlotte-Mecklenburg	NC	141,061	5,423	3.8
Philadelphia	PA	137,020	−4,442	−3.2
San Diego	CA	130,271	−1,513	−1.2
Duval County	FL	125,662	1,667	1.3

Note: Estimates are from the Proximity One webpage "Largest 100 U.S. School Districts" (http://proximityone.com/lgsd.htm).

As we have noted, a few scholars compare two or more cases. Grant (2009) looks at Raleigh and Syracuse, New York. His two contrasting examples are signaled by the title of his book *Hope and Despair in the American City*. Ryan (2010) juxtaposes a single school in the city of Richmond, Virginia, with a single school in the larger Henrico County, while Portz, Stein, and Jones (1999) discuss urban school change in three cities: Boston, Pittsburgh, and St. Louis. Other authors cover multiple but similar cases so as to provide a basis for generalization. Smrekar and Goldring's (2009a) chapters trace the evolution of desegregation and resegregation in several districts, with a particular eye toward the role of legal opinions in influencing these dynamics. Ravitch (2010), focusing on testing and school choice, draws insights from several jurisdictions, while Frankenberg and Orfield (2012) provide a very helpful set of case studies of suburban educational settings.

Instead of focusing attention on one case, contrasting two, or drawing common themes from a number of similar examples, we compare Wake to a large number of school districts from across the country, selecting jurisdictions from the literature on suburban and urban school districts' student assignment policies.[2] We have content-analyzed these cases to explore their commonalities and differences.

We begin with a typology of school districts based upon two characteristics that are critical to an explanation of the Wake case. First, as noted above, Wake has a *heterogeneous*—in terms of socioeconomic status and race—student population. Other large districts that meet this condition are often found in the South and West (Grant 2009, 30), although, as Ryan notes, they are sometimes made more homogeneous by "white flight" and "bright flight" brought about by middle-class parents who exploit the opportunities and resources available to them to find what they perceive to be the best schools for their children (2010, 17). These districts then become much less heterogeneous and thus unlikely to seek diverse schools. Small districts are often *homogeneous* because of uniform housing stock and, possibly, the manipulation of housing selection through subtle or explicit forms of discrimination. Under these circumstances, even if the district leadership wanted to create schools with a socioeconomic or racial mix, its options would be limited. Nassau County on Long Island, New York, reveals just how small districts can be; the county has over 209,000 students in fifty-six districts that contain between two and ten schools each, suggesting significant within-district homogeneity.[3]

Second, Wake County has what we believe to be a *robust civic life*. Its relatively affluent, well-educated, and cosmopolitan population ought to provide the kind of reservoir of social capital and support for public enterprises necessary for support of diversity. The concept borrows heavily from what Portz, Stein, and Jones describe as "civic capacity," which for them includes "governmental structures, institutional arrangements, leadership and political culture" sufficient to allow collective action in cities to improve school effectiveness (1999, 1). It is also similar to Rahn and Rudolph's (2005) "civic capacity" and Rice and Sumberg's (1997) "civic culture," which has four components—what the authors label "engagement," "equality," "solidarity, trust, and tolerance," and "social structures of cooperation." We believe that civic capacity and civic culture are both forms of social capital (Rahn and Rudolph 2005). We have noted that social capital operates at multiple levels of social organization and, in our case, involves networks of actors creating resources used to improve civic life. Clearly, governmental structures supported by public trust would be included in this definition. Of course civic capacity can be used to change and improve

Table 7.2 Fourfold Typology of School Districts

	Homogeneous district	Heterogeneous district
Limited civic life	Denver, CO Richmond, VA Syracuse, NY Hartford, CT St. Louis, MO Metropolitan Nashville, TN San Antonio, TX	Miami–Dade County, FL Broward County, FL Hillsborough County, FL Orange County, FL "Azalea," Orange County, CA Osseo Area, MN
Robust civic life	Henrico County, VA Austin, TX Suburban districts near Harford, CT	Wake County, NC Charlotte-Mecklenburg, NC "Sewall" County, GA Waltham, MA Montgomery County, MD San Jose, CA Jefferson County, KY

several aspects of communities. Although Portz, Stein, and Jones (1999) focus on its implications for schools, Smith (2004) argues that Charlotte's civic capacity was directed more toward economic development than toward school desegregation. We treat the important Charlotte case in more detail below.

Jurisdictions with robust civic lives also vary in terms of which educational outcomes they seek. They have cultures supportive of vibrant public debate about and political competition over public school policies. All likely desire effective schools with improving educational outcomes such as test scores and graduation rates. Some of these districts, however, also want diverse student bodies, that is, schools integrated by socioeconomic status or race. In these cases those in leadership may view purposive integration as a vehicle to promote positive educational outcomes, and their communities can support this because of the trust they place in public institutions and the social capital and other resources residents enjoy.

We recognize that other typologies are useful. Frankenberg (2012, 36) deploys cluster analysis to create a framework to study over 2,300 suburban school districts. She finds that only thirteen are countywide, while more than 1,100 are relatively stable mixed-income districts, typically located far from urban areas, and more than 700 are exclusive enclaves, predominantly white with low rates of poverty and racial change. Our choice is to use a more conceptual, as opposed to statistical, approach.

Many of the cases we examine have common themes, but there are also unique elements that challenge our ability to generalize from them. In placing jurisdictions into cells, we frequently have been required to make judgment calls, particularly with regard to the kind of civic life a jurisdiction has. Moreover, we recognize that many districts change over time, again making cell placement difficult. Indeed, many of the case studies we have consulted vividly describe changes in both demographics and political dynamics, sometimes over many years. This means that although we have placed a case in a given cell based on the era in which the data are available, the jurisdiction likely continued to change after that, suggesting it might be placed in a different cell given more recent information. Table 7.2 shows the typology we have developed and summarizes the districts we placed in each cell.

Homogeneous District/Limited Civic Life

We start with the type that is the polar opposite of Wake. These jurisdictions, with high minority and poor populations, are typically large and urban and have struggled to provide quality schooling because of low revenue, a preponderance of high poverty households, cumbersome bureaucracies, or some combination of these (Darling-Hammond 2010; Grant 2009; Portz, Stein, and Jones 1999; Ryan 2010). Their schools have little diversity, and there is little political debate about policy.

A good example is majority-black Richmond, Virginia. Using a comparison of two high schools—urban and 82 percent African American Thomas Jefferson (or "Tee-Jay") and suburban Freeman in majority-white, middle-class Henrico County—Ryan (2010) provides a rather gloomy view of the city's schools. He reports that initial "massive resistance" to school desegregation in Richmond rapidly gave way to token compliance that resulted in very little progress. While a court decree in 1970 ordered the integration of Richmond city schools with those of Henrico County, this ruling was eventually overturned on appeal. Suburban residents therefore did not concern themselves particularly with improvements in urban education. Later programs supporting school choice in the Richmond area did not result in notable changes by race and class in school composition, in part because choices were restricted to certain areas, which were themselves homogeneous (Ryan 2010). The Richmond-Henrico case illustrates how potent school district boundaries are in determining which populations attend which schools.

Syracuse, New York, is another case of this type. Like many large northern cities, it still had a varied industrial base in the years following World War II

(Grant 2009). The city enjoyed 80 percent of Onondaga County's taxable base, with the surrounding suburbs receiving the remainder (Grant 2009, 10). Schools in the city represented its diverse ethnic groups, mostly of European origin. Deep recessions in the 1980s and early 1990s, however, hurt Syracuse. U.S. Census sources show it lost 15 percent of its population and 11 percent of its jobs between 1980 and 2010. Today its top employers are in services and education, and it relies heavily on state aid.[4]

Redlining became a significant problem for Syracuse in the 1970s, and the local Home Owners Loan Corporation made it easier to purchase suburban property, where businesses were increasingly locating in order to access cheaper land and to maintain proximity to middle-class workers and customers (Grant 2009, 14–20). The placement of new urban highways destroyed existing city neighborhoods, and public housing replaced integrated communities with segregated ones. Arguing explicitly in terms of social capital, Grant suggests that as neighborhoods became more racially and economically segregated, civic life declined. Drawing on his personal experience with the neighborhood of Westcott, he argues that the closing of an elementary school removed a key resource for bringing together parents across race and class lines, thus attenuating social trust (44). The departure of additional businesses further weakened the community's social capital. By the 1980s there were some successful efforts to revitalize civic life in Westcott, with attendant positive effects on families and schools. Across the city, however, the trend was toward increased joblessness, poverty, and failing schools (67). Rahn and Rudolph (2005) found Syracuse's citizens to have lower than average levels of political trust, another indicator of low social capital.

Hartford, Connecticut, is a similar case. Dougherty, Wanzer, and Ramsay (2009, 104) note that in 1989 the city was 91 percent minority and its suburbs 88 percent white, indicating extreme segregation (Farley et al. 1978).[5] In 1996, however, the Connecticut Supreme Court ordered the city and its adjoining suburbs to support student transfers across district lines, something that was unusual for court orders (Frankenberg 2005).[6] Recognizing that the capacity to create diverse schools would occur only if the demographics were conducive, the ruling made district boundaries permeable. The results have done little to change the status quo, however. Strategies involving voluntary assignment to magnet schools have produced only slight change, and the results of a five-year plan begun in 2008 are not yet clear (Dougherty, Wanzer, and Ramsay 2009).

St. Louis is located in a state with both southern and midwestern characteristics, its schools, public accommodations, housing, and employment heavily segregated through the middle of the twentieth century (Portz, Stein, and

Jones 1999). U.S. Census sources suggest the city lost close to 63 percent of its residents between 1950 and 2010, when its population dropped to 319,000. After the 1954 *Brown v. Board of Education* decision, housing patterns brought about school segregation. Portz, Stein, and Jones argue that Missouri's preferences for lower taxes and fewer state services combined with St. Louis's lack of political will dampened an impulse to change education policy. Moreover, with a considerable Catholic population, almost half of all St. Louis children were enrolled in private schools (1999, 142). This greatly reduced the proportion of its citizens with a stake in the success of public education. Roughly 80 percent of the children left in city schools were African American. The authors argue St. Louis lacked a robust civic life and was characterized not so much by political conflict as by inertia and an absence of involvement by key actors, including the business community.

Denver is an interesting case to consider because like Wake, it has experienced recent population growth (Horn and Kurlaender 2009). U.S. Census sources show that, having grown nearly 30 percent since 1990, it contained over 600,000 people in 2010. They also show that Denver has an educated population—43 percent of residents have a college degree—but it is also young and transient and therefore probably less capable of invigorating civic life. It is also not particularly affluent and has been majority-minority for some time. Specifically, Denver schools were 66 percent white in 1967, but by 1976, whites constituted a minority of students, and by 1994, 21 percent of its population was African American and 45 percent Latino (Horn and Kurlaender 2009, 228). By 2006, just 20 percent of students were white (228). Denver schools were formally desegregated in 1973 and achieved enough integration to be declared unitary—or integrated to acceptable levels under federal law—in 1995.[7] The city's growth may have had some effect on assignment policies. By 2009, 19 percent of its children attended charter, magnet, or other schools of choice as a result of changes in district policies.[8] Its schools, however, are still ranked poorly by assessors and are as racially homogeneous as they have ever been.[9]

San Antonio, Texas, is in this category as well. Holme, Welton, and Diem (2012) describe it as containing a system of "separate but equal" schools. Another majority-minority district, San Antonio is also characterized by considerable racial and socioeconomic segregation, owing in part to the significant influx of Latino and lower socioeconomic households. Many of its schools have become increasingly segregated with district officials unwilling to move away from reliance on the neighborhood model. Educational segregation therefore mirrors residential patterns. San Antonio schools have, however, devoted resources to differentiated instruction for at-risk students and have renovated school buildings, both in middle-class and lower-class neighborhoods, so as to effectively equalize schools' physical plants. The jurisdiction's leadership has therefore worked hard to improve educational outcomes, although it has done little to diversify schools (Holme, Welton, and Diem 2012).

We also place Metropolitan Nashville Public Schools in this category. This is a large countywide district that has been growing rapidly—by 16 percent between 2002 and 2012.[10] It is also majority-minority, and in 2012–13 the student population was close to 46 percent African American, 16 percent Latino, and 33 percent white. About two-thirds of children receive free or reduced-price lunches. Smrekar and Goldring (2009b) show how Nashville schools became segregated after the district was declared unitary in 1998. In response the district allowed children to attend schools closer to home, resulting in a replication of the city's residential segregation. Even the district's magnet schools became less diverse. Nashville remains formally committed to diversity, but with its wealthier residents having fled the system, it is finding it very difficult to meet its goals.[11]

Homogeneous District/Robust Civic Life

Included in this next category are suburban districts like Henrico County, Virginia (Ryan 2010), and those around Hartford (Dougherty, Wanzer, and Ramsay 2009). Here, because of elevated property values, populations tend to be white and middle class. This homogeneity renders the question of diversification in assignments moot, and citizens often do not see it as their responsibility to address educational challenges in adjacent urban jurisdictions.

Cuban (2010) claims that Austin, Texas, is "as good as it gets" in urban education. Like many other southern municipalities, Austin's twentieth-century history was characterized by strong racial segregation, in this case separating not only African American and white residents from one another but also Mexican Americans from both groups. These divisions applied not only to housing but also to schools, parks, transportation, and medical services. Like Richmond noted above, piecemeal efforts at desegregation prior to the 1970s resulted in little change in school composition (35). Although integration policies and magnets did produce some progress, many of Austin's residents resisted busing. Its schools were eventually declared unitary in 1986, but, if anything, the following years were characterized by increased segregation.

Some things changed in the late 1990s with the appointment of Superintendent Pascal P. Forgione Jr. Assisted by the state's increased emphasis on producing educated workers for an increasingly technological and white-collar economy, Forgione is credited with some successes in changing Austin's schools. But although he closed failing institutions and improved test scores, Forgione altered Austin's assignment policies only at the margins. Today U.S. Census sources indicate Austin is a relatively homogeneous—even with a population of about 850,000—university city with a strong civic life and little ideological conflict. By 2009 Austin had more than 82,000 students but was 73 percent minority and 60 percent poor, with many students being English language learners (Cuban 2010, 21).

Heterogeneous District/Limited Civic Life

The countywide school districts in many of Florida's urban areas have diverse populations, racially, ethnically, and socioeconomically. Table 7.1 shows Miami-Dade to be the fourth most populous district in the country; Broward (Fort Lauderdale), Hillsborough (Tampa), and Orange (Orlando) Counties are also large. Their growth is generated by migration of a magnitude similar to Wake's.

What perhaps differentiates these Florida jurisdictions from Wake are their civic lives and racial mixes. Although all four Florida counties are larger in total population, Wake's principal city (Raleigh) houses a considerably greater proportion of the parent county's aggregate population than does Miami, Fort Lauderdale, Tampa, or Orlando (U.S. Census Bureau 2014). Wake's residents are also more educated than those of the Florida counties, and Wake has a significantly lower proportion of minorities. Orange, Hillsborough, and Wake have similar proportions of African Americans, yet the percentage of Latino residents in Orange and Hillsborough is about 2.5 times greater than in Wake.

School board politics in the four Florida counties appear energetic, but in no case does there appear to have been a strong debate about school assignment policies. Our study of these districts' policies suggests, for example, that Miami-Dade uses neighborhood schools as a basis for assignments but offers choice for those who want it. There are over 340 such programs in 100 schools that enroll over 43,000 students.[12] Hillsborough students are assigned to schools based on their home addresses, but there are substantial options for magnet and choice schools. Magnet choices in elementary and middle schools are made randomly via computer. In Broward County, students are assigned to schools based on physical address; they can request transfers, which are available if the chosen places have space. Siblings are not automatically enrolled in a particular school, thus raising the potential for families to have children of similar ages receiving their education in different places. Finally, Orange County also bases attendance on a student's home address, but there are a number of magnet options as well as elaborate rules regarding student transfers.[13] Florida's jurisdictions use many assignment policies, therefore, but diversity does not play a particularly prominent role in them (Brown and Knight 2005).

We should briefly note two other cases of this type, both from outside Florida. Frasure-Yokley (2012) describes the "Azalea" school district in Orange County, California.[14] A majority-minority district, Azalea has a very low percentage of African American students but large and increasing proportions of Latinos. District investments in education were reduced by severe budget cuts dating back to the 1970s. While some believe increasing proportions of middle-class Latino parents will provide greater impetus for diversification, Frasure-Yokley argues that such activity has yet to reach a critical mass.

Gumus-Dawes, Orfield, and Luce (2012) describe the Osseo Area school district, north of Minneapolis. Although, with only 20,000 students, the district is quite small, it is ethnically diverse—it has a slim white majority and, at 16 percent, a relatively large Asian and Pacific Island population—and the northern part of Hennepin County that it occupies has grown rapidly over the past two decades. The system is not particularly segregated by social class, but students tend to attend schools with children of their own race or ethnicity, and the western municipalities have a greater proportion of whites. The use of magnet schools in Osseo has not resulted in substantial improvement in diversity, a matter reinforced by Minnesota state law that permits districts to promote integration but does not mandate or offer financial support for such policies. This district provides evidence that a heterogeneous population is not a sufficient condition for diverse schools.

Heterogeneous District/Robust Civic Life

Waltham, Massachusetts, a working-class suburban district just west of Boston, has had added to its traditional mix of European immigrants a recent influx of Latinos and Southeast Asians—although the municipality has grown slowly, even for urban New England (Eaton 2012). Public schools, however, have low levels of segregation by both race and class. Eaton argues that while new immigrants are wary of institutions such as government and the police, the community has built trust between families and the schools, thus strengthening bridging social capital. One district program, Waltham Family School, promotes family literacy with services for both preschoolers and their mothers and acquaints new residents with the public school system, involving them in the classrooms as advocates for their children. Eaton suggests that Waltham's efforts constitute a model that could be applied elsewhere (see also Tough 2009). The jurisdiction's experience may suggest that a robust civic life, at least as it is related directly to education, is important to diversity policies.

There are other districts with heterogeneous populations that also have strong civic lives. DeBray and Grooms (2012) give the pseudonym "Sewall" County to a jurisdiction west of Atlanta where the local chamber of commerce and school system have worked together to manage significant population growth and provide high-quality education for its students. African American residents are more educated than whites. It is notable that the county has relied entirely on neighborhood schools, with no magnets or charters, and very few approved transfers across neighborhood boundaries. In this case, deep public concern for education has been used to manage the effects of population growth and improve student achievement and race relations generally, without formally promoting integration. The effort has been assisted by the jurisdiction's residential patterns. In 2009–10, the average African American student attended a school that was about 55 percent African American, the average white student one that was about 37 percent African American. The average free or reduced-price lunch student attended a school that was about 50 percent African American and about 40 percent white (166). In contrast to Wake, this district appears to have achieved integrated schools while adhering to the neighborhood schools model.

Montgomery County, Maryland, in suburban Washington, D.C., has grown quickly as well—it had 20 percent more residents in 2010 than in 1990 (U.S. Census 1990, 2010). U.S. Census sources show it is a wealthy county with the tenth highest median income in the country and a highly educated population—over 50 percent of residents have a bachelor's degree, and many work in government or in technical fields. Its total population is close to Wake County's, although it has many more Latino and foreign-born residents. The county invests heavily in public schools and from all sources spends more than $15,000 a year per student, a figure that is nearly twice as large as Wake's, which is closer to $8,000 (Hui 2013c). Ayscue et al. (2013, 5) show how the county required builders to sell or rent a certain proportion of new homes below value to be used for public housing. In the areas where this occurred, socioeconomic diversity in schools increased, although more recent accounts suggest that Montgomery County's level of school segregation, although relatively low at 25 percent, is growing as a result of greater residential segregation and white flight. The district's schools very recently became majority-minority.[15] This case underscores the likelihood of changes in school diversity over time as a function of district population change.

Koski and Oakes (2009) trace the recent history of San Jose schools. Often called the capital of Silicon Valley, the city more than doubled in size between 1950 and 1960 and then again by 1970, when it reached close to 500,000 residents, according to U.S. Census sources. By 2010 its population numbered 946,000, with substantial communities of Asians and Latinos. In recent years, money from technology companies has boosted civic life tremendously, and the city boasts a vibrant culture. San Jose is quite wealthy and, for a municipality of its size, has a low crime rate.

San Jose schools were highly segregated in the 1960s and 1970s, but intervening court orders followed by visible political will by Latino parents and the use of magnet schools furthered integration efforts through 1994 (Koski and Oakes 2009). This was followed by a strengthening focus on improving educational outcomes for Latino students, who by the end of the 1990s constituted a majority. Although the district pursued a variety of strategies, including voluntary integration by social class, the emphasis was on improving Latino educational outcomes rather than on diversification. San Jose's may be a story of policy change like Wake's, but the district remains quite segregated by ethnicity. The case illustrates that a robust civic life need not always generate diversification policies.

Finally, Jefferson County, Kentucky, has grown by about 10 percent since 1990 and currently has approximately 250,000 residents (U.S. Census 1990, 2010). It is majority white, with almost the same population of Latinos as Wake County. Its system was created from a merger with Louisville city schools under a court order in the 1970s. Phillips and her colleagues (2009) find that despite a rocky start to desegregation efforts in the mid-1970s, by 1978 the district embraced integration, a path it continued to follow through the early 2000s. Setting assignment policies that promised stability and proximity to home, Jefferson County was still able to maintain heterogeneous schools. In 1996 it adopted a diversification plan that required each school to have at least 15 percent but no more than 50 percent of its students African American. In June 2007, in a decision best known for its more famous companion *Parents Involved in Community Schools v. Seattle*, the U.S. Supreme Court determined that Jefferson's racial assignment plan was unconstitutional.[16] The board then moved the following year to adopt an approach, first conceived in 2002, to provide diversity by assigning students to schools based upon their parents' income (Garland 2013). Although smaller than Wake, this district shows similarities in terms of its persistence in successful school desegregation and use of socioeconomic status to continue desegregation efforts.

A Comparison of Wake with Charlotte-Mecklenburg

It is logical to wonder whether Wake might have another obvious peer in Charlotte, North Carolina's largest city. As Table 7.3 demonstrates, in 2010 Mecklenburg and Wake had populations of similar size, with the former's being slightly greater. But Wake is a much larger county in terms of area, and Charlotte is considerably more populous than Raleigh. This means Wake is less densely populated than the more centrally concentrated Mecklenburg. If both counties were to use busing to pursue school desegregation, Wake children would likely be transported farther than Mecklenburg children.

The two counties also have a different history of population growth. In 1980, Charlotte-Mecklenburg's population was 34 percent higher than Wake's. By 2000, it was only about 11 percent higher, a difference that had decreased to about 2 percent by 2010. While both counties have grown notably, Wake's rate of growth at 43.5 percent between 2000 and 2010 outstripped Mecklenburg's 32.2 percent. Moreover, residential segregation by race, as measured by dissimilarity indices, is more pronounced in Mecklenburg (University of Michigan Population Studies Center 2013). Given the reciprocal relationship between residential and school segregation, this means the jurisdiction would probably need more aggressive strategies to reach the same levels of desegregation. Wake is less diverse than Mecklenburg, which had close to 44 percent African Americans and Latinos in 2010 compared to Wake's 31.3 percent. Wake also has higher rates of high school and college completion, more home ownership, higher housing values, and lower rates of poverty.

Table 7.4 helps us to compare the two school districts. Their demographic and social characteristics mirror those of the counties as a whole: Wake has a higher percentage of white students, while Charlotte-Mecklenburg Schools (CMS) have a higher proportion of African Americans. Wake's percentage of students qualifying for free or reduced-price lunches is lower. Wake is also the larger district in terms of numbers of students, reflecting, at least in part, CMS's rates of private school attendance. However, Wake has more homeschooled children and slightly more charter schools. Despite Wake's extensive use of magnet schools, CMS actually has more magnet programs. CMS's dropout rate is higher, its per-pupil expenditure greater. These different characteristics are an integral part of the story of the two districts' divergent experiences with integration (see Mickelson, Smith, and Hawn Nelson 2015 for details on CMS).

To be sure, the processes of desegregation in the two jurisdictions show key similarities. Both have countywide districts, have been committed to improving educational outcomes generally, and have experienced success in deseg-

Table 7.3 Comparison of Charlotte-Mecklenburg County and Wake County on Population Characteristics

	Charlotte-Mecklenburg County	Wake County
Land area in square miles	523.84	835.22
Population (2010)	919,268	900,993
Population (2000)[a]	695,454	627,846
Population (1980)[b]	404,270	301,327
% population change (2000–10)[c]	+32.2	+43.5
% population change (2010–12)	+5.4	+5.7
% white (2010)	60.7	70.0
% African American (2010)	31.5	21.3
% Latino (2010)	12.4	10.0
% high school grads (2007–11)	88.6	91.8
% bachelor's degree (2007–11)	40.4	47.9
Homeownership rate (2007–11)	61.8	66.6
Median value of owner-occupied housing units (2007–11)	$187,300	$227,600
Median household income (2007–11)	$55,194	$65,289
% below the poverty level (2007–11)	13.6	10.1
Dissimilarity index (white– African American, 2010)[d]	61.1	56.2
Dissimilarity index score (white-Latino, 2010)[d]	57.9	53.9

Note: All estimates, unless otherwise noted, are from the 2010 U.S. Census.
[a]Information is from the 2000 U.S. Census.
[b]Information is from the 1980 U.S. Census.
[c]Information to compute this estimate comes from the 2000 U.S. Census and the 2010 U.S. Census.
[d]Information is from the U.S. Census Scope (http://www.censusscope.org/). The dissimilarity index measures the relative separation or integration of groups across neighborhoods. These estimates are not available for counties, so our estimates indicate dissimilarity scores for Charlotte and Raleigh. For example, a white–African American dissimilarity score of 56.2 for Raleigh means that 56.2 percent of whites would have to relocate to another neighborhood to make whites and African Americans evenly represented across all neighborhoods.

regation and improved educational outcomes in the 1980s. Both historically have had at least nominally nonpartisan school boards that, by around 2000, were becoming more partisan. Their school funding models are also similar, with each district dependent on county commissioners to authorize operating budgets and bond issuances for capital projects. At times each district had pro-diversity school boards and strong superintendents who pursued policies supporting integration. Both also used busing to achieve these objectives, with

Table 7.4 Comparison of Charlotte-Mecklenburg County and Wake County on School District Characteristics

	Charlotte-Mecklenburg	Wake County
Number of schools in district (2012)[a]	159	165
Number of students in school district (2012)[a]	135,000	149,508
Student body: % white (2012)[b]	32	49
Student body: % African American (2012)[b]	42	24
Student body: % other (2012)[b]	23	27
% free or reduced-price lunch eligibility (2012)[c]	56.8	34.8
Number of private school enrollments (2012)[d]	19,545	16,135
Number of home schools (2012)[e]	4,041	4,913
Number of charter schools (2012)[f]	12	14
Number of magnet programs (2012)[a]	40	31
Per pupil expenditure (2012)[g]	2,424	2,007
High school graduation rate (2012)[a]	74	80.4
High school dropout rate (2012)[a]	3.20	2.83

[a]Information comes from the district websites for Charlotte-Mecklenburg (http://www.cms.k12.nc.us/Pages/default.aspx) and Wake County (http://www.wcpss.net/).

[b]Estimates for Charlotte-Mecklenburg are from Mickelson, Smith, and Hawn Nelson (2015, chapter 2); estimates for Wake County are from the Wake County district website (http://www.wcpss.net/).

[c]Estimates are from the North Carolina Department of Public Instruction, Division of Financial and Business Services, "Free & Reduced Meal Application Data" (http://www.ncpublicschools.org/fbs/resources/data/).

[d]Estimates are from the North Carolina Department of Administration annual report, available at http://www.ncdnpe.org/documents/11-12CSStats.pdf.

[e]Estimates are from the Division of Non-public Education (http://www.ncdnpe.org/documents/hhh238.pdf).

[f]Estimates for Charlotte-Mecklenburg are from the MeckEd website (http://www.mecked.org/index.php/advocacy/charter-schools/charter-data/); estimates for Wake County are from the Wake County Economic Development website (http://www.raleigh-wake.org/page/private-charter-and-international-schools).

[g]Estimates are from the Public School Forum of NC (http://www.ncforum.org/).

more recent assignment plans in the jurisdictions featuring the language of choice. Finally, both have garnered national acclaim as models of large urban districts committed to education (Grant 2009; Kahlenberg 2001).

Differences occur in the strategies used to achieve integration, as well as in the timing of important historical events. CMS was created as a countywide school district earlier (1959 as opposed to 1976), while Wake consolidated after most of the dust from the school desegregation battles of the 1960s and early 1970s had settled, thus avoiding the early conflicts and turbulence that characterized CMS's efforts to desegregate. In terms of desegregation and student achievement, it would seem that the post-1974 period in CMS and the post-1976 period in Wake were very similar. Both districts achieved relatively rapid school desegregation as well as improved educational outcomes. However, while Wake used a system of magnets to entice white parents to place their children in urban, minority schools, CMS's primary strategy paired elementary schools with differing racial concentrations and bused between them. In CMS, the burden of busing fell disproportionately on African Americans, a development that caused racial tension (Mickelson 2001). In Wake, there was busing both to and from central Raleigh; arguments regarding African Americans bearing more of the burden of busing were present but muted by comparison (Silberman 2001).

The differing experiences continued. In 1991 CMS began a program of controlled choice, thus moving away from the use of paired schools. During 1996–97, when CMS had completed this process, Wake was still actively pursuing diversity in assignments and seeing some improved educational outcomes. CMS also made a series of decisions about siting schools in areas of strong population growth that resulted in increased housing segregation. The location of the Charlotte-Mecklenburg I-485 outer belt exacerbated this trend. In contrast, while Wake also built new schools, it used year-round facilities as an additional mechanism to contain costs and, at least later, continue its push for diversity. Wake's persistent and global use of diversity discouraged residential segregation.

CMS was declared unitary in 1999 with a declaration in the Capacchione case that race could not be used as a basis for children's school assignment. This decision took the pressure off CMS to further desegregate schools, since much of the argument for integration was based upon court mandate. In the aftermath of the ruling, the commitment of Charlotte's business elite to diverse schools waned, while in Wake, elite support remained strong. It was ironic that it was in reaction to CMS being declared unitary that Wake shifted from using race to socioeconomic status as a basis for school integration. Wake's policy change allowed it to continue to pursue diversity, while in CMS, schools became more racially and socioeconomically homogeneous. By 2006 CMS's policy focused on providing all children with the best education possible (Mickelson, Smith, and Hawn Nelson 2015, chapter 2). Instead of decoupling these, Wake continued to pursue both diversity and student achievement.

A stronger Republican and conservative political history in Mecklenburg may help to explain why support for diversity was lower there. So may the relatively low levels of political trust researchers have detected among Charlotte residents (Rahn and Rudolph 2005). Mecklenburg also became majority-minority sooner than Wake. This challenging demographic situation may have decreased the incentive to pursue desegregation in the county even more. In addition, despite CMS's notable use of magnet schools, Wake's magnet schools improved diversity more effectively. By the time CMS really tried magnet schools, its residents' political attitudes were shifting away from desegregation. The choice models CMS devised did not allow parents much latitude in assignments because schools in newer, white areas quickly became crowded. Few slots were therefore available for minorities who wished to transfer there. Development arguments in Charlotte also typically trumped support for desegregation (Smith 2004).

Critically, unlike CMS, the integration of Wake's schools was not undertaken by court order.[17] Pressure from federal administrators and judges to mix schools by race certainly exerted considerable influence over Wake's policy makers both before and after the merger. But policies designed to bring about desegregation, like magnet schools and the 15/45 plan, were established without the formal supervision of a court. The broad if tacit support of a majority of the county's residents and business and political leaders was sufficient to bring about a degree of racial integration that prevented federal intervention (Silberman 2001). After 1999 there was little to compensate for the loss of judicial imprimatur for desegregation in Charlotte. Finally, the African American community in Wake appears to have been less conspicuous in education politics than its Mecklenburg counterpart (see Smith 2004, 31–32, 71–72, for discussion of Mecklenburg).

Wake was able to sustain racial and socioeconomic diversity policies for far longer than CMS. Its people are more heterogeneous—in that they more closely resemble the broader state and national population—and it has traditionally enjoyed a stronger civic life. Despite their many similarities and geographic proximity to one another, Wake and CMS are not exactly peers.

Is Wake Unique?

We have argued that Wake is not alone in having a diverse population and robust civic life capable of undergirding policies of school desegregation. However, we believe Wake is alone among large districts across the nation in persisting with a diversity policy as a central feature. Indeed, as of 2012, analysis identifies the top twelve most segregated districts as Chicago, Dallas, New York City, Philadelphia, Houston, Los Angeles, Phoenix, San Diego, San Antonio, Indianapolis, San Francisco, Jacksonville, and San Jose.[18] Of the large school districts listed in Table 7.1, Los Angeles and Houston are majority-minority, thus decreasing the potential for school desegregation based on either race or social class. Clark County, Nevada, has been growing quickly and is racially and ethnically diverse but relies heavily on neighborhood schools. Fairfax County, Virginia, contains about 80 percent white and Asian populations. In 2012 it had a median household income of over $108,000 and a poverty rate of about 1 percent; it stresses student achievement, essential life skills, and responsibility to the community, not diversity. Its capacity to achieve diverse schools is therefore limited for reasons quite unlike majority-minority districts. We have already documented that the Florida districts, despite being demographically diverse, rely on neighborhood schools. And Hawaii schools, which make up a statewide school system, are not useful in comparison with Wake given their unique ethnic and geographical character.

Perhaps a more meaningful comparison would be Gwinnett County, part of the Atlanta region, with 44 percent non-Latino whites and close to 44 percent African American and Latino populations, the most racially diverse county in Georgia and among the most diverse counties in the United States. If Gwinnett has integrated schools, it is not by design but because housing segregation is modest. Children there are assigned to schools within clusters. The five districts just slightly smaller than Wake include Montgomery County, Maryland, and Charlotte-Mecklenburg, both of which we have discussed, as well as Duval County (Jacksonville), also in Florida and the twelfth most segregated large district in the country. Philadelphia and San Diego schools are majority-minority and heavily segregated.

In sum, of all the large jurisdictions nationally, only Gwinnett and Montgomery have schools that are as diverse as Wake's. As we have noted, Montgomery uses housing policy to pursue school desegregation, although a diversity policy has played a supportive role at times. Gwinnett's neighborhoods appear naturally integrated, and it does not use a school diversity policy as such. These realities place Wake in a unique position among large districts. Its combination of a heterogeneous population—that is, not too white, not too minority—and rich civic life, we believe, make a crucial difference.

We should note that the recent and significant dynamism in its policies regarding assignment also makes Wake different. Our study of policy change above has been necessarily cross-sectional. However, as far as we can tell, in the cases that are Wake's opposites—those with homogeneous populations and minimal civic life—there is little debate about school assignments, and observers often lament educational outcomes. Despite this, it is often the case that dominant political forces effectively kill proposed policy changes. Shrinking populations, principally caused by middle-class residents fleeing urban areas, also reduce the resources necessary to make such changes.

Two characteristics, dramatic population growth and competitive partisan politics, seem to explain Wake schools' rather unusually intense and fluid policy making. Newcomers of all types are likely to be attracted to a jurisdiction with a robust civic life. This combination creates a vibrant and broadly participatory debate about public schools. Diverse populations may provide energy for integrative assignment policies, but they also bring about political heterogeneity and a challenge to them.

8 ▸ An Epilogue and Conclusion

The central purpose of this book has been to explain the end of a consensus surrounding public school governance in Wake County. We found that explosive population growth, elevated partisanship and politicization of local matters, and a growing and increasingly coordinated opposition to the existing school board majority and its decisions, particularly those surrounding diversity in student assignments, brought about tremendous change in board composition and many policies. The board elected in 2009 found governing difficult, and Republican control lasted only two years. Despite the establishment of a pro-diversity majority after 2011, however, the old policy was not immediately or completely revived. It is against this backdrop that we first describe events between 2011 and 2014 in more detail and then reflect on our findings.

The 2011 Election and Another New Board

The 2011 school board election campaign focused intently on the performance of the Republican majority and the policies it had issued or was intending to issue—recall that the final approval of the "controlled choice" assignment plan did not take place until two weeks after voters went to the polls in early October. Five seats were contested, all four that Democrats were defending in and immediately surrounding the city of Raleigh—Kevin Hill's third district, Keith Sutton's fourth, Anne McLaurin's fifth, and Carolyn Morrison's sixth—as well as the seat of the board's chair, Ron Margiotta, in the eighth district covering Apex and parts of Cary and Holly Springs. To regain the majority, therefore, candidates affiliated with the Democrats needed to win every race. Again, as in 2009, significant sums were raised and spent on the campaign—approximately $500,000 this time around (Stover 2012). There was a palpable sense that the stakes were high.

As expected, the Democrats quite comfortably held on to the seats in the fourth, fifth, and sixth districts, where Sutton and newcomers Jim Martin and Christine Kushner won. Control of the board therefore effectively came down to two races, between incumbent Hill and Heather Losurdo and between Margiotta and his challenger, Susan Evans. On election night, Evans was able to eke out a narrow and dramatic victory by winning most of the eighth's precincts outside of Margiotta's hometown of Apex. Her supporters attributed the victory to a repudiation of Margiotta's leadership and the board's policies (Goldsmith and Hui 2011), although the geographical pattern in returns suggest that Margiotta may have been viewed as less attentive to the needs of constituents outside the area of Apex where he lived.[1] Regardless, the Evans victory meant the Hill-Losurdo contest would decide who controlled the board and likely the future direction of public schools in the county. Hill won a plurality in October but with 49.7 percent of the vote came fifty-one votes shy of a majority. As the second-place finisher, Losurdo invoked her right to request a runoff.

The race had already attracted a great deal of attention and money. By the end of the runoff campaign, the candidates had raised around $125,000 between them, about two-thirds of it going to Losurdo (Hui 2011; Stover 2012). It was also acrimonious. Hill was boosted by thousands of dollars spent by the Democrat-affiliated 527 group Common Sense on fliers attacking his opponent (Hui, Goldsmith, and Garfield 2011). Comments made by Losurdo about President Obama on Facebook became a subject of debate, and she was considered unfit for office by opponents who questioned her past—which included a stint as a waitress in a strip club—and accused her of exaggerating her midlevel responsibilities at a bank. Fliers linking Hill to a liberal machine led by Obama mysteriously ended up in mailboxes. The odds were stacked against Losurdo, but she was assisted by elevated public interest that was sure to increase turnout for the rematch four weeks later. This was indeed the case; nearly 4,000 more voters went to the polls. Hill managed to win narrowly with 52.3 percent, and the county's experiment with a Republican and conservative school board majority was over.

The new Democratic-majority school board inherited the controlled choice assignment plan adopted just weeks earlier. It moved to examine the policy with the intention of changing it. This kind of work was, as the Republican majority discovered two years earlier, tough sledding as staff collected and analyzed mountains of data and the legal foundations of possible approaches. In June 2012 the board, after heated debate and a "party-line" 5–4 vote, altered the assignment policy to return to an address-based plan with expanded magnet school options (Goldsmith and Hui 2012). In May 2013 it amended this new policy to make it more consistent with principles of diversity. Efforts would be made in assignments to minimize concentrations of poor-performing and low income students, and in schools where optimal amounts of diversity were unattainable, a new office would work to promote equity (Hui 2013b).

Unsurprisingly, partisan disputes dominated in 2012 and 2013. Superintendent Tony Tata's relationship with the Democratic majority and its first chair,

Kevin Hill, rapidly deteriorated (Hui 2012). Tata was eventually fired in the late summer of 2012 after widespread problems with bus services brought on by state spending cuts and, possibly, the new controlled choice assignment plan that lengthened many routes.[2] The board majority, several of whom had challenged Tata's legitimacy because of his professional background outside of education, hired Jim Merrill, superintendent in Virginia Beach and a former assistant superintendent in Wake, as permanent replacement in June 2013.

In control of the state's General Assembly, Republicans attempted to undermine Democratic governance of the board. They were able to pass legislation in 2013 that reapportioned the school board's seats to produce two "regional" districts that covered the entire county and seven smaller, more conventional districts. Elections were also moved to coincide with federal and state contests in even-numbered years. The idea was to improve future Republican candidates' chances of being elected (Hui 2013d). The state legislature was less successful in its attempt to have responsibility for school construction and land acquisition transferred from the board to county commissioners. The bill, defeated in the House, was representative of a strained relationship, generally over funding issues, between the two countywide governing bodies.

The Republican position on the school board was damaged beyond immediate repair by the efforts of three members to run for higher office in 2012. John Tedesco won a primary for the state superintendent's office but lost in the November general election to incumbent Democrat June Atkinson. Just before their elections, Debra Goldman, who was the Republican nominee for state auditor, and Chris Malone, who was chasing a state House seat centered around his hometown of Wake Forest, were the subject of bizarre stories in the media suggesting they had been involved romantically and that Goldman had reported Malone to the police for burglarizing her residence. Malone won his election and left the board, replaced by Tom Benton, a Democrat and former principal. Goldman lost hers, and with her position on the board effectively untenable, she took a job elsewhere in the state and resigned. She was replaced by Bill Fletcher, a moderate Republican and realtor who had been on the board from 1993 to 2005. When Tedesco said he would not run for reelection in 2013, the only remaining member of the original five in the Republican majority was Deborah Prickett.

The board's new membership prohibited any kind of coalition of conservatives from seizing back control after the October 2013 election. As a result the campaign was relatively subdued and the money raised was considerably less than what it had been in 2009 and 2011. There were conservative challengers to Benton and Fletcher—Don McIntyre in the first district, Nancy Caggia in the ninth—and they ran the incumbents very close. But a Democrat, Monika Johnson-Hostler, won Tedesco's old second district seat and Prickett lost hers in the seventh. This defeat, by a considerable fifteen percentage points, cemented Democratic control. Now there would be just one Republican on the board, old hand Fletcher, who had a long history of working with Democrats.

A construction bond worth $810 million was also quite handily approved by 58 percent of the county's voters that day. Most of Wake's political and business leadership supported the effort; the county Republican Party and Taxpayers' Association were two of the very few groups to oppose it. Added to the school board election and particularly Prickett's resounding defeat, the bond result constituted a significant setback for conservative interests in Wake public school politics. It also suggested a shift in the party's strength in the county. Residents in the western suburbs who—somewhat inaccurately, as our analysis shows—had been accused of leading the fight against liberal initiatives like the diversity assignment policy and mandatory year-round schools strongly supported the bond. Opposition was most robust in the far outlying rural areas and the small towns of eastern Wake.

Despite this victory, the Democratic board had still not fully reestablished a diversity assignment policy. As of early 2015, it continued to wrestle with the codification and implementation of assignment rules that balanced principles like student heterogeneity and proximity. Just as the Republican board had not overhauled the old diversity policy in as rapid and comprehensive a manner as the intense politics of the time suggested it would, the new Democratic majority seemed unwilling to return fully to the traditional diversity policy and its former implementation strategies.

How Are Attitudes toward School Assignment Policies Configured?

One major finding from our qualitative research is that of polarization. Community elites we interviewed portrayed themselves as in favor of either diversity or neighborhood schools. Although some acknowledged the legitimacy of the opposing viewpoint, interviewees characterized themselves as solidly in one camp or the other. Media coverage also framed the two positions as diametrically opposed. Our survey, however, revealed a more nuanced picture. We discovered that support for neighborhood schools and diversity did not occupy each end of a single continuum but rather constituted two separate dimensions of sentiment. Although inverse, the relationship between the two was not perfectly so. Our findings suggest that many individuals favored neighborhood schools, but a subset of them were also strongly committed to diversity, rendering the structure of attitudes around the issue considerably more complex than a purely polarized model would imply. These findings are important and suggest that our initial hunch had been correct: Wake citizens favored both diversity and neighborhood schools and would likely support a policy that incorporated elements of each. This may explain the delayed and tempered assignment policies made in 2011 and 2013.

We were also able to discern three specific problems that respondents saw in reassignments: they suggested that transferring children between schools presented significant challenges for parents; they worried about the dangers to learning and friendships, a form of social capital, from repeated reassignments; and they fretted about the uncertainties generated by frequent transfers and the seemingly arbitrary reassignment process. Wake County residents' attitudes about student assignment policies were not only multidimensional but also clouded by the practice of frequent reassignment.

Beyond Description: What about Race, Gender, and Politics?

For many on the left side of the political spectrum, African American or white, Wake's story has strong racial overtones. Even after the assignment policy was overhauled to account for students' socioeconomic status, many equated diversity entirely with race. Supporters frequently claimed that critics' embrace of neighborhood schools was motivated by skin color; their opposition often argued the new approach using income was a thinly veiled effort to engineer racial heterogeneity. We have shown that there are many reasons why county residents supported or opposed diversity. It is undeniably true, however, that African Americans approved of the approach appreciably more than did whites, even after controlling for things such as gender and ideology. They, more than whites, seemed to view diversity as beneficial to their children.

On further inspection, however, race's role is complex. African American attitudes about diversity were not monolithic. Affluent African American residents with large reserves of social capital were the principle's most vocal supporters. Poorer African Americans who lived in central Raleigh were considerably more ambivalent. It was children in their neighborhoods who were often bused long distances in the policy's implementation. Our interview data suggest that African American parents felt that wealthier whites were using them as pawns in a broader political struggle and wondered why the county could not place good schools in their communities.

Race, moreover, played no role in resident attitudes about mandatory year-round schooling. Its influence on views about the ad hoc reassignment process that had become an annual event is interesting as well. Whites were demonstrably more sensitive to the challenges, dangers, and uncertainties of annual reassignments. We speculate that one reason for the difference might be that African Americans were acutely aware that reassignments had been an integral part of the effort to keep schools diversified. Another might be that by living in the most rapidly growing parts of the county, whites were more frequently exposed to board-mandated transfers.

We detected some polarization by age, with older respondents more supportive of neighborhood schools and less so of diversity. They were also more likely to approve of the school board's actions. Unsurprisingly, political ideology was quite clearly a powerful predictor as well. The story here is consistent with the general trend of increased partisanship and polarization in American politics at all levels, as we described in chapter 2. Conservatives were appreciably less supportive of diversity and more likely to favor neighborhood schools and the Republican-controlled board, as well as to fret about the challenges and dangers of reassignments. They were also more critical of the year-round calendar, a finding that is presumably attributable to the ideological framing of the schools debate in Wake and not particularly consistent with conservative philosophy that generally appreciates the lower costs of year-round schooling.

We found gender to be a major dimension of polarization. Women were demonstrably more supportive of diversity in public school assignments than were men, while, interestingly, men and women were equally supportive of neighborhood schools. This discovery reinforced our conclusion that diversity and neighborhood schools are not polar opposites. We also found women to be more worried than men about the challenges, dangers, and uncertainties of reassignment. These results place women's greater support for diversity in broader perspective. They suggest that the strength of the position is such that it can resist the costs women disproportionately pay for school assignments that frequently change or that are distant from home. Such costs involve the actual work of understanding the assignment process and how it may affect children, advocating for the family, and availing oneself of children's schooling options should they be targeted for transfer. They may also require "emotional capital" (Reay 2000) to deal with children who are upset with the prospect of changing schools and the associated disruption to their lives.

We also uncovered interesting features of whites' attitudes toward diversity. Those with an attitude of racial animus did not, unsurprisingly, favor a policy imposing socioeconomic or racial integration. Those who lived in urban Raleigh were more supportive, a position that might have reflected the policy's effect of actually making the city's schools less diverse as low-income children were assigned to more affluent suburban schools.

In all, both our qualitative and quantitative findings suggest that within each racial group, there was a variation of opinion regarding school assignment. As the effects of knowledge about busing demonstrate, this is somewhat attributable to a lack of information, but it also is a function of each respondent's proximity to the policy. Whites and African Americans with school-age children tended to oppose diversity and mandatory year-round schools and display significant concerns for the challenges, dangers, and uncertainties of reassignments. This, in turn, suggests that the salience of the effects of the board's decisions, as well as self-interest, played a strong role in the formation of attitudes. We return to this idea below.

The Importance of Social Class and Social Capital in Attitude Formation

Social class and affluence are powerful protectors from concerns generated by assignment policies. Those with higher incomes and more education were less likely to worry about challenges, dangers, and uncertainties; they were also more likely to support year-round schools. In addition, the better educated were less likely to advocate neighborhood schools. Such social and economic resources seemed to allow residents to cope with the anxieties and manage the costs of their children transferring to schools that were more distant or attended by students of different backgrounds. Greater trust in government is a powerful insulator as well. Elevated levels of trust in government led to a heightened acceptance of policies that could undermine stability in school assignments and interfere with traditional educational arrangements. Higher levels of organizational involvement, another mechanism through which people can build bridging social capital, did not have comparable effects—although, as was expected, those with higher levels of organizational involvement were less supportive of neighborhood schools and, among African Americans, more supportive of diversity.

Implications for Social Capital: Neighborhood Schools as a Cultural Model

Wake's residents probably attended a variety of types of schools growing up. Our evidence suggests that despite variation in these individual experiences, the idea of what neighborhood schools are and how they function retained a powerful grip on citizen expectations for K–12 education. We saw this in the general agreement that such schools are best for parents and children and when residents worried about long bus rides, protested children's repeated transfers, and actively resisted mandatory assignment to year-round schools. Although families tended to adjust quickly to the changes in board policy that affected their families, initial reactions were frequently deeply negative.

We have speculated that some of these reactions were tied to the notion that neighborhood schools help households manage both work and family demands. Our findings show that longer household work hours did indeed increase criticism of diversity and support for neighborhood schools, although longer commutes had the opposite effect. Our qualitative evidence also suggests that having children attend schools farther from home was a particular challenge for single-headed households.

We believe these findings have implications for social capital theory generally. We have argued that neighborhood schools facilitate both bonding social capital within families as well as bridging social capital between parents and teachers, between children and teachers, and among children themselves. The neighborhood schools model also promotes time closure, in that successive children within families often attend the same schools, possibly learning from the same teachers as older siblings. We have noted that frequent reassignments disrupt stability of bonds for individual students and require that both parents and children invest in a different stock of capital for the future. Year-round schools potentially place children from the same family on different school calendars, thus disrupting family bonding social capital further.

These forces were indeed at work in Wake County. For example, stability in school assignments was a recurrent theme with the people we interviewed. The board elected in 2011 understood that. By assuring greater stability in future school assignments, the board favored a policy that would improve the time closure of relationships between families and schools. Stability in assignments would also reduce the work that households, and often mothers, must do to sift among school choices to make the best decisions for their families. The policy would facilitate the paths of younger children who are allowed to attend their elder siblings' schools. This "placement inheritance" would strengthen the social capital linking families and schools by encouraging parental involvement in education. In short, stability and proximity in assignments should facilitate the work-life balance many families seek.

At the same time, adhering more closely to the policy of neighborhood schools places at risk the types of social capital than can be built within diverse schools. For advocates of diversity, the notion that children from different backgrounds will learn to work with one another is an important one. Evidence suggesting that children of lower socioeconomic status gain disproportionately from such arrangements is welcome news to those who would like to see schools ameliorate social inequality. School assignment policies that blend these two models may therefore generate the greatest public support.

What Does the Wake Case Say about School Assignment Policies Generally?

We have described how the consensus around the diversity policy broke down in Wake, particularly after 2000. Conversely, we should also ask why consensus lasted so long. We argue that comparing Wake to Charlotte-Mecklenburg provides important insights to this question because, in contrast to Wake, Charlotte-Mecklenburg's diversity policy for school assignments was not long-lived. We have noted that Charlotte-Mecklenburg grew in population earlier than did Raleigh, and its school district became majority-minority sooner. Its policy makers made different decisions regarding the use of magnet schools, and its Republican Party was traditionally stronger than Wake's. We have suggested that differences in civic life and elite leadership have been consequential as well.

But we also have looked at cases beyond North Carolina. Large jurisdictions that become majority-minority do not often have the demographic characteristics necessary to create socioeconomically diverse schools. Very small communities may, because of their homogeneous housing stocks, lack the capacity to create such heterogeneity too. Proponents of diversity may therefore take comfort in a long-term trend in the United States toward school district consolidation. Howell (2005, 4) finds that from 1936 to 1997, the number of jurisdictions fell from 118,892 to 15,178. Current debates regarding consolidation in order to reap economies of scale (Waters 2012) may provide additional opportunity for communities to organize schools with diversity as a principle.

However, and as we have seen, particularly with the Florida cases, the demographic capacity to diversify districts does not necessarily lead to diverse schools. Florida stands somewhat in contrast to other areas that utilize neighborhood schools in small jurisdictions because it uses this model on a large, countywide scale. At least for the districts we studied, the civic lives of Florida's counties seemed less robust than elsewhere. Assuming this, we would expect them to have less debate about school assignment policies.

Is There a New Consensus Forming? Will Wake Go Back?

Prediction is difficult. As of this writing, however, it appears that a new consensus may be forming, one that is different from that prior to 2009. Having rejected the approach of the Republican-backed board of 2009–11, the new Democratic majorities have returned to neither frequent reassignments nor an assignment plan based largely on mandatory year-round schools. They have not fully reimplemented the old diversity policy. The newer boards have appeared more responsive to the importance of stability in children's school assignments and to proximity between children's homes and schools than the Democratically controlled boards of the past. They appear to have heard parents' concerns regarding what we have termed challenges, dangers, and uncertainties. They have been assisted by a slight infusion of resources, particularly from a recent bond referendum, and, during the recession, a short respite from strong population growth. A basic if ambiguous commitment to use socioeconomic heterogeneity as a feature of the assignment policy remains. If the end of consensus produced anything, it was a complicating of the debate between the neighborhood schools and diversity models. With the resumption of population growth in the past year or so, these complications have only intensified.

By November 2013 it was therefore clear that the board would not return to precisely the same diversity policy the county had held prior to 2009. Increased numbers of schools were struggling with student achievement. Recognizing that two-thirds of the student body growth between 2009 and 2013 had been low-income and that parents have educational choices other than traditional public schools, the board was discussing a multipronged approach to improving student learning (Hui 2013a). As Keith Sutton, then chair, stated, "We can't rely solely on assignment to balance student achievement. We can't rely solely on magnet programs to balance student achievement. You can't rely only on an infusion of additional money. There's not a single bullet" (Hui 2013a).

These findings underscore the importance of the typology we developed in chapter 7 yet provide cautionary evidence regarding Wake's placement within it. As of 2014, the county's public schools are majority-minority, if one counts students of more than one race as minority. Its capacity to rely on student reassignment to mix most schools socioeconomically has therefore declined. The county may also look increasingly like other urban districts we have discussed. Given social, economic, and political developments that make the county increasingly Democratic as well—55 percent of its voters supported Barack Obama in the 2012 presidential election—there may be little organized opposition to Democratic-majority school boards. Wake's relatively affluent citizenry will need to maintain the county's robust civic life if they are to promote a strong educational system for all children.

When Institutions Collide

Much of the literature on the relationship between families and schools advocates for cooperation between these two institutions. It is intuitive that when families and schools work in tandem, with the same values and goals, academic performance is enhanced. The evidence for this notion, however, is mixed, with some studies finding that parental involvement supports child academic achievement (Comer and Haynes 1991; Dufur, Parcel and Troutman 2013; Jeynes, 2005, 2007), while others present mixed or negative findings (Fan and Chen 2001; Robinson and Harris 2014). These debates, however, neglect the fact that conflict between these institutions is a reality of modern life.

The family retains enormous power in modern society, especially with regard to education. Families begin preparing their offspring even before children enter school, and they do much to determine educational success (Hart and Risley 1995; Heckman 2008; Tough 2009). There is considerable variance in how much effort parents put into this, however. Socioeconomic status seems to be the key determinant here, and the results of socialization continue to be felt through the childhood and adolescent years, with middle-class children being prepared for adult roles via "concerted cultivation" and the less affluent through the more laissez-faire "accomplishment of natural growth" (Lareau 2011). Although Schaub (2010) argues that the relationship between socioeconomic status and adult nurturance of early verbal ability has declined over time and Sui-Chu and Willms (1996) find that parents of lower socioeconomic status are involved in children's schooling, strong evidence remains that class undergirds the nature and amount of parental investment in children (Parcel and Hendrix 2014).

Middle-class families have considerable latitude to decide where they will reside, while less affluent households are more constrained. If the school district in which families locate uses neighborhood schools, which is currently the case for about 73 percent of jurisdictions (Lareau 2014, 169), then the selection of homes and schools is simultaneous. Similarly, when children attend private schools or are homeschooled (Lois 2013), their parents have considerable control over their education. Some public school systems like Wake, however, are increasingly steering participating children to particular schools and interfering with what has traditionally been considered largely a family's choice. Given parents' investment in and influence over children's education, conditions are ripe for conflict when officials promulgate policies to shape school assignments, especially if these policies conflict with long-established cultural models.

Lareau and Muñoz (2012) provide one illustration of family-school conflict where the administration was able to prevail. The Wake case, however, reveals a dispute on a much larger scale. As we have noted, although parental control over assignments can have negative effects (Ravitch 2010), it also can be helpful in generating support for public schools. Regardless, governing bodies should anticipate the potential for conflict with families when their policies are at variance with parental expectations and wishes.

Community, Individualism, and Cultural Models of Public School Assignments

The debate between those favoring diversity and those favoring neighborhood schools reflects different conceptualizations of community. Those who support the neighborhood model view community in traditional terms, where children's residential ties are reinforced by school attendance. Parental involvement is enhanced by proximity between home and place of education, as are connections among parents and among children within the same neighborhood. Logical and stable feeder patterns have children from the same family attending the same institutions from elementary school through high school. But citizens who favor diversity conceptualize community differently. For them it is broader. They see socioeconomic diversity in schools as a moral obligation to promote the educational well-being of all children and to advance important national democratic and meritocratic principles. In Wake, supporters of diversity saw the policy as a mechanism to promote the prosperity of the entire community. Many of the county's business leaders argued that it was difficult to sell the area to relocating firms and to recruit skilled workers if they could not advertise strong public schools and citizen consensus supporting education. Although the events of 2013 may seem to have at least temporarily resolved the underlying debate regarding how broadly community should be conceptualized, it is sure to be revived. Those with strong adherence to traditional neighborhood schools will likely find Wake too large and heterogeneous to favor a countywide assignment policy.

At the same time, another divide looms, that between community and the individual. The twenty-first century has seen increased global competition, a worldwide recession, and a furthering of economic inequality in the

United States. Parents attuned to these dynamics are likely placing even more importance on education as a vehicle for ensuring their children's financial futures. Our interviews revealed some parental sentiment stressing that their responsibility was first to their own children. As one conservative interviewee put it, "I don't like the concept of a healthy school; I want a healthy child."[3]

For many parents, the neighborhood schools model might be viewed as a way of maximizing their children's success. Others believe private schools or homeschooling are better options. We have even suggested that the support of some white middle-class urban residents for diversity assignments might be explained by a desire to move poorer children from schools where they live out to the suburbs. Wake has traditionally been able to present the county as a single community, but broad political, social, and economic trends suggest this idea remains under significant threat.

Methodological Appendix

Ours appears to be a unique study of district-level policy making in that it combines traditional case study methods such as interviewing and archival research with a probability-based survey of a large number of community residents. Survey questions were framed following initial interviews and focus groups. We believe the survey data are valuable because they reflect the underlying values of adults in Wake County, the group from whom voters for school board elections are drawn. Even though the survey was not part of a panel, we believe themes we uncovered in both the survey and in our interviews are long-standing ones that were relevant for many years prior to and following the 2009 election. We did not confine our study to Wake County parents, although we asked additional questions of these particular adults to enable future analyses. We have further innovated by designing the survey to include an oversample of African Americans so that we would have sufficient cases in order to study racial effects on relevant values and to present cross-race comparisons.

Elite Interviewing and Archival Research

We completed twenty-four interviews between October 2010 and April 2012 with Wake County elites such as current or former school board members, community activists, and business leaders. We also ran two focus groups: one included community activists who were pro-diversity, and the second focused on African Americans. The process was approved by North Carolina State University's Institutional Review Board for the Protection of Human Subjects in Research, and all participants signed consent forms. We closely analyzed media accounts of Wake County schools from the early 1970s through the present.

The Survey

The survey was conducted via Interactive Voice Response during the second full week of March 2011 by Public Policy Polling (PPP), based in Raleigh, North Carolina. PPP was founded in 2001 and works primarily with Democratic and left-of-center political candidates and clients. PPP provided considerable survey data to various news media prior to the 2012 presidential election and won acclaim for the accuracy of its polling results.

For our study, the firm purchased two lists of phone numbers from Aristotle, Inc. in Washington, D.C. The first list consisted of a simple random sample of 20,000 landline phone numbers identified as households in Wake County, drawn from the company's overall list of 200,000 Wake County numbers, for a sampling rate of 10 percent. The second list consisted of a simple random sample of 20,000 landline phone numbers in Wake County that Aristotle, Inc. had identified as African American. This constituted 76 percent of the total identified population of African American households with landlines. After the numbers were selected, the firm tried to reach a respondent at each number eight times across a five-day period so that households with different work and personal schedules would be fairly represented. These times were Wednesday evening, Thursday morning, Thursday evening, Friday afternoon, Saturday morning, Saturday afternoon and twice on Sunday afternoon. From the two lists the firm was able to reach 21,177 numbers; numbers not reached included those that had been disconnected, numbers that were fax machines, and numbers that were not answered during the time the survey was in the field. Calls that did not reach someone twenty-one years of age or older resulted in a non-interview.

Table A.1 includes the variables we used in this study along with the range of values, means, and standard deviations of each. Table A.2 includes the relevant questions from the survey. The survey consisted of fifty closed-ended questions, plus another fourteen that were posed only to respondents who had children in the Wake County public schools (data not shown). It took between fifteen and twenty minutes to complete.

Sample Weighting and Missing Data

The number of respondents to the survey was 1,706, for a response rate of 8.1 percent. This response rate is good considering the automated nature of the poll and the length of the survey. Perhaps inevitably, the sample was biased. Respondents were disproportionately married, had more postgraduate degrees, and were more likely to have household incomes higher than $75,000 compared with the 2010 census results from Wake County. They were also disproportionately female and, by design, African American. We used the results of the 2010 census to post-weight the data so that for the analyses involving all 1,706 respondents, the sample would reflect Wake County proportions of women, African Americans, and married respondents and be representative of Wake County in terms of education and household income. To accomplish this, we used a procedure known as raking ratio estimation or sample balancing. The raking procedure assigns a weight value to each survey respondent so that marginal totals of the adjusted weights on specified characteristics are in line with the corresponding totals for the population. A major advantage of the raking procedure is its ability to produce respondent weights that are based on multiple control totals, such as marital status, race, sex, income, and education (Battaglia et al. 2004; Kalton 1983). We used the same strategy in analyses for whites and blacks separately, except in these cases the weights by race were not needed. The bottom section of Table A.1 shows that our weighted proportions and means match the 2010 census along these dimensions.

To compensate for missing data on independent variables, we used a data augmentation approach to estimate a multiple imputation procedure using SAS, which relies on a sequential chain of data augmentation cycles (see Little and Rubin 2002). We used a series of five imputations to predict the missing values of independent variables. The procedure estimated a set of plausible values for missing data and replaced the missing values with these estimates and produced appropriate standard errors. The estimates were analyzed using standard regression procedures, and then results from these analyses were combined. The resulting estimates reflect statistically valid inferences that take into account the uncertainty owing to missing values (Allison 2002).

Deriving Common Sentiments Underlying Attitudes and Values

There were nineteen items tapping general attitudes toward school assignment policies. We subjected these items to principal components analysis to reveal the relationships among them and to reduce the data to a smaller number of underlying dimensions (Kim and Mueller 1978). Five dimensions met eigenvalue criteria and include those we have named: challenges, neighborhood schools, diversity, dangers, and uncertainty (see also chapters 3 and 4). We created additive indices for each of the dimensions using the sixteen items that met statistical criteria; these are shown in Tables A1 and A2. An advantage of this principle components procedure is that because its results reflect intercorrelations among the survey items, it promotes the construction of reliable indices. Table A.1 shows that our resulting measures are indeed of good to excellent reliability.

We used ordinary least-squares regression to evaluate the determinants of continuous dependent variables and ordered logistic regression in the cases of ordinal dependent variables. Tables present the signs of the effects; a positive coefficient means that an increase in the explanatory variable led to an increase in the dependent variable and a decrease in the former led to a decrease in the latter. A negative sign means the opposite, and the measures move in different directions. Only coefficients that are statistically significant—or have low standard errors relative to their size—reflect findings worth having any confidence in. We define statistical significance as a p value of .05 or lower, meaning that the direction of the relationship between the explanatory and dependent variables can be accepted with at least 95 percent certainty. Where this is not the case we entered "NS" to designate that the coefficient in that cell was not significant.

Placing Wake County in National Context

A key issue for us was to understand more about whether Wake was relatively unique in the national context. We wondered whether there were other large urban districts that had been or were currently struggling with how to assign children to public schools and where there was also public debate regarding the relative importance of diversity versus neighborhood schools. To address this, we identified from an extensive literature review a number of monographs, book chapters, and scholarly articles that told stories of various districts that had experienced policy change regarding public school assignments. A number of these involved districts that had been subjected to court orders to desegregate public schools. We included other districts not under such court orders and those that had been declared unitary subsequent to court-ordered desegregation. A complicating factor was that the United States organizes schools along several lines of jurisdiction, most typically using county, city, or township units. Thus, our cases included districts of varying size. In addition, we needed to derive a parsimonious number of dimensions along which we could compare Wake with these other districts. After detailed content analysis of the cases, we settled on two: population heterogeneity and what we call "civic capacity," or the robustness of civic life. Toward the end of this analysis we came to the tentative conclusion that Wake was the largest public school district that had been able to sustain a diversity policy for children's school assignments for an extended period of time, events of 2009 notwithstanding. To evaluate this hypothesis, we studied the policies of U.S. school districts larger than Wake. Analysis confirmed this conclusion. We described the results in chapter 7.

Table A.1 Variable Descriptions, Measurement, Means, and Standard Deviations (N = 1,706)

Variable description	Range	Mean	SD
Dependent variables			
DIVERSITY SUPPORT: Four items measuring respondents' support for racial and economic diversity in classrooms and schools. Higher scores indicate greater support. α = .94	4–20	14.45	4.69
NEIGHBORHOOD SCHOOL SUPPORT: Four items measuring respondents' support for neighborhood schools. Higher scores indicate greater support. α = .73	4–20	14.59	3.81
CHALLENGES OF REASSIGNMENT: Two items measuring respondents' perceptions of the challenges posed by elementary school and middle school reassignment. Higher scores indicate a greater perception of challenges. α = .93	2–10	7.81	2.22
DANGER OF REASSIGNMENT: Four items measuring respondents' perceptions of the dangers that reassignment poses for children's learning and friendship experiences during elementary and middle school. Higher scores indicate a greater perceived danger. α =.90	3–15	10.84	3.40
REASSIGNMENT UNCERTAINTY: Two items measuring respondents' perceptions of problems for parents and children as a result of reassignment. Higher scores indicate greater uncertainty about reassignment. α = .74	2–10	8.23	1.95
RATING OF WAKE PUBLIC SCHOOLS' YEAR-ROUND CALENDAR: Continuous item indicating how favorably the respondent views the year-round calendar (higher score indicates greater favorability).	1–9	5.86	2.31
RATING OF WAKE COUNTY SCHOOL BOARD: Continuous item indicating how favorably the respondent views the school board (higher score indicates greater favorability).	1–9	4.08	2.89
Key concepts and independent variables			
SEX: Dummy variable indicating whether respondent is male (0) or female (1).	0–1	.50	.50
AGE: Continuous item indicating respondents' age.	21–99	56.58	14.25
RACE: Three dummy variables to represent whether the respondent is white, African American, or Latino/other.			
African American	0–1	.20	.40
Latino/other	0–1	.07	.26
White	0–1	.73	.44

Table A.1 (*continued*)

Variable description	Range	Mean	SD
ANNUAL HOUSEHOLD INCOME: Item with six intervals representing household income (under $25,000, $25–50,000, $50–75,000, $75–100,000, $100–150,000, more than $150,000).	1–6	3.26	1.51
EDUCATIONAL ATTAINMENT: Ordinal item with five categories indicating respondents' educational attainment (some high school, high school diploma, some college, college degree, postgraduate degree).	1–5	3.41	1.13
TOTAL HOUSEHOLD COMMUTE: Continuous item indicating total number of daily household commuting minutes.	0–120	17.83	20.19
TOTAL HOUSEHOLD WORK HOURS: Continuous item indicating total number of weekly household work in a job in hours.	0–100	34.72	32.12
SCHOOL-AGE CHILDREN: Dummy variable indicating whether respondent has school-age children (yes = 1).	0–1	.26	.44
NUMBER OF SCHOOL-AGE CHILDREN: Continuous item indicating number of school-age children belonging to respondent. 4 refers to four or more children.	0–4	.47	.91
CHILDREN IN YEAR-ROUND SCHOOLS: Dummy variable indicating whether the respondent has a child in a year-round school (yes = 1).	0–1	.06	.24
CHILDREN WITH REASSIGNMENTS: Dummy variable indicating whether respondent has children who have been reassigned (yes = 1).	0–1	.08	.27
LENGTH OF RESIDENCE IN WAKE COUNTY: Item with six intervals indicating how long respondent has lived in Wake County (a year or less, 1–3 years, 4–7 years, 8–15 years, more than 15 years, entire life).	0–5	3.72	1.03
AREA OF RESIDENCE IN WAKE COUNTY: Three dummy variables indicating whether the respondent lives in western Wake/north Raleigh/Wake Forest; central/east Raleigh; or south or east Wake.			
Western Wake/north Raleigh/Wake Forest	0–1	.43	.50
Central/east Raleigh	0–1	.39	.49
South/east Wake	0–1	.18	.38

Variable description	Range	Mean	SD
NEIGHBORHOOD MINORITY PERCENTAGE: Continuous item indicating the percentage of respondent's neighborhood (defined by zip code) that is African American or Latino.	7.4–84.5	32.67	21.82
PERCEPTION OF BUSING: Continuous item indicating respondent's perception of what percentage of children in Wake County are bused for the purpose of diversity.	0–96	27.52	20.13
TRUST IN LOCAL GOVERNMENT: Item with four categories indicating how often the respondent trusts the local government (never, hardly ever, some of the time, most of the time).	1–4	2.78	.73
TRUST IN GOVERNMENT: Three items tapping respondent's trust in local, state, and federal government. Higher scores indicate greater trust in government. α = .82	3–12	8.27	1.88
NUMBER OF ORGANIZATIONS: Continuous item indicating the number of organizations the respondent belongs to.	1–6	2.32	1.56
ATTITUDES TOWARD MLK: Dummy variable indicating respondent's view of Martin Luther King Jr. (0 = "somewhat favorable"/ "somewhat unfavorable"/ "very unfavorable," 1 = "very favorable").	0–1	.58	.50
CONSERVATIVE IDEOLOGY: Ordinal item with three categories to indicate the extent to which the respondent reports a conservative political ideology (1 = liberal, 2 = moderate, 3 = conservative).	1–3	2.14	.68

Note: Our sample is weighted so that estimates for race, sex, marital status, income, and education levels match actual proportions in Wake County.

Race (2010 Census):
  White .73
  African American .20
  Other .07
Sex (2010 Census):
  Male .50
  Female .50
Marital status (2010 Census):
  Married .53
  Not married .47

Annual household income (2010 Census):
  Under $25,000 .144
  $25–50,000 .233
  $50–75,000 .212
  $75–100,000 .154
  $100–150,000 .161
  $150,000+ .097

Educational attainment (Wake County Government Health Report 2012):
  High school or less .269
  Some college .179
  Associate's or bachelor's degree .383
  Graduate or professional degree .168

Table A.2 Survey Questions

Variable	Survey question(s) / statement(s)	Response choices
Diversity support	Children learn best when they attend schools that are racially diverse. Children learn best when they attend schools that are economically diverse. Children learn best when they are in classrooms that are racially diverse. Children learn best when they are in classrooms that are economically diverse.	1. Strongly disagree 2. Somewhat disagree 3. Neutral 4. Somewhat agree 5. Strongly agree
Neighborhood school support	Having children in neighborhood schools makes it easier for parents. School bus rides over 45 minutes are too hard on young children. Children learn best when they attend school with children from their own neighborhoods. I am willing to pay higher taxes to build more schools so more children can attend school closer to home.	Same as diversity support
Challenges of reassignment	Reassigning children even once during elementary school creates challenges for parents. Reassigning children even once during middle school creates challenges for parents.	Same as diversity support
Dangers of reassignment	Reassigning children even once during elementary school inhibits learning. Reassigning children even once during middle school inhibits learning. Reassigning children even once during elementary school inhibits child friendships. Reassigning children even once during middle school inhibits child friendships.	Same as diversity support

Variable	Survey question(s) / statement(s)	Response choices
Reassignment uncertainty	The uncertainty surrounding possible school reassignments creates problems for children. The uncertainty surrounding possible school reassignments creates problems for parents.	Same as diversity support
Sex of respondent	What is your gender?	1. Male 2. Female
Age of respondent	What is your age?	Respondent inputs age
Race of respondent	What is your race?	1. Latino 2. White 3. African American 4. Other
Annual household income	What is your approximate annual household income?	1. Less than $25,000 2. $25–50,000 3. $50–75,000 4. $75–100,000 5. $100–150,000 6. More than $150,000
Educational attainment	What is the highest level of education you have completed?	1. Some high school 2. Graduated from high school 3. Some college 4. Graduated from college 5. Postgraduate training or degree
Total household commute hours	Approximately how long is your/your spouse's commute to work on a typical day? (Questions asked separately, scores tallied.)	1. 15 minutes or less 2. 15–30 minutes 3. 30–45 minutes 4. More than 45 minutes
Total household work hours	Approximately how many hours a week do you/your spouse work for pay? (Questions asked separately, scores tallied.)	1. 1–20 2. 21–34 3. 35–40 4. More than 40

Variable	Survey question(s) / statement(s)	Response choices
School-age children	Do you have school-age children?	1. No 2. Yes
Number of school-age children	How many school-age children do you have?	1–9
Children in year-round schools	Is your youngest child on a traditional or year-round calendar?	1. Traditional 2. Year-round
Children with reassignments	Has Wake County ever reassigned any of your children from one school to another?	1. No 2. Yes
Length of residence in Wake County	How long have you lived in Wake County?	1. A year or less 2. 1–3 years 3. 4–7 years 4. 8–15 years 5. More than 15 years 6. All of your life
Area of residence in Wake County	What are the last three digits of your zip code? (Measure calculated from respondent's zip code.)	3-digit zip code
Neighborhood minority percentage	What are the last three digits of your zip code? (Measure calculated from respondent's zip code.)	3-digit zip code
Perception of busing	What percentage of children in Wake County public schools do you think are bused for the purpose of the diversity policy?	0–99
Rating of WCPSS year-round calendar	On a scale of 1–9, how would you rate Wake County's year-round calendar for elementary and middle schools?	1 (most unfavorable) to 9 (most favorable)
Rating of Wake County school board	On a scale of 1–9, how would you rate the job Wake County's current school board is doing?	1 (most unfavorable) to 9 (most favorable)
Trust in local government	Generally speaking, how often do you think you can trust the local government to do what is right?	1. Never 2. Hardly ever 3. Some of the time 4. Most of the time

Variable	Survey question(s) / statement(s)	Response choices
Trust in state government	Generally speaking, how often do you think you can trust the state government to do what is right?	1. Never 2. Hardly ever 3. Some of the time 4. Most of the time
Trust in federal government	Generally speaking, how often do you think you can trust the federal government to do what is right?	1. Never 2. Hardly ever 3. Some of the time 4. Most of the time
Member of organizations	Are you a member of any civic, religious, or political organizations?	1. No 2. Yes
Number of organizations	How many civic, religious, or political organizations do you belong to?	0–9
Attitudes toward MLK	What are your impressions of Martin Luther King?	1. Very favorable 2. Somewhat favorable 3. Somewhat unfavorable 4. Very unfavorable
Conservative ideology	What would you consider is your political ideology?	1. Liberal 2. Moderate 3. Conservative

Note: Many items allowed respondents to record a "don't know" response.

Notes

Chapter 1

1. We use the term "school board" throughout the book to describe the system's governing body. We do so because that is how it is generally described by the public and local media. Its formal name, however, is the Wake County Board of Education.

2. Scholars recognize that close connections among actors may not lead to positive outcomes. If the prevailing norms within the group are antisocial, then greater access to this form of capital will have negative effects. See Portes (1998) regarding these possibilities. Despite these important dynamics, our emphasis is on the positive effects social capital may have for promoting desirable social outcomes at several levels of social organization.

3. This model neglects the reality that some parents choose to send their children to private schools, another long-standing cultural model in our society. If parents make this choice, then students might be transported out of their neighborhoods, thus potentially disrupting the social capital both children and parents have already developed. These social forces will be lessened if many neighbors make decisions to send their children to the same private schools.

4. Blair-Loy (2003) develops analogous arguments regarding work-family conflict among women executives. In her work, devotion to family and devotion to work compete among executive women, with these schemas coming into conflict, thus creating moral dilemmas or moral distress. Trying to fulfill the goals of both compromises valued goals in each sphere. Our argument is related but different, in that the conflict for Wake parents is created by the disjuncture between the abstract neighborhood schools model that they have in their minds and the reality of the Wake County assignment model as we describe it. Still, Blair-Loy's work is relevant because it provides guidance for considering how cultural models with moral significance may conflict, causing distress and, in the Wake case, political change.

5. Political scientists have begun to detect connections between commute lengths and participation in public life and what are commonly regarded as the responsibilities of citizenship. Long commutes reduce interest in politics, particularly among those with low incomes (Newman, Johnson, and Lown 2014).

Chapter 2

1. This segregation can be attributed somewhat to a federal court's ruling in *Holt v. City of Raleigh Schools* (265 F.2d 95 (4th Cir. 1959)). This is the only federal court case affecting the desegregation of Wake County schools. The decision upheld an administrative promulgation denying the student's transfer, although it did so on what was effectively a technicality. Despite the U.S. Supreme Court's *Brown* decisions, the city and county schools largely resisted integration. For more on how little immediate effect *Brown* had on desegregation, see Clotfelter (2004, 23–25).

2. Raleigh and county schools did not see much of this, but there was significant unrest and some violence in Orange County, where Chapel Hill is located. For more, see McElreath (2002, 473–93).

3. For more on HEW's influence on the merger process, see McElreath (2002, 327–70, 392–401, 417–42).

4. The work that led to the report, "The Raleigh-Wake Public Schools: A Survey," was conducted in 1968–69. It is impressively thorough and was widely distributed and cited as the merger battle heated up.

5. For more on the growth of private schools in Raleigh at this time, see McElreath (2002, 402–16).

6. A 1972 study by North Carolina State University economist Richard King suggested merger would have negligible effects on assignments. The county board disagreed and suggested 6,800 of its students would have to be reassigned. The county was, however, already busing 19,000 of its 29,000 students, even if it was not ostensibly for the purposes of racial desegregation (McElreath 2002, 400).

7. In 1973, some on the Wake County board initiated an effort to equalize per-student spending with Raleigh, where property taxes were higher and the schools received commensurately more money. They also pushed for a $40 million bond referendum for new facilities. In both cases they were rebuffed, although a bond issuance half the size was approved, over the objections of the Raleigh board, by voters in November of that year (Carroll 1973).

8. There are a number of comprehensive treatments of the social, cultural, political, and economic developments of the 1970s. They include Borstelmann (2012), Carroll (2000), and Frum (2000).

9. There were disputes, of course. The complexion of the nine districts that would elect the members of the new board caused some disagreement (Cohodas 1976).

10. Due to changes in tracts and definitional issues, the census does not make it easy to compare the 1970s population of Raleigh and the rest of Wake County by race and age. However, the proportion of Raleigh five- to nineteen-year-olds who were African American rose by about nine percentage points to roughly 34 percent from 1970 to 1980. The data suggest the figure in the remainder of the county was stagnant and possibly decreased.

11. Murphy had been doing a considerable amount of outside consulting and admitted to private use of his work phone.

12. The article is in the journal *Theory into Practice*.

13. If anything, Marks's final year or so as superintendent was more scandalous than Murphy's. He had a rather ostentatious style—driving around in a Lincoln Continental, living in a large house, and demanding his wife be given an assistant principal position in the county (Celis 1991).

14. Schools of choice had seven official goals. They were to improve facility utilization; establish consistent elementary, middle, and high school systems; provide racially balanced population in schools; make the transportation system more effective and economical; expand the curriculum; make educational opportunities equitable; and generate increased parental participation in their child's schooling.

15. Judge Larkins's 1971 order calling on Raleigh city schools to integrate further was ruled inapplicable to the new Wake County school district in 1979.

16. It is difficult to get precise figures on where Wake County's migrants come from. In the 1990s, however, census data show people migrated from New York to North Carolina in greater numbers than they did from between any other two states.

17. These results were also attributed to the inability of Gentry and Carawan to supervise Superintendent Marks appropriately (Krueger 1985).

18. The race was so close that there was a recount and a lawsuit. It was decided by the state's General Assembly in August 2005.

19. Interview, November 12, 2010.

20. In 1986 Ann Koonce held off a challenge from Republican vice chair Henry C. Knight. Knight then defeated Koonce's vice chair, Linda B. Johnson, the next year. Both were 5–4 votes but hardly partisan. There were just not enough Republicans on the board in the 1980s to make party an issue. Moreover, the coalition that supported Knight in 1986 was quite different from the one that supported him the following year.

21. Interview, August 11, 2011.

22. The descriptions of this kind of position, prevalent in North Carolina among business leaders, are from two prominent modern histories of North Carolina politics. Luebke (1998) uses the term "modernizer"; Christensen (2008) "business progressives."

23. The ABC program constitutes an effort to measure academic progress made by students in North Carolina schools. Based largely on end-of-year tests for children in certain grade levels, they are designed to hold schools accountable and to assist in the distribution of resources to teachers and institutions.

24. The Wake Education Partnership assessments are done every two years. The 2000 report is not available online and was obtained directly from the organization.

25. The figures are calculated from a Wake County Public School System document, http://www.wcpss.net/about-us/our-students/demographics/reports/Growth2005.pdf.

26. Such fees were struck down by the North Carolina Supreme Court in 2011 (*Anward Homes v. Town of Cary, Tradition at Stonewater I v. Town of Cary*).

27. The first quote is Bill Fletcher's, chair of the board at the time. The second is Wake resident Dennis Keller's. Both can be found in Hui and Silberman (2000).

28. The cases were *Cappachione v. Charlotte-Mecklenburg Schools* and *Eisenberg v. Montgomery County Schools*.

29. Descriptions of and results from these surveys can be found at http://www.wakeed partnership.org/publications/d/CommunityAssessment04.pdf.

30. For more on this, see Houck and Williams (2010). They show that the coefficient of variation (the standard deviation divided by the mean) for the percentage of African American students in Wake County schools was just about the same in 2007 as it was in 1999.

31. For more on the Helms-Hunt race, see Luebke (1998, 173–79).

32. Much twentieth-century political history shows this. In 1960, for example, Wake gave 59 percent of its vote to John F. Kennedy; Mecklenburg County, Charlotte's home, gave 55 percent to Richard M. Nixon. However, Charlotte currently has a Democratic mayor and played host to the party's national convention in 2012. It gave Obama a larger share of its vote than did Wake in 2008.

33. For much more on the National Congressional Club, see Christensen (2008, 219–27).

34. It is a testament to those skills that Fetzer became the state party chair in 2009 and guided Republican legislative candidates to the majority in both the House and Senate in 2010—the first time that had happened since Reconstruction.

35. As Lassiter (2006, 225–41) notes, Nixon talked about other issues like law and order and respect for traditional values.

36. This was despite the fact that Roxie Cash was chair and that she, Fletcher, Fisher, O'Neal, and former chair Judy Hoffman theoretically constituted a Republican majority.

37. See, for example, Pendleton's efforts in promotion of charter schools (Silberman and Rawlins 1995).

38. After the 2002 election, the North Carolina House had a very narrow 61–59 Republican majority. Sitting Speaker, Democrat Jim Black, then arranged a deal in which a Republican defected to the Democrats, and he orchestrated a shared speakership with Republican Richard Morgan. The resolution that established the unusual arrangement gained only five Republican votes.

39. The Wake County Taxpayers' Association did launch a very late and somewhat half-hearted campaign against the 2003 bond issuance (Hui 2003b).

40. Direct Instruction uses such techniques as choral group responses and individual turns in response to teacher directives.

41. A significant amount of social science research demonstrates that growing and diversifying communities have lower amounts of "generalized trust"—that is, in others, including policy makers (Brehm and Rahn 1997; Hero 2007; Putnam 2000).

42. We do not have data for Wake County, but a national NBC News/*Wall Street Journal* poll taken in December 2009 revealed 66 percent of respondents were "not confident" that "life for their children's generation will be better than it is for us." This was the highest proportion since September 1993.

43. As noted earlier, school board elections are ostensibly nonpartisan. If formal partisan affiliation is based upon party registration, then the new board that came in after the November 2009 elections was officially made up of four Republicans, four Democrats, and one independent. Deborah Prickett, who had been a Republican, changed her voter registration to unaffiliated in November 2007 but back to Republican in January 2010. She said she had done this as a result of her getting a job at the Department of Public Instruction (Hui 2010c).

It may also have been the case that there was a Republican majority in the early 1990s. It is difficult to tell because many members kept their personal party affiliations to themselves. Regardless, Republican members like Cash, Hoffman, and Fletcher generally worked closely with Democratic colleagues and were not nearly as interested in changing the direction of board policies as were those elected in 2009.

Chapter 3

1. *Capacchione v. Charlotte-Mecklenburg Schools*, 57 F. Supp. 2d 228 (W.D.N.C. 1999), 291.

2. The Maryland and Virginia cases were *Eisenberg v. Montgomery County Public Schools* (197 F.3d 123 (4th Cir. 1999)) and *Tuttle v. Arlington County Schools* (195 F.3d 698 (4th Cir.

1999)). In effect, many legal analysts argued, the decisions unambiguously prohibited the use of race as a means to determine magnet school and transfer requests and likely meant that race could not be used to direct jurisdictions' general student assignment policies (Boger and Bower 2001).

3. Recent rulings had declared cities like Atlanta, Denver, Nashville, and San Diego unitary.

4. For more on Goal 2003, see Grant (2009, 122–25).

5. For more on these figures, see WCPSS's November 2003 "Measuring Up" report (E&R Report No. 03.32). It can be found at http://www.wcpss.net/evaluation-research/reports/2003/0332outcomes_summary.pdf.

6. The scores in Charlotte were from the mid-40s to mid-50s. For more, see Mickelson (2005).

7. The ABC program was established to meet federal requirements enacted in the No Child Left Behind Act of 2001. The figures are from Wake County Public Schools' January 2011 "Measuring Up" report (E&R Report No. 10.20). It can be found at https://www.wcpss.net/results/reports /2011/1020abc-aypo9–10.pdf.

8. Interview, December 20, 2010.

9. Interview, December 10, 2010

10. Focus group, November 22, 2010.

11. Ibid.

12. Interview, November 23, 2010.

13. Interview, November 19, 2010.

14. Interview, February 10, 2011.

15. Interview, April 4, 2011.

16. Interview, November 23, 2010.

17. Interview, November 17, 2010.

18. Focus group, February 26, 2011.

19. Focus Group, November 22, 2010.

20. Interview, March 1, 2011.

21. This can be found at http://www.newsobserver.com/2010/03/07/372652/the-long-view-on-diverse-schools.html.

22. The measure adds a respondent's answers to separate questions about their trust in the federal, state, and local governments. Each question asks the subject if he or she trusts that government "never," "hardly ever," "some of the time," or "most of the time."

23. Some of these themes are consistent with arguments made by African American residents who opposed racial integration efforts in Louisville, Kentucky, schools (Garland 2013).

24. Focus group, February 26, 2011.

Chapter 4

1. A 2000 report by the Brookings Institution's Center on Urban and Metropolitan Policy is a prime example of this criticism (see http://www.brookings.edu/~/media/research/files/reports/2000/7/north-carolina/ncreport.pdf).

2. This is WCPSS's own figure; see http://www.wcpss.net/about-us/our-students/demographics/reports/Growth2005.pdf.

3. For more on the history of the annual reassignment process, see Hui (2009a).

4. Interview, December 10, 2010.

5. Interestingly, there were few lawsuits brought by parents challenging these reassignments. Probably the most publicized of these was David and Rhonda Bailey's effort to get the courts to block the transfer of their daughter, Brittany, whose new school's hours prevented her from attending an early morning class run by the Mormon Church. The Baileys claimed the new assignment violated their freedom of religion (Hui 2006d).

6. Interview, February 10, 2011.

7. Interview, March 1, 2011.

8. Focus group, February 26, 2011.

9. Interview, November 19, 2010.

10. Interview, November 17, 2010. Not everyone, however, agreed that lack of proximity discourages child or parental involvement. A liberal board member said in an interview on December 13, 2010: "Parents feel as their kids get older that they want their kids involved in extracurricular [activities] and depending on where they are, they do not feel they can stay after school to get involved. I have not really seen that as a major deterrent, though. I think parents can become involved to the degree that they choose to or not to participate in the schools."

11. Interview, April 4, 2011.

12. Focus group, February 26, 2011.

13. Interview, November 12, 2010.

14. Interview, February 10, 2011.

15. Interview, April 4, 2011.

16. Focus group, February 26, 2011.

Chapter 5

1. Although often run on single tracks and with different calendars, there were year-round schools in the United States well before Wake County had them. The earliest such schools, some of which emerged in the 1800s, were in urban areas that were not tied to the agricultural economy (Shepard and Baker 1977).

2. The only exception to this in the 1990s was Wilburn Elementary, where students were assigned the school as their "base."

3. The inflated cost of child care outside of the summer was continually cited by board members as the reason why low-income families did not apply for year-round schools. In the words of one of our interviewees, "Year-round schools . . . were all entirely voluntary, entirely magnet, and you did not tend to get low-income applicants because of daycare, [which was a] big problem, with that different schedule and kids out for three weeks and nobody to take care of them" (interview, December 2, 2010). We could find no systematic empirical evidence consistent with the claim, however.

4. Interview, November 17, 2010.

5. Interview, February 10, 2011.

6. Focus group, November 22, 2010.

7. Interview, November 15, 2010.

8. Interview, November 23, 2010.

9. Interview, February 10, 2011.

10. Interview, November 15, 2010.

11. Interview, February 10, 2011.

12. Interview, January 25, 2011.

13. Interview, January 27, 2011.

14. The Civitas poll can be found at http://www.nccivitas.org/2009/wake-county-schools-survey/.

15. Interview, January 27, 2011.

Chapter 6

1. The North Carolina General Assembly changed Wake County school board elections by law in 2013. Starting in 2016, elections will be in even-numbered years and the county divided into seven equally sized districts and two "regional" districts that will each cover half of the county. Apart from lengthening the tenures of some sitting members as a result of the adjustment, terms will remain for four years.

2. Of course, we cannot provide systematic evidence to this effect, but there were numerous websites set up during the first decade of the 2000s to discuss Wake County public school issues. The sites of various local media outlets also provided a platform for the many hundreds of people who seemingly wished to sound off. Even the most perfunctory of examinations would have demonstrated the vitriolic nature of some of the language.

The evidence is mixed on whether the Internet actually intensifies polarization. Garrett, Carnahan, and Lynch (2013) and Gentzkow and Shapiro (2011) have shown that it does not segregate ideologues from one another and that they at least seek to read, see, or hear what their opponents are doing.

3. This was particularly the case in our interviews with those who organized against the board.

4. Interview, November 15, 2010.

5. Ibid.

6. Several opponents of the Democratic majority stated they had been accused of being or labeled as "racist." One African American activist said he had been called an "Uncle Tom" for questioning the diversity assignment policy (interview, November 17, 2010).

7. Interview, December 20, 2010.

8. This theme was repeated frequently—and we discuss it a little in chapter 2 and later here in chapter 6.

9. For more on the Civitas poll, see http://www.nccivitas.org/2009/voters-divided-obama-health-care-plan/. For more on PPP's poll, see http://www.publicpolicypolling.com/pdf/2009/PPP_Release_NC_910.pdf.

10. For more on the poll, see http://www.publicpolicypolling.com/main/2009/12/north-carolinians-on-the-issues.html.

11. For more on the Civitas poll, see http://www.nccivitas.org/2009/wake-county-schools-survey/.

12. To say that Goldman helped produce a great deal of news copy during her time on the board is probably an understatement. The most bizarre media story probably came when she was running as the Republican nominee for state auditor in the fall of

2012. The press divulged statements made by Goldman to local police that her home had been burglarized by board colleague Chris Malone, with whom, it seemed to many, she was having some kind of romantic relationship. In fact, the police had been called to the Goldman home on a number of occasions to respond to what she had reported as thefts—her husband, whom she was divorcing at the time of the stories, had begun but later aborted an insurance claim in the amount of $43,000. The police did not follow up on her accusations, suggesting to some that she had made false reports. Some Republicans pointed to the stories as evidence of her instability and as an explanation for why she toppled the majority's general assignment policy in October 2010 (Hui, Goldsmith, and Blythe 2011).

13. Interview, November 12, 2010.

14. Interview, January 25, 2011.

15. Focus group with "liberal" activists, November 22, 2010.

16. Interview, January 27, 2011.

17. Interview, January 25, 2011.

18. Interview, November 12, 2010.

19. Interview, December 20, 2010.

20. Interview, November 15, 2010. Another conservative suggested that Margiotta did not have a good relationship with female activists who supported the majority's agenda and that "his people skills" were problematic (interview, March 30, 2011).

21. The relationship between Goldman and Tedesco produced plenty of entertainment. After the defeat of his zonal plan, Tedesco called his colleague "Benedict Goldman" on his Facebook page. In June 2011 they ran against each other to be Margiotta's vice chair. It took fifty-six separate ballots and the very possible victory of a Democratic member before Goldman relented and supported her rival.

22. The "imbalance index" uses school assignments that mirror a jurisdiction's entire population perfectly and those that segregate completely as the poles of a 0–1 scale. At 0.12 in 2004–05, Wake's were 12 percent shy of perfectly mixed and therefore quite well integrated compared to most districts across the country.

Chapter 7

1. For the last several years, Wake and Montgomery County, Maryland, have had school districts of similar sizes. Depending upon the year observed, either might be the fifteenth largest.

2. We stop short of claiming ours is a meta-analysis. Meta-analysis is essentially a technique used to combine the quantitative findings of large numbers of existing studies on a topic to see whether they reveal patterns, a precondition we do not meet.

3. These data are taken from the Nassau County Public Schools website, http://www.newyorkschools.com/counties/nassau.html.

4. These data are from a publication of the New York State Controller's office, "New York Cities: An Economic and Fiscal Analysis, 1980–2010," and accessed at http://www.osc.state.ny.us/localgov/pubs/fiscalmonitoring/pdf/nycreport2012.pdf.

5. Farley et al. (1978) uses an "index of dissimilarity" in which districts where all schools are perfectly balanced racially and therefore reflect the exact proportions of

the entire population are given a score of 0 and those where all schools are completely segregated and there is absolutely no racial mixing given a 100.

6. The case was *Sheff v. O'Neill* (238 Conn. 1, 678 A.2d 1267).

7. Denver schools were desegregated by the U.S. Supreme Court's decision in *Keyes v. School District No. 1, Denver, Colorado* (413 US 189 (1973)).

8. See a report by the Institute for Innovation in Public School Choice, "An Assessment of Enrollment and Choice in Denver Public Schools," at http://getsmartschools .hotpressplatform.com/services/Report%20with%20ESG%20edits.pdf.

9. See, especially on assessments, ColoradoSchoolGrades.com. Chungmei Lee of the Civil Rights Project provides data in a 2006 report to demonstrate the level of segregation. See http://civilrightsproject.ucla.edu/research/k-12-education/integration-and-diversity/denver-public-schools-resegregation-latino-style/lee-denver-public-school-resegregation-2006.pdf.

10. These data were taken from http://www.mnps.org/assetFactory.

11. Houston (2012) provides a more historical account of Nashville schools.

12. For more on this particular policy, see http://yourchoicemiami.org.

13. For more on the assignment policies in Broward, Hillsborough, and Orange Counties, see the websites of the respective districts.

14. Sociologists, particularly, often wish to retain the anonymity of their subjects. Some of the school districts studied are therefore given pseudonyms. In these instances, although we can report the authors' findings, we cannot, with any real confidence, add accurate information to the cases ourselves.

15. For more on this, see Dan Reed, "De Facto Segregation Threatens Montgomery Public Schools," which can be accessed at http://greatergreaterwashington.org/post/19285/de-facto-segregation-threatens-montgomery-public-schools/.

16. The case is *Meredith v. Jefferson County Board of Education* (547 U.S. 1178).

17. As noted earlier, the only federal court case affecting the desegregation of Wake schools was *Holt v. City of Raleigh Schools* (265 F.2d 95 (4th Cir. 1959)), in which circuit and district courts upheld an administrative promulgation denying an African American high school student a transfer to an all-white school. The decision was narrowly drawn and effectively technical. A 2004 report by the U.S. Department of Education's Office for Civil Rights notes that Wake County was under a "court-ordered desegregation plan until the district achieved unitary status in 1982" (http://www2.ed.gov/about/offices/list/ocr/edlite-raceneutralreport2.html). This is incorrect. There was no order and Wake County has therefore never been eligible to achieve unitary status.

18. This information comes from a 2012 study done by the *New York Times* in conjunction with a series of articles about segregation in New York City schools. It can be found at http://www.nytimes.com/interactive/2012/05/11/nyregion/segregation-in-new-york-city-public-schools.html?ref=education.

Chapter 8

1. Margiotta did very well in Democratic precincts around where he lived in north Apex but was heavily defeated in some Republican districts in the southern part of the district. There is also evidence that efforts to label him as a "Tea Party extremist" had

some effect. See http://blogs.newsobserver.com/wakeed/ppp-on-using-ron-margiottas-defeat-as-a-national-model-for-democrats.

2. The problem was that children were picked up and dropped off much later than scheduled. It began when year-round schools started the 2012–13 year and only escalated when students on the traditional calendar went back to school. Tata repeatedly denied that the assignment plan had contributed to the problem (Hui 2013a).

3. Interview, March 30, 2011.

References

Abramowitz, Alan I. 2010. *The Disappearing Center: Engaged Citizens, Polarization, and American Democracy*. New Haven: Yale University Press.

Aldrich, John H., and James S. Coleman Battista. 2002. "Conditional Party Government in the States." *American Journal of Political Science* 46 (January): 164–72.

Alesina, Alberto, Reza Baqir, and William Easterly. 1999. "Public Goods and Ethnic Divisions." *Quarterly Journal of Economics* 114 (November): 1243–84.

Alexander, Karl L., Doris R. Entwisle, and Linda S. Olson. 2007. "Lasting Consequences of the Summer Learning Gap." *American Sociological Review* 72 (April): 167–80.

Alexander, Karl L., and Aaron M. Pallas. 1985. "School Sector and Cognitive Performance: When Is Little a Little?" *Sociology of Education* 58 (April): 115–28.

Allatt, Patricia. 1993. "Becoming Privileged: The Role of Family Processes." In *Youth and Inequality*, edited by I. Bates and G. Riseborough, 139–59. Buckingham, UK: Open University Press.

Allison, Paul D. 2002. *Missing Data*. Thousand Oaks, Calif.: Sage.

Allport, Gordon W. 1954. *The Nature of Prejudice*. Reading, Mass.: Addison-Wesley.

Armor, David J., and Christine H. Rossell. 2002. "Desegregation and Resegregation in the Public Schools." In *Beyond the Color Line: New Perspectives on Race and Ethnicity*, edited by Abigail Thernstrom and Stephan Thernstrom, 219–58. Stanford: Hoover Institution Press.

Ayscue, Jennifer B., Greg Flaxman, John Kucsera, and Genevieve Siegel-Hawley. 2013. *Settle for Segregation or Strive for Diversity: A Defining Moment for Maryland's Public Schools*. Los Angeles: Civil Rights Project, University of California at Los Angeles.

Banks, Antoine J., and Nicholas A. Valentino. 2012. "Emotional Substrates of White Racial Attitudes." *American Journal of Political Science* 56 (April): 286–97.

Battaglia, Michael, David Izrael, David Hoaglin, and Martin Frankel. 2004. "Tips and Tricks for Raking Survey Data (A.K.A. Sample Balancing)." Paper presented at the annual meeting of the American Association for Public Opinion Research, Phoenix, Ariz., May.

Beckwith, Ryan. 2007. "Vote Would Stall Year-Rounds." *News and Observer*, January 9.

Berg, Steve. 1972. "Anti-Merger Spokesman: Busing Not Prime Issue." *News and Observer*, October 12.

———. 1973. "Twiggs Vows to Bring School Boards Together." *News and Observer*, February 27.

Berkman, Michael B., and Eric Plutzer. 2005. *Ten Thousand Democracies: Politics and Public Opinion in America's School Districts*. Washington, D.C.: Georgetown University Press.

Bianchi, Suzanne M., and Melissa A. Milkie. 2010. "Work and Family Research in the First Decade of the 21st Century." *Journal of Marriage and Family* 72 (June): 705–25.

Black, Earl, and Merle Black. 2003. *The Rise of Southern Republicans*. Cambridge, Mass.: Harvard University Press.

Blair-Loy, Mary. 2003. *Competing Devotions: Career and Family among Women Executives*. Cambridge, Mass.: Harvard University Press.

Blalock, Hubert M. 1967. *Toward a Theory of Minority-Group Relations*. New York: John Wiley and Sons.

Blau, Judith R. 2003. *Race in the Schools: Perpetuating White Dominance?* Boulder: Lynne Rienner Publishers.

Blau, Peter, and Otis Dudley Duncan. 1967. *The American Occupational Structure*. New York: John Wiley and Sons.

Blumer, Herbert. 1958. "Race Prejudice as a Sense of Group Position." *Pacific Sociological Review* 1 (Spring): 3–7.

Bobo, Lawrence. 2001. "Racial Attitudes and Relations at the Close of the Twentieth Century." In *America Becoming: Racial Trends and Their Consequences*, edited by N. Smelser, W. J. Wilson, and F. Mitchell, 262–99. Washington, D.C.: National Academy Press.

Bobo, Lawrence, and Vincent L. Hutchings. 1996. "Perceptions of Racial Group Competition: Extending Blumer's Theory of Group Position to a Multiracial Social Context." *American Sociological Review* 61 (December): 951–72.

Boger, John Charles, and Elizabeth Jean Bower. 2001. "The Future of Educational Diversity: Old Decrees, New Challenges." *Popular Government* 66 (Winter): 2–17.

Boger, John Charles, and Gary Orfield, eds. 2005. *School Resegregation: Must the South Turn Back?* Chapel Hill: University of North Carolina Press.

Borstelmann, Thomas. 2012. *The 1970s: A New Global History from Civil Rights to Economic Inequality*. Princeton: Princeton University Press.

Bourdieu, Pierre. 1998. *Practical Reason: On the Theory of Action*. Cambridge: Polity Press.

Bowles, Samuel, and Herbert Gintis. 2002. "The Inheritance of Inequality." *Journal of Economic Perspectives* 16 (Summer): 3–30.

Braddock, Jomills Henry, II, and T. M. Eitle. 2004. "The Effects of School Desegregation." In *Handbook of Research on Multicultural Education*, edited by J. A. Banks and C. A. McGee, 828–46. New York: John Wiley and Sons.

Braddock, Jomills Henry, II, and Amaryllis Del Carmen Gonzalez. 2010. "Social Isolation and Social Cohesion: The Effects of K–12 Neighborhood and School Segregation on Intergroup Orientations." *Teachers College Record* 112: 1631–53.

Branton, Regina P., and Bradford S. Jones. 2005. "Examining Racial Attitudes: The Conditional Relationship between Diversity and the Socio-Economic Environment." *American Journal of Political Science* 49 (April): 359–72.

Breen, Richard, and Jan O. Jonsson. 2005. "Inequality of Opportunity in Comparative Perspective: Recent Research on Educational Attainment and Social Mobility." *Annual Review of Sociology* 31 (August): 223–43.

Brehm, John, and Wendy Rahn. 1997. "Individual-Level Evidence for the Causes and

Consequences of Social Capital." *American Journal of Political Science* 41 (July): 999–1023.

Brown, Arlene K., and Karen W. Knight. 2005. "School Boundary and Student Assignment Procedures in Large, Urban Public School Systems." *Education and Urban Society* 37 (August): 398–418.

Brown, Beverly. 1993. "Parents Face Bad News." *News and Observer*, March 11.

Campbell, Richard T. 1983. "Status Attainment Research: End of the Beginning or Beginning of the End?" *Sociology of Education* 56 (January): 47–62.

Carroll, Ginny. 1973. "Growing Black Student Ratio Is a Factor in Bond Campaign." *News and Observer*, November 2.

Carroll, Peter N. 2000. *It Seemed Like Nothing Happened: America in the 1970s.* New Brunswick, N.J.: Rutgers University Press.

Celis, William. 1991. "Educator's Legacy: Success, and Shaky Finances, in Several Districts." *New York Times*, May 8.

Chafe, William H. 1980. *Civilities and Civil Rights: Greensboro, North Carolina, and the Black Struggle for Freedom.* New York: Oxford University Press.

Charmaz, Kathy. 2006. *Constructing Grounded Theory: A Practical Guide through Qualitative Analysis.* Thousand Oaks, Calif.: Sage.

Christensen, Rob. 1973. "City, County Boards Trade School Bond Issue Views." *News and Observer*, July 23.

———. 2008. *The Paradox of Tar Heel Politics: The Personalities, Elections, and Events That Shaped Modern North Carolina.* Chapel Hill: University of North Carolina Press.

———. 2010. "Art Pope: A One-Man Republican Equalizer." *News and Observer*, October 27.

Clotfelter, Charles T. 2001. "Are Whites Still 'Fleeing'? Racial Patterns and Enrollment Shifts in Urban Public Schools, 1987–1996." *Journal of Policy Analysis and Management* 20 (Spring): 199–221.

———. 2004. *After* Brown: *The Rise and Retreat of School Desegregation.* Princeton: Princeton University Press.

Clotfelter, Charles T., Helen F. Ladd, and Jacob L. Vigdor. 2013. "Racial and Economic Diversity in North Carolina's Schools: An Update." *Sanford Working Paper Series* 13: 1–45.

Cohodas, Nadine. 1976. "School Districts Plan Gives Edge to County." *News and Observer*, December 16.

Coleman, James S. 1988. "Social Capital in the Creation of Human Capital." *American Journal of Sociology* 94 (Suppl.): 95–120.

———. 1990. *Foundations of Social Theory.* Cambridge, Mass.: Harvard University Press.

Coleman, James S., Earnest Q. Campbell, Carol J. Hobson, James McPartland, Alexander M. Mood, Frederick D. Weinfeld, and Robert L. York. 1966. *Equality of Educational Opportunity.* Washington, D.C.: U.S. Government Printing Office.

Coleman, James S., Thomas Hoffer, and Sally Kilgore. 1982. *High School Achievement: Public, Catholic, and Private Schools Compared.* New York: Basic Books.

Coleman, Toby. 2006. "Support Weak for School Bonds." *News and Observer*, March 15.

———. 2009. "Black Voices Quiet." *News and Observer*, October 3.

———. 2010. "NAACP Renews Schools Crusade." *News and Observer*, January 10.

Collins, Kristin. 2009. "Black Voices Quiet." *News and Observer*, October 3.

———. 2010. "NAACP Renews Schools Crusade." *News and Observer*, January 10.

Collins, Kristin, and T. Keung Hui. 2009. "School Policy in Voters' Hands." *News and Observer*, October 6.

Comer, James P., and Norris M. Haynes. 1991. "Parent Involvement in Schools: An Ecological Approach." *Elementary School Journal* 91 (January): 271–77.

Cook, Karen S., Margaret Levi, and Russell Hardin. 2009. *Whom Can We Trust? How Groups, Networks, and Institutions Make Trust Possible.* New York: Russell Sage.

Cooper, Harris, Barbara Nye, Kelly Charlton, James Lindsay, and Scott Greathouse. 1996. "The Effects of Summer Vacation on Achievement Test Scores: A Narrative and Meta-analytic Review." *Review of Educational Research* 66 (Fall): 227–68.

Crosnoe, Robert. 2004. "Social Capital and the Interplay of Families and Schools." *Journal of Marriage and Family* 66 (May): 267–80.

Cuban, Larry. 2010. *As Good as It Gets: What School Reform Brought to Austin.* Cambridge, Mass.: Harvard University Press.

Cullen, Robert B. 1972. "Galfianakis, Helms Agree Busing Undesirable." *News and Observer*, October 10.

D'Alessio, Stewart, Lisa Stolzenberg, and David J. Eitle. 2002. "The Effect of Racial Threat on Interracial and Intraracial Crimes." *Social Science Research* 31 (September): 392–408.

Darling-Hammond, Linda. 2010. *The Flat World and Education: How America's Commitment to Equity Will Determine Our Future.* New York: Teachers College Press.

David, Miriam, Anne West, and Jane Ribbens. 1994. *Mother's Intuition? Choosing Secondary Schools.* London: Falmer Press.

Davis, Angela. 1972. "Merge Remark Rebuttal." *News and Observer*, November 4.

Debray, Elizabeth, and Ain Grooms. 2012. "High Civic Capacity, Low Demand for Integration: Rapid Demographic Transition in Suburban Atlanta." In Frankenberg and Orfield 2012, 163–84.

Deckman, Melissa M. 2004. *School Board Battles: The Christian Right in Local Politics.* Washington, D.C.: Georgetown University Press.

DeLuca, Stefanie, and Elizabeth Dayton. 2009. "Switching Social Contexts: The Effects of Housing Mobility and School Choice Programs on Youth Outcomes." *Annual Review of Sociology* 35 (August): 457–91.

Dixon, John, Linda R. Tropp, Kevin Durrheim, and Collin Tredoux. 2010. "'Let Them Eat Harmony': Prejudice-Reduction Strategies and Attitudes of Historically Disadvantaged Groups." *Current Directions in Psychological Science* 19 (April): 76–80.

Dougherty, Jack, Jesse Wanzer, and Christina Ramsay. 2009. "*Sheff v. O'Neill*: Weak Desegregation Remedies and Strong Disincentives in Connecticut, 1996–2008." In Smrekar and Goldring 2009a, 103–27.

Downey, Douglas B., Paul T. von Hippel, and Beckett A. Broh. 2004. "Are Schools the

Great Equalizer? Cognitive Inequality during the Summer Months and the School Year." *American Sociological Review* 69 (October): 613–35.

Dufur, Mikaela, Toby L. Parcel, and Benjamin A. McKune. 2008. "Capital and Context: Using Social Capital at Home and at School to Predict Child Social Adjustment." *Journal of Health and Social Behavior* 49 (June): 146–61.

Dufur, Mikaela J., Toby L. Parcel, and Kelley Troutman. 2013. "Does Capital at Home Matter More than Capital at School? Social Capital Effects on Academic Achievement." *Research in Social Stratification and Mobility* 31 (March): 1–21.

Duncan, Otis Dudley, David L. Featherman, and Beverley Duncan. 1972. *Socioeconomic Background and Achievement.* New York: Seminar Press.

Eaton, Susan. 2012. "Help Wanted: The Challenges and Opportunities of Immigration and Cultural Change in a Working-Class Boston Suburb." In Frankenberg and Orfield 2012, 91–112.

Edsall, Mary D., and Thomas B. Edsall. 1991. *Chain Reaction: The Impact of Race, Rights, and Taxes on American Politics.* New York: W. W. Norton.

Eisley, Matthew. 1995. "GOP Activists Gather for Convention." *News and Observer,* March 10.

Epps, Kinea White. 2007. "Wake Schools Delay Diversity Policy." *News and Observer,* October 10.

Fan, Xitao, and Michael Chen. 2001. "Parental Involvement and Students' Academic Achievement: A Meta-analysis." *Educational Psychology Review* 13, no. 1: 1–22.

Farley, Reynolds, Howard Schuman, Suzanne Bianchi, Diane Colasanto, and Shirley Hatchet. 1978. "Chocolate City, Vanilla Suburbs: Will the Trend toward Racial Separate Communities Continue?" *Social Science Research* 7 (December): 319–44.

Federico, Christopher M. 2004. "When Do Welfare Attitudes Become Racialized? The Paradoxical Effects of Education." *American Journal of Political Science* 48 (April): 374–91.

Finder, Alan. 2005. "As Test Scores Jump, Raleigh Credits Integration by Income." *New York Times,* September 25.

Firebaugh, Glenn, and Kenneth E. Davis. 1988. "Trends in Antiblack Prejudice, 1972–1984: Region and Cohort Effects." *American Journal of Sociology* 94 (September): 251–72.

Flinspach, Susan E., and Karen E. Banks. 2005. "Moving beyond Race: Socioeconomic Diversity as a Race-Neutral Approach to Desegregation in the Wake County Schools." In Boger and Orfield 2005, 261–80.

Ford, Steve. 2010. "The Long View on Diverse Schools." *News and Observer,* March 7.

Frankenberg, Erica. 2005. "The Impact of School Segregation on Residential Housing Patterns: Mobile, Alabama, and Charlotte, North Carolina." In Boger and Orfield 2005, 164–84.

———. 2012. "Understanding Suburban School District Transformation: A Typology of Suburban Districts." In Frankenberg and Orfield 2012, 27–43.

Frankenberg, Erica, and Gary Orfield, eds. 2012. *The Resegregation of Suburban Schools: A Hidden Crisis in American Education.* Cambridge, Mass.: Harvard Education Press.

Frasure-Yokley, Lorrie. 2012. "Holding the Borderline: School District Responsiveness

to Demographic Change in Orange County, California." In Frankenberg and
Orfield 2012, 69–90.

Frum, David. 2000. *How We Got Here: The '70s*. New York: Basic Books.

Fukuyama, Francis. 1995. *Human Nature and the Reconstitution of Social Order*.
New York: Free Press.

Furstenberg, Frank F. 2005. "Banking on Families: How Families Generate and
Distribute Social Capital." *Journal of Marriage and Family* 67 (November): 809–21.

Gamoran, Adam. 1992. "The Variable Effects of High School Tracking." *American
Sociological Review* 57 (December): 812–28.

———. 2001. "American Schooling and Educational Inequality: Forecast for the
21st Century." *Sociology of Education* 34 (Extra Issue): 135–53.

Garland, Sarah. 2013. *Divided We Fail: The Story of an African-American Community
That Ended the Era of School Desegregation*. Boston: Beacon Press.

Garreau, Joel. 1991. *Edge City: Life on the New Frontier*. New York: Anchor Books.

Garrett, R. Kelly, Dustin Carnahan, and Emily K. Lynch. 2013. "A Turn toward
Avoidance? Selective Exposure to Online Political Information, 2004–2008."
Political Behavior 35, no. 1: 113–35.

Gentzkow, Matthew, and Jesse M. Shapiro. 2011. "Ideological Segregation Online
and Offline." *Quarterly Journal of Economics* 126: 1799–1839.

George Peabody College for Teachers. 1969. *Raleigh–Wake County Public Schools:
A Survey Report*. Nashville: Division.

Gewirtz, Sharon, Stephen J. Ball, and Richard Bowe. 1995. *Markets, Choice and Equity
in Education*. Buckingham, UK: Open University Press.

Gibbins, Neil, and Robert Bickel. 1991. "Comparing Public and Private High Schools
Using Three SAT Data Sets." *Urban Review* 23 (June): 101–15.

Giles, Micheal W. 1977. "Percent Black and Racial Hostility: An Old Assumption
Reexamined." *Social Science Quarterly* 58 (December): 412–17.

Goldsmith, Thomas. 2009a. "Election Could Reshape Diversity in Wake Schools."
News and Observer, September 7.

———. 2009b. "Neighborhood Schools' Issue Tapped Anger." *News and Observer*,
October 7.

———. 2010a. "Rallying Cry Is Wake Schools." *News and Observer*, April 27.

———. 2010b. "Idea Intrigues Board Factions." *News and Observer*, July 22.

Goldsmith, Thomas, and T. Keung Hui. 2011. "Margiotta Ousted; Democrats Win
Four School Board Seats in Wake." *News and Observer*, October 12.

———. 2012. "Wake County School Board Votes to Pursue Diversity-Based Student
Assignment Plan." *News and Observer*, June 19.

Graetz, Brian. 1990. "Private Schools and Educational Attainment: Cohort and
Generational Effects." *Australian Journal of Education* 34 (August): 174–91.

Grant, Gerald. 2009. *Hope and Despair in the American City: Why There Are No Bad
Schools in Raleigh*. Cambridge, Mass.: Harvard University Press.

Griffin, Larry J., and Kenneth A. Bollen. 2009. "What Do These Memories Do?
Civil Rights Remembrance and Racial Attitudes." *American Sociological Review* 74
(August): 594–614.

Griffith, Alison, and Dorothy E. Smith. 1991. "Constructing Cultural Knowledge:

Mothering as Discourse." In *Women and Education: A Canadian Perspective*, edited by Jane Gaskell and Arlene Mclaren, 87–103. Calgary: Detseilig Enterprises.

Grubb, W. Norton. 2009. *The Money Myth: School Resources, Outcomes, and Equity*. New York: Russell Sage.

Gumus-Dawes, Baris, Myron Orfield, and Thomas Luce. 2012. "Dividing Lines: East Versus West in Minneapolis Suburbs." In Frankenberg and Orfield 2012, 113–38.

Gurin, Patricia, Eric L. Dey, and Sylvia Hurtado. 2002. "Diversity and Higher Education: Theory and Impact on Educational Outcomes." *Harvard Educational Review* 72 (Fall): 330–67.

Haberman, Martin. 2005. *Star Teachers: The Ideology and Best Practice of Effective Teachers of Diverse Children and Youth in Poverty*. Houston: Haberman Education Fund.

Hallinan, Maureen T. 1988. "Equality of Educational Opportunity." *Annual Review of Sociology* 14 (August): 249–68.

Hart, Betty, and Todd R. Risley. 1995. *Meaningful Differences in the Everyday Experience of Young American Children*. Baltimore: Paul H. Brookes.

Hayes, Sharon. 1996. *The Cultural Contradictions of Motherhood*. New Haven: Yale University Press.

Heckman, James J. 2008. "Schools, Skills, and Synapses." *Economic Inquiry* 46 (June): 289–324.

Hero, Rodney E. 2007. *Racial Diversity and Social Capital: Equality and Community in America*. New York: Cambridge University Press.

Hess, Frederick M., and David L. Leal. 2005. "School House Politics: Expenditures, Interests and Competition in School Board Elections." In *Besieged: School Boards and the Future of Education Politics*, edited by William G. Howell, 228–53. Washington, D.C.: Brookings Institution Press.

Hetherington, Marc. 2005. *Why Trust Matters: Declining Political Trust and the Demise of American Liberalism*. Princeton: Princeton University Press.

Hochschild, Arlie R. 2000. "Global Care Chains and Emotional Surplus Value." In *On the Edge: Living with Global Capitalism*, edited by Will Hutton and Anthony Giddens, 130–46. London: Jonathan Cape.

Hoffmann, John P. 2002. "The Community Context of Family Structure and Adolescent Drug Use." *Journal of Marriage and Family* 64 (May): 314–30.

Holme, Jennifer Jellison, Anjale Welton, and Sarah Diem. 2012. "Pursuing 'Separate but Equal' in Suburban San Antonio: A Case Study of a Southern Independent School District." In Frankenberg and Orfield 2012, 45–67.

Horn, Catherine L., and Michal Kurlaender. 2009. "The End of *Keyes*: Resegregation Trends and Achievement in Denver Public Schools." In Smrekar and Goldring 2009a, 221–38.

Houck, Eric A., and Sheneka M. Williams. 2010. "'To Turn Back Now Would Be a Huge Mistake': Race, Class, and Student Assignment in Wake County Public Schools." Paper presented at the annual meeting of the American Educational Research Association, Denver, Colo., May.

Houston, Benjamin. 2012. *The Nashville Way: Racial Etiquette and the Struggle for Social Justice in a Southern City*. Athens: University of Georgia Press.

Howell, Susan E., and Christine L. Day. 2000. "Complexities of the Gender Gap." *Journal of Politics* 62 (August): 858–74.

Howell, William G., ed. 2005. *Besieged: School Boards and the Future of Education Politics*. Washington, D.C.: Brookings Institution Press.

Howell, William G., and Paul E. Peterson. 2002. *The Education Gap: Vouchers and Urban Schools*. Washington, D.C.: Brookings Institution Press.

Hoxby, Caroline M., and Gretchen Weingarth. 2006. "Taking Race out of the Equation: School Reassignments and the Structure of Peer Effects." Unpublished manuscript, Harvard University.

Hughes, Michael, and Steven A. Tuch. 2003. "Gender Differences in Whites' Racial Attitudes: Are Women's Attitudes Really More Favorable?" *Social Psychology Quarterly* 66 (December): 384–401.

Hui, T. Keung. 1999a. "Cary's New Slow-Growth Law Draws Scrutiny." *News and Observer*, July 27.

———. 1999b. "Wake, Durham, Have Eye on Other Cases." *News and Observer*, September 11.

———. 2001. "Year-Round Expansion a Challenge." *News and Observer*, August 30.

———. 2002a. "Wake Alters School Plan." *News and Observer*, March 1.

———. 2002b. "Reassignment Ruckus." *News and Observer*, March 16.

———. 2003a. "Reassignment Plan Adopted." *News and Observer*, April 2.

———. 2003b. "Wake School Bonds Succeed." *News and Observer*, October 8.

———. 2005. "Election Marks Win for Wake's Diversity Policy." *News and Observer*, November 9.

———. 2006a. "Wake School Decision Looms." *News and Observer*, January 4.

———. 2006b. "Teachers Split on Calendar Shift." *News and Observer*, May 3.

———. 2006c. "Year-Round Foes Demand Schools Seek More Funds." *News and Observer*, May 3.

———. 2006d. "A New School, a New Lawsuit." *News and Observer*, July 18.

———. 2006e. "Wake Voters Say 'Yes': Build More Schools." *News and Observer*, November 8.

———. 2007. "Schools Offer Option, 'Warning.'" *News and Observer*, May 9.

———. 2008a. "Reassignment OK'd, Largely Intact." *News and Observer*, February 6.

———. 2008b. "Year-Round School Shuffle Possible." *News and Observer*, February 7.

———. 2008c. "Year-Round Schools Don't Work for Some." *News and Observer*, February 26.

———. 2009a. "Parents Seek Changes in Plan." *News and Observer*, January 6.

———. 2009b. "Wake Candidates Split on Year-Round Stance." *News and Observer*, September 24.

———. 2009c. "Truitt: 'Forced Busing Is Dead.'" *News and Observer*, October 8.

———. 2009d. "From Gadfly to Take Charge Guy." *News and Observer*, December 7.

———. 2010a. "Survey Shows Most Wake Parents Satisfied with Wake Calendar." *News and Observer*, February 2.

———. 2010b. "Two Businessmen Invested Big in Schools Race." *News and Observer*, February 9.

————. 2010c. "School Board Member Says She's Republican." *News and Observer*, February 13.

————. 2010d. "NAACP to Margiotta: Resign." *News and Observer*, March 10.

————. 2011. "Losurdo Campaign Outpaces Hill, Hits School Board Record." *News and Observer*, November 2.

————. 2012. "Board Chairman Kevin Hill Says Tony Tata's Leadership Style Wasn't a Good Fit." *News and Observer*, October 6.

————. 2013a. "Wake May Spend $2.25 Million to Fix School Bus Problems." *News and Observer*, February 4.

————. 2013b. "Wake Schools Look to Promote Diversity." *News and Observer*, April 23.

————. 2013c. "Wake Schools, Struggling to Lead State, Haven't Caught Regional Targets." *News and Observer*, June 2.

————. 2013d. "New Wake County School Board Election Districts Appear to Favor GOP." *News and Observer*, June 14.

————. 2013e. "In Wake County, a Growing Number of High-Poverty Schools." *News and Observer*, November 23.

Hui, T. Keung, and Kinea White Epps. 2008. "Wake Schools Regain Control over Year-Round Assignments." *News and Observer*, May 7.

Hui, T. Keung, and Thomas Goldsmith. 2009. "Party Money Pours In." *News and Observer*, October 2.

————. 2010a. "Goldman Goes a Wee Bit Rogue." *News and Observer*, October 5.

————. 2010b. "Diversity Policy Voted Down in Tense Meeting." *News and Observer*, March 3.

————. 2012. "School Change Timing Debated." *News and Observer*, January 5.

Hui, T. Keung, Thomas Goldsmith, and Anne Blythe. 2011. "Wake School Board's Goldman Named Colleague Malone in Theft." *News and Observer*, October 20.

Hui, T. Keung, Thomas Goldsmith, and Matt Garfield. 2011. "Hill Win Puts Dems in Charge." *News and Observer*, November 13.

Hui, T. Keung, and Todd Silberman. 2000. "Wake Voters Give Big OK to Schools." *News and Observer*, November 8.

————. 2006. "'Yes' Vote on School Bonds No Fast Fix." *News and Observer*, January 31.

Hutchings, Vincent L., Hanes Walton Jr., and Andrea Benjamin. 2010. "The Impact of Explicit Racial Cues on Gender Differences in Support for Confederate Symbols and Partisanship." *Journal of Politics* 72 (October): 1175–88.

Jackl, Andrew, and Aimee Lougee. 2012. "Wake County Public School System Professional Learning Teams: 2010–11 to 2011–12 School-Based Policy Study." D&A Report No. 12–02, April, http://webarchive.wcpss.net/results/reports/2012/1202plt10–11sbp.pdf.

Jackman, Mary R., and Marie Crane. 1986. "'Some of My Best Friends Are Black . . .': Interracial Friendship and Whites' Racial Attitudes." *Public Opinion Quarterly* 50 (Winter): 459–86.

Jensen, Gary F. 1986. "Explaining Differences in Academic Behavior between Public-

School and Catholic-School Students: A Quantitative Case Study." *Sociology of Education* 59 (January): 32–41.

Jeynes, William H. 2005. "Effects of Parental Involvement and Family Structure on the Academic Achievement of Adolescents." *Marriage and Family Review* 37, no. 3: 99–116.

———. 2007. "The Relationship Between Parental Involvement and Urban Secondary School Student Academic Achievement." *Urban Education* 42 (January): 82–110.

Johnson, Monica K., Robert Crosnoe, and Glen H. Elder. 2001. "Students' Attachment and Academic Engagement: The Role of Race and Ethnicity." *Sociology of Education* 74 (October): 318–40.

Jordan, Keith. 1995. "Parents Challenge Reassignment Proposals." *News and Observer*, March 30.

Kahlenberg, Richard D. 2001. *All Together Now: Creating Middle-Class Schools through Public School Choice*. Washington, D.C.: Brookings Institution Press.

———. 2007. "Rescuing *Brown vs. Board of Education*: Profiles of Twelve School Districts Pursuing Socioeconomic School Integration." New York: Century Foundation.

Kalton, Graham. 1983. "Compensating for Missing Survey Data." Survey Research Center, Institute for Social Research, University of Michigan.

Katsillis, John, and Richard Rubinson. 1990. "Cultural Capital, Student Achievement, and Educational Reproduction: The Case of Greece." *American Sociological Review* 55 (April): 270–79.

Kenny, Lawrence W., and Amy B. Schmidt. 1994. "The Decline in the Number of School Districts in the U.S.: 1950–1980." *Public Choice* 79 (April): 1–18.

Kent, Stephanie L., and David Jacobs. 2004. "Social Divisions and Coercive Control in Advanced Societies: Law Enforcement Strength in Eleven Nations from 1975 to 1994." *Social Problems* 51 (August): 343–61.

———. 2005. "Minority Threat and Police Strength from 1980 to 2000: A Fixed-Effects Analysis of Nonlinear and Interactive Effects in Large US Cities." *Criminology* 43 (August): 731–60.

Key, Vladimir O. 1949. *Southern Politics in State and Nation*. New York: Knopf.

Kim, Doo H., and Barbara Schneider. 2005. "Social Capital in Action: Alignment of Parental Support in Adolescents' Transition to Postsecondary Education." *Social Forces* 84 (December): 1181–1206.

Kim, Jae-On, and Charles W. Mueller. 1978. *Introduction to Factor Analysis: What It Is and How to Do It*. Beverly Hills: Sage.

Kirst, Michael W., and Frederick M. Wirt. 2009. *The Political Dynamics of American Education*. 4th ed. Richmond, Calif.: McCutchan.

Knack, Stephen. 2002. "Social Capital and the Quality of Government: Evidence from the States." *American Journal of Political Science* 46 (October): 772–87.

Kneese, Carolyn Calvin. 1996. "Review of Research on Student Learning in Year-Round Education." *Journal of Research and Development in Education* 29 (Winter): 60–72.

Koski, William S., and Jeannie Oakes. 2009. "Equal Educational Opportunity, School

Reform, and the Courts: A Study of the Desegregation Litigation in San Jose." In Smrekar and Goldring 2009a, 71–102.

Kozol, Jonathan. 2005. *The Shame of the Nation: The Restoration of Apartheid Schooling in America*. New York: Crown.

Krueger, Bill. 1985. "Newcomers Topple Incumbents in Two Wake School Board Races." *News and Observer*, October 9.

Kruse, Kevin M. 2005. *White Flight: Atlanta and the Making of Modern Conservatism*. Princeton: Princeton University Press.

Kuklinski, James H., Michael D. Cobb, and Martin Gilens. 1997. "Racial Attitudes and the 'New South.'" *Journal of Politics* 59 (May): 323–49.

Ladwig, James. 2010. "Beyond Academic Outcomes." *Review of Research in Education* 34 (March): 113–41.

Lareau, Annette. 2011. *Unequal Childhoods: Class, Race, and Family Life*. 2nd ed. Berkeley: University of California Press.

———. 2014. "Schools, Housing, and the Reproduction of Inequality: Experiences of White and African-American Suburban Parents." In *Choosing Homes, Choosing Schools*, edited by Annette Lareau and Kimberly Goyette, 169–206. New York: Russell Sage Foundation.

Lareau, Annette, and Vanessa Lopes Muñoz. 2012. "'You're Not Going to Call the Shots': Structural Conflicts between the Principal and the PTO at a Suburban Public Elementary School." *Sociology of Education* 85 (July): 201–18.

Lassiter, Matthew. 2006. *The Silent Majority: Suburban Politics in the Sunbelt South*. Princeton: Princeton University Press.

Lauen, Douglas Lee, and S. Michael Gaddis. 2013. "Exposure to Classroom Poverty and Test Score Achievement: Contextual Effects or Selection?" *American Journal of Sociology* 118 (January): 943–79.

Levendusky, Matthew. 2009. *The Partisan Sort: How Liberals Became Democrats and Conservatives Became Republicans*. Chicago: University of Chicago Press.

Lindstrom, Matthew J., and Hugh Bartling. 2003. *Suburban Sprawl: Culture, Theory, and Politics*. Lanham, Md.: Rowman and Littlefield.

Linn, Robert, and Kevin Welner. 2007. *Race Conscious Policies for Assigning Students to Schools: Social Science Research and Supreme Court Cases*. Washington, D.C.: National Academy of Education.

Little, Roderick, and Donald B. Rubin. 2002. *Statistical Analysis with Missing Data*. New York: John Wiley and Sons.

Lleras, Christy. 2008. "Race, Racial Concentration, and the Dynamics of Educational Inequality across Urban and Suburban Schools." *American Educational Research* 45 (December): 886–912.

Logan, John R., Elisabeta Minca, and Sinem Adar. 2012. "The Geography of Inequality: Why Separate Means Unequal in American Public Schools" *Sociology of Education* 20 (July): 287–301.

Lois, Jennifer. 2013. *Home Is Where the School Is*. New York: New York University Press.

Lopez, Linda, and Adrian A. Pantoja. 2004. "Beyond Black and White: General

Support for Race-Conscious Policies among African Americans, Latinos, Asian Americans and Whites." *Political Research Quarterly* 57 (December): 633–42.

Lublin, David. 2004. *The Republican South: Democratization and Partisan Change*. Princeton: Princeton University Press.

Luebke, Paul. 1998. *Tar Heel Politics 2000*. Chapel Hill: University of North Carolina Press.

MacDonald, Douane. 1999. "Teacher Attrition: A Review of Literature." *Teaching and Teacher Education* 15 (November): 839–48.

Marlowe, Gene. 1972. "Group Opposes Schools Merger." *News and Observer*, March 14.

Marshall, Melissa J., and Dietlind Stolle. 2004. "Race and the City: Neighborhood Context and the Development of Generalized Trust." *Political Behavior* 26 (2004): 125–54.

Mayer, Jane. 2011. "State for Sale." *New Yorker*, October 10, 90–103.

McElreath, Jack M. 2002. "The Cost of Opportunity: School Desegregation and Changing Race Relations in the Triangle since World War II." PhD diss., University of Pennsylvania.

McMahan, Karen. 2007. "Garner Opposes School Growth Plan." *Carolina Journal*, April 19, http://www.carolinajournal.com/exclusives/display_exclusive.html?id=4019.

McMullen, Steven C., and Kathryn E. Rouse. 2012. "The Impact of Year-Round Schooling on Academic Achievement: Evidence from Mandatory School Calendar Conversions." *American Economic Journal: Economic Policy* 4 (November): 230–52.

McNeal, William R., and Thomas B. Oxholm. 2009. *A School District's Journey to Excellence: Lessons from Business and Education*. Thousand Oaks, Calif.: Corwin.

Meyer, John W. 1977. "The Effects of Education as an Institution." *American Journal of Sociology* 83 (July): 55–77.

Mickelson, Roslyn A. 2001. "Subverting *Swann*: First- and Second-Generation Segregation in the Charlotte-Mecklenburg Schools." *American Educational Research Journal* 38 (Summer): 215–52.

———. 2005. "The Incomplete Desegregation of the Charlotte-Mecklenburg Schools and Its Consequences, 1971–2004." In Boger and Orfield 2005, 87–110.

———. 2014. "The Problem of the Color Lines in Twenty-First-Century Sociology of Education: Researching and Theorizing Demographic Change, Segregation, and School Outcomes. *Social Currents* 1 (June): 157–65.

Mickelson, Roslyn A., Martha Bottia, and R. Lambert. 2013. "Effects of School Racial Composition on K–12 Mathematics Outcomes: A Metaregression Analysis." *Review of Educational Research* 83 (March): 121–58.

Mickelson, Roslyn A., Stephen S. Smith, and Amy Hawn Nelson. Eds. 2015. *Yesterday, Today, and Tomorrow: Desegregation and Resegregation in Charlotte*. Cambridge, Mass.: Harvard Education Press.

Miller, John J. 2009. "The Fisherman's Friend." *National Review*, December 21, 22–24.

Mintz, Stephen, and Susan Kellogg. 1988. *Domestic Revolutions: A Social History of American Family Life*. New York: Free Press.

Moody, James. 2001. "Race, School Integration, and Friendship Segregation in America." *American Journal of Sociology* 107 (November): 679–716.

Morgan, Stephen L., and Aage B. Sørensen. 1999. "Parental Networks, Social Closure, and Mathematics Learning: A Test of Coleman's Social Capital Explanation of School Effects." *American Sociological Review* 64 (October): 661–81.

Murphy, John. 1978. "Magnet School Proposal, Exhibit A." From Wake County Public School System Board meeting minutes, March 20, 255.

Murray, Charles. 2012. *Coming Apart: The State of White America, 1960–2010.* New York: Crown.

Nasaw, David. 1979. *Schooled to Order: A Social History of Public Schooling in the United States.* New York: Oxford University Press.

Newman, Benjamin, Joshua Johnson, and Patrick Lown. 2014. "The 'Daily Grind'— Work, Commuting, and Their Impact on Political Participation." *American Politics Research* 42 (January): 141–70.

Norfleet, Erin S. 2002. "Wake County's Negotiated Agreement on School Funding: Has It Worked?" *Popular Government* 68 (Fall): 34–39.

Nowotny, Helga. 1981. "Women in Public Life in Austria." In *Access to Power: Cross-National Studies of Women and Elites,* edited by C. Fuchs Epstein and R. Laub Coser, 147–56. London: George Allen and Unwin.

Oliver, J. Eric, and Tali Mendelberg. 2000. "Reconsidering the Environmental Determinants of White Racial Attitudes." *American Journal of Political Science* 44 (July): 574–87.

Orfield, Gary. 1988. "School Desegregation in the 1980s." *Equity and Choice* 4 (February): 25–28.

Orfield, Gary, Susan E. Eaton, and the Harvard Project on School Desegregation. 1996. *Dismantling Desegregation: The Quiet Reversal of* Brown v. Board of Education. New York: New Press.

Orfield, Gary, and Chungmei Lee. 2005. *Why Segregation Matters: Poverty and Educational Inequality.* Cambridge, Mass.: Civil Rights Project, Harvard University.

Orfield, Gary, and John T. Yun. 1999. "Resegregation in American Schools." Cambridge, Mass.: Civil Rights Project, Harvard University.

Parcel, Toby L., and Mikaela J. Dufur. 2001a. "Capital at Home and at School: Effects on Child Social Adjustment." *Journal of Marriage and Family* 63 (February): 32–47.

———. 2001b. "Capital at Home and at School: Effects on Student Achievement." *Social Forces* 79 (March): 881–912.

Parcel, Toby L., Mikaela J. Dufur, and Rena Cornell Zito. 2010. "Capital at Home and at School: A Review and Synthesis." *Journal of Marriage and Family* 72 (August): 828–46.

Parcel, Toby L., and Joshua A. Hendrix. 2014. "Family Transmission of Social and Cultural Capital." In *Sociology of Families,* edited by Jackie Scott, Martin Richards, and Judith Treas, 361–81. Malden, Mass.: Wiley-Blackwell.

Pettigrew, Thomas F., and Linda R. Tropp. 2004. "Intergroup Contact and the Central Role of Affect in Intergroup Prejudice." In *The Social Life of Emotion: Studies in Emotion and Social Interaction,* edited by L. Tiedens and C. W. Leach, 246–69. New York: Cambridge University Press.

———. 2006. "A Meta-analytic Test of Intergroup Contact Theory." *Journal of Personality and Social Psychology* 90 (May): 751–83.

Phillips, Kristie J. R., Robert J. Rodosky, Marco A. Muñoz, and Elisabeth S. Larsen. 2009. "Integrated Schools, Integrated Futures? A Case Study of School Desegregation in Jefferson County, Kentucky." In Smrekar and Goldring 2009a, 239–69.

Portes, Alejandro. 1998. "Social Capital: Its Origins and Applications in Modern Sociology." *Annual Review of Sociology* 24 (August): 1–24.

———. 2000. "The Two Meanings of Social Capital." *Sociological Forum* 15 (March): 1–12.

Portz, John, Lana Stein, and Robin R. Jones. 1999. *City Politics and City Schools.* Lawrence: University Press of Kansas.

Putnam, Robert D. 2000. *Bowling Alone: The Collapse and Revival of American Community.* New York: Simon and Schuster.

Rahn, Wendy M., and Thomas J. Rudolph. 2002. "Trust in Local Governments." In *Understanding Public Opinion,* 2nd ed., edited by Barbara Norrander and Clyde Wilcox, 281–300. Washington, D.C.: CQ Press.

———. 2005. "A Tale of Political Trust in American Cities." *Public Opinion Quarterly* 69 (Winter): 530–60.

Raudenbush, Stephen W., and Anthony Bryk. 1986. "A Hierarchical Model for Studying School Effects." *Sociology of Education* 59 (January): 1–17.

Raudenbush, Stephen W., and J. Douglas Willms. 1995. "The Estimation of School Effects." *Journal of Educational and Behavioral Statistics* 20 (Winter): 307–35.

Ravitch, Diane. 2010. *The Death and Life of the Great American School System.* New York: Basic Books.

Rawlins, Wade. 1993. "Elevating the GOP By His Own Boot Straps." *News and Observer,* November 14.

———. 1995. "Wake GOP Aims to Widen Its Influence." *News and Observer,* February 7.

———. 1996. "Big Cut Proposed in School Request." *News and Observer,* January 30.

Reay, Diane. 2000. "A Useful Extension of Bourdieu's Conceptual Framework? Emotional Capital as a Way of Understanding Mothers' Involvement in Their Children's Education." *Sociological Review* 4 (November): 568–85.

Reay, Diane, and Stephen J. Ball. 1998. "'Making Their Minds Up': Family Dynamics of School Choice." *British Educational Research Journal* 24 (September): 431–48.

Reisel, Liza. 2011. "Two Paths to Inequality in Educational Outcomes: Family Background and Educational Selection in the United States and Norway." *Sociology of Education* 84 (October): 261–80.

Reynolds, David R. 1999. *There Goes the Neighborhood: Rural School Consolidation at the Grass Roots in Early Twentieth-Century Iowa.* Iowa City: University of Iowa Press.

Rice, Tom W., and Alexander F. Sumberg. 1997. "Civic Culture and Government Performance in the American States." *Publius: The Journal of Federalism* 27, no. 1: 99–114.

Robinson, Keith, and Angel L. Harris. 2014. *The Broken Compass: Parental Involvement with Children's Education.* Cambridge, Mass.: Harvard University Press.

Roksa, Josipa, and Daniel Potter. 2011. "Parenting and Academic Achievement." *Sociology of Education* 84 (October): 299–321.

Roscigno, Vincent J., Donald Tomaskovic-Devey, and Martha Crowley. 2006. "Education and the Inequalities of Place." *Social Forces* 84 (June): 2121–45.

Rossell, Christine, and David J. Armor. 1996. "The Effectiveness of School Desegregation Plans, 1968–1991." *American Politics Quarterly* 24 (July): 267–302.

Rossell, Christine H., Davis J. Armor, and Herbert J. Walberg. 2002. *School Desegregation in the 21st Century.* Westport, Conn.: Praeger Publishers.

Rudolph, Thomas J., and Jillian Evans. 2005. "Political Trust, Ideology, and Public Support for Government Spending." *American Journal of Political Science* 49 (July): 660–71.

Rudolph, Thomas J., and Elizabeth Popp. 2010. "Race, Environment, and Interracial Trust." *Journal of Politics* 72 (January): 1–16.

Rumberger, Russell W., and Gregory J. Palardy. 2005. "Does Segregation Still Matter? The Impact of Student Composition on Academic Achievement in High School." *Teachers College Record* 107: 1999–2045.

Ryan, James E. 2010. *Five Miles Away, a World Apart: One City, Two Schools, and the Story of Educational Opportunity in Modern America.* New York: Oxford University Press.

Schaub, Maryellen. 2010. "Parenting for Cognitive Development from 1950 to 2000: The Institutionalization of Mass Education and the Social Construction of Parenting in the United States." *Sociology of Education* 83 (January): 46–66.

Scher, Richard K. 1997. *Politics in the New South: Republicanism, Race, and Leadership in the Twentieth Century.* 2nd ed. Armonk, N.Y.: Sharpe.

Schuman, Howard, Charlotte Steeh, Lawrence Bobo, and Maria Krysan. 1997. *Racial Attitudes in America: Trends and Interpretations.* Rev. ed. Cambridge, Mass.: Harvard University Press.

Shafer, Byron, and Richard Johnston. 2006. *The End of Southern Exceptionalism: Class, Race, and Partisan Change in the Postwar South.* Cambridge, Mass.: Harvard University Press.

Shepard, Morris, and Keith Baker. 1977. *Year-Round Schools.* Lexington, Va.: Lexington Books.

Shober, Arnold. 2012. *The Democratic Dilemma of American Education: Out of Many, One?* Boulder: Westview Press.

Shor, Boris, Christopher Berry, and Nolan McCarty. 2010. "A Bridge to Somewhere: Mapping State and Congressional Ideology on a Cross-Institutional Common Space." *Legislative Studies Quarterly* 35 (August): 417–48.

Sigelman, Lee, and Susan Welch. 1993. "The Contact Hypothesis Revisited: Black-White Interaction and Positive Racial Attitudes." *Social Forces* 71 (March): 781–95.

Silberman, Todd. 1992. "Year-Round Schools Need More Blacks." *News and Observer,* July 24.

———. 1995. "School Board Hopefuls Tout GOP Platform." *News and Observer,* August 24.

———. 1996a. "Parents Hot Over School Switches." *News and Observer,* February 8.

———. 1996b. "Wake Board Appears Ready to Relent on Some Reassignments." *News and Observer*, February 28.

———. 1997a. "School Board Wants New Fee to Offset Costs." *News and Observer*, March 5.

———. 1997b. "School Board Scales Back Reassignments." *News and Observer*, April 9.

———. 1997c. "Fliers Misleading, School Board Chairwoman Says." *News and Observer*, September 27.

———. 1999. "Schools Facing Diversity Dilemma." *News and Observer*, December 26.

———. 2000a. "Wake School Board Talks of Stepping Back, Defining Its Role." *News and Observer*, April 6.

———. 2000b. "Schools' Plan Adopted." *News and Observer*, January 11.

———. 2001. "Wake County Schools: A Question of Balance." In *Divided We Fail: Coming Together through Public School Choice*, 146–66. Washington, D.C.: Century Foundation.

Silberman, Todd, and T. Keung Hui. 1999. "Wake Rejects School Bonds." *News and Observer*, June 9.

Silberman, Todd, and Wade Rawlins. 1995. "Commissioners, School Board Members Drift into One Another's Turf." *News and Observer*, September 19.

———. 1996. "Wake Says 'Yes' to School Bonds." *News and Observer*, June 5.

Skocpol, Theda, and Vanessa Williamson. 2012. *The Tea Party and the Remaking of Republican Conservatism*. Oxford: Oxford University Press.

Slemrod, Joel, and Peter Katuscak. 2005. "Do Trust and Trustworthiness Pay Off?" *Journal of Human Resources* 40 (Summer): 621–46.

Smith, Stephen S. 2004. *Boom for Whom? Education, Desegregation, and Development in Charlotte*. Albany: State University of New York Press.

Smrekar, Claire E., and Ellen B. Goldring, eds. 2009a. *From the Courtroom to the Classroom: The Shifting Landscape of School Desegregation*. Cambridge, Mass.: Harvard Education Press.

———. 2009b. "Neighborhood Schools in the Aftermath of Court-Ended Busing: Educator's Perspectives on How Context and Composition Matter." In Smrekar and Goldring 2009a, 157–90.

Sniderman, Paul M., Richard A. Brody, and Phillip E. Tetlock. 1991. *Reasoning and Choice: Explorations in Political Psychology*. New York: Cambridge University Press.

Sniderman, Paul M., and Thomas Piazza. 1993. *The Scar of Race*. Cambridge, Mass.: Belknap Press.

Spanierman, Lisa B., Jaclyn C. Beard, and Nathan R. Todd. 2012. "White Men's Fears, White Women's Tears: Examining Gender Differences in Racial Affect Types." *Sex Roles* (August): 174–86.

Stearns, Elizabeth. 2010. "Long-Term Correlates of High School Racial Composition: Perpetuation Theory Reexamined." *Teachers College Record* 112: 1654–78.

Stolle, Dietlind, Stuart Soroka, and Richard Johnston. 2008. "When Does Diversity Erode Trust? Neighborhood Diversity, Interpersonal Trust and the Mediating Effect of Social Interactions." *Political Studies* 56 (March): 57–75.

Stover, Del. 2012. "Pay to Play?" *American School Board Journal* 199 (March): 14–18.

Strang, David. 1987. "The Administrative Transformation of American Education:

School District Consolidation, 1938–1980." *Administrative Science Quarterly* 32 (September): 352–66.

Sui-Chu, Esther Ho, and J. Douglas Willms. 1996. "Effects of Parental Involvement on Eighth-Grade Achievement." *Sociology of Education* 69 (April): 126–41.

Taylor, Marylee C., and Peter J. Mateyka. 2011. "Community Influences on White Racial Attitudes: What Matters and Why?" *Sociological Quarterly* 52 (Spring): 220–43.

Teixeira, Ruy A. 1992. *The Disappearing American Voter*. Washington, D.C.: Brookings Institution.

Theriault, Sean M. 2008. *Party Polarization in Congress*. New York: Cambridge University Press.

Tough, Paul. 2009. *Whatever It Takes: Geoffrey Canada's Quest to Change Harlem and America*. New York: Houghton Mifflin Harcourt.

Tropp, Linda R., and Thomas F. Pettigrew. 2005. "Differential Relationships between Intergroup Contact and Affective and Cognitive Dimensions of Prejudice." *Personality and Social Psychology Bulletin* 31 (August): 1145–58.

Tuch, Steven A., and Michael Hughes. 1996. "Whites' Racial Policy Attitudes." *Social Science Quarterly* 77 (December): 723–45.

Tyack, David. 1974. *The One Best System*. Cambridge, Mass.: Harvard University Press.

University of Michigan Population Studies Center. 2013. "Segregation." http://www.psc.isr.umich.edu/dis/census/segregation.html, accessed November 20.

U.S. Census Bureau. State and County Quickfacts, Broward, Hillsborough, Miami-Dade and Orange Counties, Florida, 2014. http://quickfacts.census.gov/qfd/states/12/1224000.html.

U.S. Census Bureau. State and County Quickfacts, Wake County, 1990, 2010, 2014. http://quickfacts.census.gov/qfd/index.html.

Vigdor, Jacob, and Jens Ludwig. 2008. "Segregation and the Test Score Gap." In *Steady Gains and Stalled Progress: Inequality and the Black-White Test Score Gap*, edited by Katherine Magnuson and Jane Waldfogel, 181–211. New York: Russell Sage Foundation.

Wake County Public School System. 2003. *Measuring Up*. Report prepared by the Evaluation and Research Department. Raleigh, N.C.: Wake County Public School System.

Wake Education Partnership. 2002. *Investing in Solutions: Community Engagement and Public-Private Partnerships to Address Goal 2003*. Raleigh, N.C.: Wake Education Partnership.

———. 2003. *Making Choices: Diversity, Student Assignment, and Quality in Wake's Schools*. Raleigh, N.C.: Wake Education Partnership.

Waters, Laura. 2012. "When Talking about School Consolidation in N.J., Let's Talk Money." NJ Left Behind Blog. http://www.newsworks.org/index.php/new-jersey-more/item/36811-when-talking-about-school-consolidation-in-nj-lets-talk-money&Itemid=248.

Welch, Susan, Lee Sigelman, Timothy Bledsoe, and Michael Combs. 2001. *Race and Place: Race Relations in an American City*. New York: Cambridge University Press.

Wells, Amy, and Robert Crain. 1994. "Perpetuation Theory and the Long-Term Effects of School Desegregation." *Review of Educational Research* 64 (Winter): 531–55.

Wells, Amy, Jacquelyn Duran, and Terrenda White. 2008. "Refusing to Leave Desegregation Behind: From Graduates of Racially Diverse Schools to Supreme." *Teachers College Record* 110: 2532–70.

Welner, Kevin. 2006. "K–12 Race-Conscious Student Assignment Policies: Law, Social Science and Diversity." *Review of Research in Education* 76 (Fall): 349–82.

Williams, Linda. 1975a. "House OKs Merger Plan." *News and Observer*, June 7.

———. 1975b. "Boards Voting Today on Merger." *News and Observer*, September 3.

Williams, Sheneka M., and Eric A. Houck. 2013. "The Life and Death of Desegregation Policy in Wake County Public School System and Charlotte-Mecklenburg Schools." *Education and Urban Society* 45 (September): 571–88.

Willms, J. Douglas. 1985. "Catholic-School Effects on Academic Achievement: New Evidence from the High School and Beyond Follow-Up Study." *Sociology of Education* 58 (April): 98–114.

Wolak, Jennifer, and Christine K. Palus. 2010. "The Dynamics of Public Confidence in the U.S. State and Local Government." *State Politics and Policy Quarterly* 10 (Winter): 421–45.

Yin, Robert K. 2008. *Case Study Research: Design and Methods*. Washington, D.C.: Sage, 2008.

Zernicke, Kate. 2010. *Boiling Mad: Inside Tea Party America*. New York: Times Press.

Index

ABC program, 22, 36, 137 (n. 23), 139 (n. 7)

Academic achievement: and diversity, 27; and neighborhood schools, 80; promoting, xi, xv, 5; and school composition, 3, 4, 33, 35; and social capital, 6; in Wake, 36. *See also* Education; Schools

Adcock, Stewart, 20

African Americans, xii–xiii, 3, 8, 14–20, 28, 34; in Charlotte-Mecklenburg schools, 102, 105; children of, 36; and dissimilarity index, 103; focus group of, xii, 123; political power of, 18; proportions of in Florida counties, 98; proportions of in Wake, 43, 48, 98, 124; and sampling of, xiii, 39, 123; and views of challenge of reassignment, 63; and views of diversity, 44, 48, 50, 81, 113–15; and views of reassignment, 64; and views of school assignments, xvi; and views of Wake school board, 88; and views of year-round schools, 75–76; whites' views of, 42. *See also* Latinos; Race

Akins, Waverly F., 16

Alexander v. Holmes, 14

Alves, Michael, 85

Americans for Prosperity, 30

Apex, N.C., 12, 14, 19, 25, 29, 42–43, 53–55, 66–72, 109–10, 143 (n. 1)

Assignment By Choice (ABC), 30, 35, 37, 55

Austin, Tex., 4, 97–98

Avila, Marilyn, 30

Ayscue, Jennifer B., 100

Backhouse, Allison, 69, 81

Barber, William, 83

Barker, Bob, 17

Benton, Tom, 111

Boger, John Charles, 2

Boston, Mass., 4, 91, 99

Bottia, Martha, 3

Brennan, Kathleen, 69

Bridges, Robert, 21

Bright flight, 2, 92

Broh, Beckett A., 65

Broward County, Fla., 98, 143 (n. 13)

Brown v. Board of Education, 96, 135 (n. 1)

Broyhill, Jim, 29

Burns, Del, 83

Busing: and academic achievement, 27; attitudes towards 30, 36, 38, 41, 58; and diversity, xv, 11; and diversity policy, 34, 49, 60; forced, 82; and magnet schools, 66; outside of Wake, 34, 102, 103, 105; perceptions of in Wake, 45, 115; and population growth, 53; Republican views of, 16, 29, 31; reverse, 26, 55, 81, 105; in Wake, 15, 116, 136 (n. 6). *See also* African Americans

Capacchione v. Charlotte-Mecklenburg Schools, 105, 138 (n.1)

Capps, Paul, 56

Capps, Russell, 30

Carawan, Roy E., 20–21, 137 (n. 17)

Cary, N.C., 12, 14, 16, 17, 21, 23, 25, 43, 54, 69; political activism of, 54, 55, 69, 72, 77, 85, 109; population growth of, 16, 17, 20, 23, 29, 42, 66, 67; school reassignments in, 25, 54; year-round schools in, 21, 70

Case study, 123

Catholic schools, 5
Census, U.S., 12, 29, 39, 51, 95–101, 124–25, 136 (n. 10), 137 (n. 16)
Century Foundation, 35
Challenge of school reassignments. *See* School reassignment: challenges of
Charlotte, N.C., xii, 15, 26–28, 37, 93, 102, 105–6, 137 (n. 32), 139 (n. 6)
Charlotte-Mecklenburg school district, xvii, 4, 14, 34–36, 102, 105, 107, 117, 137 (n. 28), 138 (n. 1)
Children: low-income, 55, 56, 115; minority, 2, 6, 23, 39, 43, 48, 49, 67
Citizens for Good Schools, 24
Citizens for the Right to Vote, 16
Civitas poll, 73, 81
Clark, Beverly, 51
Clark County, Nev., 107
Coble, Paul, 28
Colbert, Stephen, xi, 83
Coleman, James S., 3–7
Coleman Report, 3
Common Sense group, 110
Commutes (commuting), 11, 27, 44, 116, 135 (n. 5)
Concerned Parents Association of Charlotte, 37
Conservatives, 8, 18, 77, 88; and political activism, 72, 89; and Republicans, 30; social and religious, 30, 37, 80; and views of diversity, 34, 41, 49, 114; and views of neighborhood schools, 33, 45; and views of reassignment, 60, 62, 64; and views of year-round schools, 70, 75, 76
Controlled Choice Assignment Plan, 86, 105, 109–11
Cuban, Larry, 4, 97

Dangers of school reassignment. *See* School reassignment: dangers of
Daniels, Frank, 16
Danielson, F. Roland, 17
Debnam, Dean, 82
DeBray, Elizabeth, 100

Delaney, Chuck, 58
Democratic Party, 8–9, 123; in Wake County, 17, 22, 27–28, 32, 78, 85, 86, 110–11, 112, 118–19, 137 (n. 32), 138 (n. 43), 141 (n. 6), 142 (n. 21), 143 (n. 1)
Denver, Colo., 96, 139 (n. 3), 143 (nn. 7, 8)
Diem, Sarah, 96
Direct instruction, 31, 138 (n. 40)
Diversity model of school assignment, xiv, 1, 2–4, 10–12, 44, 94–99, 101, 103, 105–7, 110–12, 114–15, 117, 120–21, 128, 130; and annual reassignments, 55–56, 57, 64; and social capital, 11–12, 46, 115, 116–17; and socioeconomic status, 35–36; and views by gender, 41, 45; and views by race, 35, 46–48, 81, 114–15; and views of citizens, 32, 39–49, 81–82, 113–14; in Wake County, 2–3, 19–20, 33–49, 51, 53, 78, 80, 83, 88–89, 118–19, 126; and year-round schools, 66–67, 71–72. *See also* Neighborhood model of school assignment; School reassignment; Social capital; Social class; Year-round schools
Dollar, Nelson, 30
Dougherty, Jack, 95
Downey, Douglas B., 65
Duncan, Dave, 69

Eaton, Susan, 2, 99
Economist, The, xi, 83
Education: and busing, 38; and children, 44, 52, 57, 58, 59; and community, 120; conservative views of, 8–9, 24, 29, 30–31, 33–34, 37–38, 41–42, 60, 78, 86, 114; diversity in, 1–2, 10–12, 34–49, 117–18; comparisons to Wake, 98–100, 104–5; and equal opportunity, xxiii; as industry, 29, 95; as institution, 119; K–12, 33, 53, 80, 90, 116; levels of, 50, 62, 63, 74, 115, 124, 125; liberal views of, 2–4, 33–34, 41–42, 44, 49, 89, 112; and parental involvement and control, 116, 119, 120; as placement mechanism in society, xiv, 1, 2, 81, 121; as profes-

sion, 111; professionalization of, 15; public, 29, 50, 70, 76, 96; and school board members, 21; and social class, 41, 43, 46, 50; urban 94. *See also* African Americans; Diversity model of school assignment; Elementary schools; Neighborhood model of school assignment; Schools

Elections, xv, 27, 111, 123

Elementary schools: child experience in, 38, 59; choice of, 86; conversion to year-round, 68, 70; and diversity, 34, 48; and feeder patterns, 58, 120; and magnets, 98; and proximity to home, 9; and reassignment, 52; and social capital, 95; in Wake, 25, 26, 51. *See also* Education; Schools

Emotional capital, 62, 114

Evans, Susan, 109–10

Fairfax County, Va., 107

Families: low-income, 81; minority, 76, 81; trust in schools, 21, 85, 99. *See also* Family life; Trust; Work hours

Family life, 31, 56, 74, 78; and education, xvi; parents' work and, xiv, 18. *See also* Families

Fetzer, Tom, 28, 30, 84, 138 (n. 34)

Fisher, Bill, 9, 138 (n. 36)

Fletcher, Bill, 21, 29–30, 52, 84, 111–12, 137 (n. 27), 138 (nn. 36, 43)

Florida, 90, 98–99, 107, 117

Focus group, xiii, xv, 36, 38, 46, 56, 58, 69, 84, 123

Ford, Steve, 42

Forgione, Pascal P., Jr., 97

Fort Lauderdale, Fla., 98

Fourth Circuit Court of Appeals, 26

Frankenberg, Erica, 3, 91, 93

Frasure-Yokley, Lorrie, 99

Friends of Wake County, 25

Fuller, Chuck, 30

Fuquay-Varina, N.C., 14, 17, 70, 77

Fussell, Aaron, 15

Gamoran, Adam, 3

Gantt, Harvey, 28

Gender, xiv, 32, 60, 88–89, 113–14

Gentry, Mary, 17, 20–21, 137 (n. 17)

George Peabody College for Teachers, 15

Gilbert, John H., 21, 67

Goal 2003, 36

Goettee, Eleanor, 30, 77, 84

Goldman, Debra, 77, 82–83, 85, 111, 141 (n. 12, chap. 6), 142 (n. 21)

Goldring, Ellen B., 91, 97

Grant, Gerald, 5, 91, 95, 139 (n. 4)

Great Recession, 8

Great Schools in Wake, 33, 80, 83

Green v. County School Board of New Kent County, 14

Grooms, Ain, 100

Gumus-Dawes, Baris, 99

Gwinnett County, Ga., 107

Hartford, Conn., 95, 97

Harvard Project on School Desegregation, 2

Hawaii, 107

Head, Patti, 68, 77

Health, Education, and Welfare, Department of (HEW), 14–16, 136 (n. 3)

Heineman, Fred, 28

Helms, Jesse, 16, 27–29, 137 (n. 31)

Hennepin County, Minn., 99

Henrico County, Va., 91, 94, 97

Hergert, Barlow, 28

Heroes Emerging Amongst Teens (N.C.HEAT), 83

Hetherington, Marc, 43

Hill, Kevin, 109–11, 136 (n. 2)

Hillsborough County, Fla., 98, 143 (n. 13)

Hochschild, Arlie R., 60

Hoffman, Judy, 24, 84, 138 (nn. 36, 43)

Holly Springs, N.C., 12, 25, 42–43, 52, 69–70, 109

Holme, Jennifer Jellison, 96

Holshouser, Jim, 27, 29

Holyrod, Casper, 16
Howell, Susan E., 117
Hunt, Jim, 28, 137 (n. 31)

Individualism, 120
Interactive Voice Response (IVR), 123

Jefferson County, Ky., 101, 143 (n. 16)
Johnson-Hostler, Monika, 112
Jones, Robin R., 4, 91–93, 96
Joslin, Stewart, 30

Kahlenberg, Richard, 35
King, George, 16
King, Martin Luther, Jr., 42, 44–45, 47
Knight, Henry C., 16, 22, 137 (n. 20)
Koski, William S., 101
Kushner, Christine, 109

Lambert, R., 3
Lareau, Annette, 9, 120
Larkins, John D., 14, 137 (n. 15)
Latinos, 34, 36, 42, 48, 67, 96–97, 98–99, 101–2
Lee, Patrice, 69
Lewis, Craig, 21
Liberals, 43, 74, 77, 81; and views of schools, 2–4, 33–34, 41–42, 44, 49, 89, 102
Losurdo, Heather, 109–10
Louisville, Ky., 101, 139 (n. 23)
Luce, Thomas, 99
Luddy, Robert L., 30–31, 80–81

Malone, Chris, 77, 82, 111, 142 (n. 12)
Malone, Vernon, 18
Manning, Howard, Jr., 70–71
Margiotta, Ron, xi, 37, 42, 69, 71–72, 77, 82–83, 109–10, 142 (nn. 20, 21), 143 (n. 1)
Marks, Walter L., 19, 21, 136 (n. 13), 137 (n. 17)
Martin, Charlotte, 22
Martin, Governor Jim, 29
Martin, Jim, 48, 109

Massey, John, 19, 21
Matson, Cynthia, 35, 55
McAlister, Ernie, 54
McLaurin, Ann, 86, 109
McNeill, Bill, 35
Merrill, Jim, 111
Miami-Dade, Fla., 98
Mickelson, Roslyn A., 3, 4, 139 (n. 6)
Middle class, 2, 97
Millberg, Lori, 77
Miner, David, 28, 30
Minority group and contact, 7–8
Montgomery County, Md., 100, 107, 137 (n. 28), 138 (n. 2), 142 (n. 1), 143 (n. 15)
Moore, Dan K., 14
Morrison, Carolyn, 86, 109
Muñoz, Vanessa Lopes, 120
Murphy, John A., 18–19, 21, 136 (nn. 11, 13)
Murray, Charles, 6

NAACP, 83
Nashville, Tenn., 97, 139 (n. 3), 143 (n. 11)
Nassau County, N.Y., 92, 142 (n. 3)
National Congressional Club, 28, 138 (n. 33)
National Education Longitudinal Study, 1988, 3
Neighborhood model of school assignment, xiv, 1, 5–6, 9–10, 33, 95, 96–97, 100, 107, 112–13, 114, 118, 120–21, 127, 130; and social capital, 4–6, 11–12, 115–16, 135 (n. 4); and views of public, 33–34, 39–49, 81–82; and Wake County policies towards, xv, 14–15, 18, 31, 37, 85
Neighborhoods: minority, 67; low-income, 67
Nelson, Amy Hawn, 4
New York City, 4, 106, 137 (n. 16)
New York Times, The, xi, 83, 143 (n. 18)
Nixon, Lois, 77–78
Nixon, Richard, 16, 28, 137 (n. 32), 138 (n. 35)

No Child Left Behind (NCLB), 2, 139
  (n. 7)
North Carolina Citizens for a Sound
  Economy, 30
North Carolina General Assembly, 16, 17,
  111, 137 (n. 18), 141 (n. 1)
North Carolina Supreme Court, 71, 76,
  137 (n. 26)

Oakes, Jeannie, 101
O'Neal, J. C., 29, 138 (n. 36)
Onondaga County, N.Y., 95
Orange County, Calif., 99
Orange County, Fla., 98–99
Orfield, Gary, 2, 3, 91, 99
Orlando, Fla., 98
Osseo Area, Minn., 99
Oxholm, Tom, 30

Palardy, Gregory J., 3
Parents, low-income, 66
Parents Involved in Community Schools v.
  Seattle School District, 34, 101
Pendleton, Gary, 30, 138 (n. 37)
Phillips, Kristie J., 101
Pittsburgh, Pa., 4, 91
Political ideology, xiv, 41, 114
Political minority, 86
Political polarization, 8, 141 (n. 2); and
  Wake County, 78, 80, 112, 114
Pope, Art, 29, 80
Pope, Claude, 31
Populations, minority, 3, 7, 94
Portz, John, 4, 91–93, 96
Potter, Robert, 34–35
Price, David, 28
Prickett, Deborah, 77–78, 82, 111–12, 138
  (n. 43)
Principal components analysis, 125
Public Policy Polling, 39, 81, 123
Putnam, Robert D., 5–7

Race, xi, xiv, 2–3, 7–8, 15, 19–20, 28, 34–37,
  42–43, 48, 49, 102, 105–6, 113–14;
  and citizens' views of, 41–42, 80, 141

(n. 6); and contact theory, 6–8, 43;
  outside of Wake, 94, 95, 99–100; and
  politics, 19–20; and sample weighting,
  125; and school assignment, 62– 63,
  75–76, 86, 105–6, 107, 138–39 (n. 2); and
  threat theory, 7–8, 43; and U.S. Census
  definition, 136 (n. 10). *See also* African
  Americans; Latinos; School assignment
Racial distribution in Wake, 92–93
Rahn, Wendy M., 92, 95
Rakestraw, Rita, 77–78, 80
Raleigh Chamber of Commerce, 22, 85
Raleigh News and Observer, 16, 39
Ramsay, Christina, 95
Ranzino, Samuel S., 17
Ravitch, Diane, 4, 91
Republican Party: in Charlotte-
  Mecklenburg, 117; in Wake County,
  xv, 27–31, 42, 57, 69, 83–84, 86, 105, 109,
  110–12, 137 (n. 20), 138 (nn. 34, 36, 38,
  43), 143 (n. 1)
Resegregation, xii–xiii, 2–3, 91
Residential segregation, 2, 10, 97, 100, 102,
  105
Rice, Tom W., 92
Richmond, Va., 4, 15, 91, 94, 97
Roberg, Tom, 28
Rudolph, Thomas J., 92, 95
Rumberger, Russell W., 3
Ryan, James E., 4, 91–92, 94

St. Louis, Mo., 4, 91, 95–96
San Antonio, Tex., 96, 106
San Diego, Calif., 4, 90, 106–7, 139 (n. 3)
San Jose, Calif., 101, 107
SAS, 125
SAT scores, 22
Save Our Summers Wake County, 69
Schaub, Maryellen, 119
Schilawski, L. Jean, 21
School choice, 60, 91, 94
School desegregation, 2, 93, 101, 102, 104,
  106; and unitary status, 143
School districts, xii, 12–13, 90–108; compo-
  sition of, 90–101; majority-minority,

95, 96, 97, 98, 106–7, 117; size of, 106–7. *See also* Education; Schools

School reassignment, 51–64; challenges of, xvi, 56–57, 59–64, 113, 114–15, 118, 125, 127, 130; dangers of, xvi, 57–58, 59–64, 113, 114–15, 127, 130; opposition to, 54–56, 72, 77–78; uncertainties of, xvi, 25, 27, 54, 58–64, 71, 125; views of citizens, 56–64, 113–14, 116, 118; in Wake County, xvi, 11, 21, 25–26, 31, 51–64. *See also* Diversity model of school assignment; Education; Neighborhood model of school assignment; Schools; Year-round schools

Schools (or schooling): high, 3, 9, 11, 34, 51, 58, 62, 70, 86, 94, 120; home, 30; magnets in Wake, xiii, xv, 11, 19, 20, 25–26, 34–35, 43, 49, 54, 56, 58–59, 65–66, 68, 71, 76, 105–6, 110, 118; magnets outside of Wake, 95–102, 104–6, 117; majority-minority, 34, 100; middle, xiv, 9, 21, 25, 26, 34, 48, 51, 57, 58, 59, 65–66, 67, 70, 72, 86, 98; minority, 34, 105; private, 70, 79, 96, 119, 121, 135 (n. 3), 136 (n. 5); Wake schools as majority-minority, 118. *See also* Diversity model of school assignment; Education; Elementary schools; Neighborhood model of school assignment; Year-round schools

School segregation, 2, 10, 96, 100, 102. *See also* School desegregation

"Sewall" County, Ga., 100

Schools of Choice, 19

Simon, Karen, 77–78

Smith, Stephen S., 4, 93

Smrekar, Claire E., 91, 97

Social capital, xi, xiv, xvi–xvii, 6–8, 10–12, 43–44, 50, 60, 92, 115–16, 135; and African Americans, 48, 49, 113; bonding, 5, 10, 12, 44, 116; bridging, 6, 10, 44, 99, 115, 116; and civic capacity, 4, 92, 126; and civic culture, 92; and civic life, xvi, xvii, 92–101, 106–8, 117, 119, 126; and

community, 93, 95; defined, 4; and friendship, 113; at home, 4–5, 10, 27, 40, 76, 89, 116; and intergenerational closure, 6; and neighborhoods, 33, 115; and networks, xiv, 6, 11, 12, 60, 92; and norms, xiv, 6, 11, 12, 60, 92; at school, 4, 33; and views of school assignment, 45–47; in school districts, 92–93, 95, 97–98, 99–100; and time closure, 5, 116. *See also* Coleman, James S.; Putnam, Robert D.; Trust

Social class, xi, 2, 41, 99, 101, 107, 115. *See also* Education: levels of; Middle class; Students

Stam, Paul "Skip," 30

Stangler, Curt, 30, 37

Staton, William E., 17

Stein, Lana, 4, 91, 92–94, 96

Stephens, Wray, 21–22, 30

Stiles, Karen, 53

Stop Mandatory Year-Round, 69, 80

Students: low-income, 66, 67, 71, 118; minority, 20, 26, 33–36, 48, 66. *See also* African Americans; Latinos

Suburban jurisdictions, xvii, 90

Sui-Chu, Esther Ho, 119

Sumberg, Alexander F., 92

Supreme Court, U.S., 14, 34, 101, 135 (n. 1), 143 (n. 7)

Surratt, Jim, 24, 35, 67

Sutton, Keith, 82, 109, 118

Swann v. Charlotte-Mecklenburg, 14

Syracuse, N.Y., 5, 91, 94–95

Take Wake Schools Back, 37, 81

Talton, Jim, 24

Tampa, Fla., 98

Tart, Horace, 37, 77–78, 82

Tata, Tony, 83, 86, 110–11, 144 (n. 2)

Teachers: investments in, 33; and school resources, 18, 137 (n. 23); and social capital, 5, 9, 10, 11, 79, 116; turnover of, 5, 70; and unions, 8, 80. *See also* Education; Schools; Social capital

Year-round schools, xvi, 20–21, 25–26, 30, 52, 55, 58, 65–76, 78, 82, 89, 105, 114, 115, 127, 140 (n. 3), 144 (n. 2); attitudes toward, xvi, 31, 89, 115; and cost saving, 20; defined, 20; and growth, 25; and low-income families, 140 (n. 3); mandatory, xvi, 24–25, 37, 55, 68, 69–74, 78, 83, 112, 113, 114, 115, 116, 118; opposition to, 69–71, 80–81; and parental consent, 25; and views of citizens 72–76; in Wake, 1990s, 21; in Wake, 2000s, 25, 30, 144 (n. 2). *See also* Education; School assignment; Schools

Youth, low-income, 3

Zebulon, N.C., 14, 17, 77